What is Consciousness?

What is consciousness and why is it so philosophically and scientifically puzzling? For many years philosophers approached this question assuming a standard physicalist framework on which consciousness can be explained by contemporary physics, biology, neuroscience, and cognitive science. This book is a debate between two philosophers who are united in their rejection of this kind of "standard" physicalism—but who differ sharply in what lesson to draw from this. Amy Kind defends dualism 2.0, a thoroughly modern version of dualism (the theory that there are two fundamentally different kinds of things in the world: those that are physical and those that are mental) decoupled from any religious or non-scientific connotations. Daniel Stoljar defends non-standard physicalism, a kind of physicalism different from both the standard version and dualism 2.0. The book presents a cutting-edge assessment of the philosophy of consciousness and provides a glimpse at what the future study of this area might bring.

Key Features

- Outlines the different things people mean by "consciousness" and provides an account of what consciousness is.
- Reviews the key arguments for thinking that consciousness is incompatible with physicalism.
- Explores and provides a defense of contrasting responses to those arguments, with a special focus on responses that reject the standard physicalist framework.
- Provides an account of the basic aims of the science of consciousness.
- Written in a lively and accessible style.
- Includes a comprehensive glossary.

Amy Kind is Russell K. Pitzer of Philosophy at Claremont McKenna College. She has authored numerous articles in philosophy of mind, as well as two books, *Persons and Personal Identity* (Polity, 2015) and *Philosophy of Mind: The Basics* (Routledge, 2020); she has also edited and co-edited four volumes, the most recent of which is *Epistemic Uses of Imagination* (Routledge, 2021).

Daniel Stoljar is Professor of Philosophy and Director of the Centre for Consciousness in the Research School of Social Sciences at the Australian National University. He is the author of many papers in philosophy of mind and related topics, as well as the books, *Ignorance and Imagination: The Epistemic Origin of the Problem of Consciousness* (OUP, 2006), *Physicalism* (Routledge, 2010), and *Philosophical Progress: In Defence of a Reasonable Optimism* (OUP, 2017).

Little Debates About Big Questions

Tyron Goldschmidt
Fellow of the Rutgers Center for Philosophy of Religion, USA

Dustin Crummett
Ludwig Maximilian University of Munich, Germany

About the series:

Philosophy asks questions about the fundamental nature of reality, our place in the world, and what we should do. Some of these questions are perennial: for example, *Do we have free will? What is morality?* Some are much newer: for example, *How far should free speech on campus extend? Are race, sex and gender social constructs?* But all of these are among the big questions in philosophy and they remain controversial.

Each book in the *Little Debates About Big Questions* series features two professors on opposite sides of a big question. Each author presents their own side, and the authors then exchange objections and replies. Short, lively, and accessible, these debates showcase diverse and deep answers. Pedagogical features include standard form arguments, section summaries, bolded key terms and principles, glossaries, and annotated reading lists.

The debate format is an ideal way to learn about controversial topics. Whereas the usual essay or book risks overlooking objections against its own proposition or misrepresenting the opposite side, in a debate each side can make their case at equal length, and then present objections the other side must consider. Debates have a more conversational and fun style too, and we selected particularly talented philosophers—in substance and style—for these kinds of encounters.

Debates can be combative—sometimes even descending into anger and animosity. But debates can also be cooperative. While our authors disagree strongly, they work together to help each other and the reader get clearer on the ideas, arguments, and objections. This is intellectual progress, and a much-needed model for civil and constructive disagreement.

The substance and style of the debates will captivate interested readers new to the questions. But there's enough to interest experts too. The debates will be especially useful for courses in philosophy and related subjects—whether as primary or secondary readings—and a few debates can be combined to make up the reading for an entire course.

We thank the authors for their help in constructing this series. We are honored to showcase their work. They are all preeminent scholars or rising-stars in their fields, and through these debates they share what's been discovered with a wider audience. This is a paradigm for public philosophy, and will impress upon students, scholars, and other interested readers the enduring importance of debating the big questions.

Published Titles:

What is Consciousness?
A Debate
By Amy Kind and Daniel Stoljar

Do We Have a Soul?
A Debate
By Eric T. Olson and Aaron Segal

Can War Be Justified?
A Debate
By Andrew Fiala and Jennifer Kling

Does Tomorrow Exist?
A Debate
By Nikk Effingham and Kristie Miller

Should Wealth Be Redistributed?
A Debate
By Steven McMullen and James R. Otteson

Do We Have Free Will? A Debate
By Robert Kane and Carolina Sartorio

For more information about this series, please visit: www.routledge.com/Little-Debates-about-Big-Questions/book-series/LDABQ

What is Consciousness?

A Debate

Amy Kind and Daniel Stoljar

NEW YORK AND LONDON

Designed cover image: © Getty Images

First published 2023
by Routledge
605 Third Avenue, New York, NY 10158

and by Routledge
4 Park Square, Milton Park, Abingdon, Oxon, OX14 4RN

Routledge is an imprint of the Taylor & Francis Group, an informa business

© 2023 Taylor & Francis

The right of Amy Kind and Daniel Stoljar to be identified as authors of this work has been asserted in accordance with sections 77 and 78 of the Copyright, Designs and Patents Act 1988.

All rights reserved. No part of this book may be reprinted or reproduced or utilised in any form or by any electronic, mechanical, or other means, now known or hereafter invented, including photocopying and recording, or in any information storage or retrieval system, without permission in writing from the publishers.

Trademark notice: Product or corporate names may be trademarks or registered trademarks, and are used only for identification and explanation without intent to infringe.

ISBN: 978-1-032-47062-7 (hbk)
ISBN: 978-0-367-33242-6 (pbk)
ISBN: 978-0-429-32401-7 (ebk)

DOI: 10.4324/9780429324017

Typeset in Sabon
by Apex CoVantage, LLC

Contents

Acknowledgments   xi
Foreword   xii
FRANK JACKSON

Opening Statements   1

1. **The Mind-Body Problem: Dualism Rebooted**   3
   AMY KIND

   Introduction 3
   1. *The Mind-Body Problem* 5
      1.1. Dualism 7
      1.2. Physicalism 11
   2. *The Consciousness Problem* 13
      2.1. Phenomenal Consciousness 14
      2.2. The Problem 18
   3. *Why Consciousness Escapes the Physicalist Net* 23
      3.1. The Bat 23
      3.2. The Color Scientist 25
      3.3. The Zombie 30
   4. *Theories of Consciousness* 35
      4.1. Representationalism 36
      4.2. Higher-Order Theory 42
      4.3. Russellian Monism 45
   5. *Dualism Rebooted* 52
      5.1. The Irreducibility of the Phenomenal 53
      5.2. What Science Does (and Doesn't) Tell Us 58
      5.3. The Way Ahead 61

2. **Non-standard Physicalism: The Epistemic Approach to the Problem of Consciousness**   63
   DANIEL STOLJAR

   Introduction 63
   1. *What Consciousness Is* 68
      1.1. Phenomenal Consciousness 68
      1.2. Complications 70
      1.3. Higher-Order Consciousness 78
      1.4. Access Consciousness 83
      1.5. Relations Among These Notions 87
   2. *Consciousness and the World* 91
      2.1. The Conceivability Argument 92
      2.2. The Epistemic View 94
      2.3. Alternatives to This View 99
      2.4. Features of This View 103
      2.5. Objections to This View 107
   3. *The Metaphysics of the Science of Consciousness* 114
      3.1. Case Study: Aaronson Versus Tononi 115
      3.2. The Laws of Consciousness Thesis 118
      3.3. Are There Laws of Consciousness? 123
      3.4. Consciousness Science Without the Laws? 128
      3.5. Consciousness Science After Ignorance 130

First Round of Replies   133

3. **Ignorance Is No Defense: Reply to Daniel Stoljar**   135
   AMY KIND

   Introduction 135
   1. *An Analogy* 136
   2. *Why Should We Believe the Epistemic View?* 138
   3. *What Does the Epistemic View Tell Us About the Metaphysics of Consciousness?* 144
   4. *Where Does the Burden of Proof Lie?* 148
      4.1. Denying Physicalism Does Not Commit One to Something Spooky or Supernatural 150
      4.2. Great Past Success Does Not Necessarily Mean Great Future Success 150

    4.3. Considerations of Simplicity Do Not
         Settle the Matter   151
    4.4. Should the Epistemic View Benefit From
         the Presumption in Favor of Physicalism? 152
 5. Where Does That Leave Us? 153

4. Taking Non-Standard Options Seriously:
   Reply to Amy Kind   155
   DANIEL STOLJAR

   Introduction 155
   1. Russellian Monism 157
   2. Kind's Critique 158
   3. Must We Say What the Properties Are? 160
   4. The Combination Problem 162
   5. False Advertising 164
   6. Non-standard and Non-Russellian? 166
   7. Kind and the Structure and Dynamics Argument 167
   8. Dualism 2.0 and the Conceivability Argument 169
   9. The Mathematics Analogy 170
   10. Reconsidering the Space of Options 171

Second Round of Replies   175

5. The Consciousness Slugathon: Reply to
   Daniel Stoljar's Reply   177
   AMY KIND

   Introduction 177
   1. The Non-Russellian Epistemic View 179
   2. Is Dualism Impossible to Believe? 186

6. Even More Seriously: Reply to Amy Kind's Reply   193
   DANIEL STOLJAR

   Introduction 193
   1. Details Don't Matter 194
   2. You're Not Done 196
   3. Burden of Proof 197
   4. Is Ignorance a Defense? 198

Suggested Further Readings 201
AMY KIND AND DANIEL STOLJAR

Glossary 203
References 209
Index 218

Acknowledgments

Amy Kind

Thanks first of all to Tyron Goldschmidt for inviting me to be a part of this excellent debate series and for his continuing editorial guidance. For discussion and helpful comments along the way, thanks to the members of the Virtual Philosophy of Mind and Language WIP. My writing was supported in part by a Research Incentivization Grant from the Gould Center for Humanistic Studies at Claremont McKenna College. I am grateful for their backing. Finally, thanks to Frank Jackson for his generous foreword and to Daniel Stoljar for the stimulating back-and-forth discussion in this debate. It's an honor to have him as an opponent.

Daniel Stoljar

I would like to thank the following for comments on previous drafts or discussions that led to improvements: Justin D'Ambrosio, Brian Garrett, Brian Hedden, Alan Hájek, Frank Jackson, Darryl Mathieson, Justin Mendelow, Hezki Symonds, and Shauna Winram. Thanks also to Tyron Goldschmidt for setting up this debate, to an anonymous referee for the press, to Frank Jackson (again) for contributing the foreword, and especially to Amy Kind for being such a great interlocutor.

Foreword

I won't try and summarize the debate between Amy Kind and Daniel Stoljar. They each do an outstanding job of telling us what they believe about consciousness, why they believe it, how their views relate to those to be found in the extensive literature on consciousness, and why they disagree with each other. What I will do is try and give a sense of what the debate is about and the nature of a key disagreement between them.

What happens when you stub your toe? One kind of answer requires no knowledge of the physical sciences, of, that is to say, physics, chemistry, neuroscience, biology, and so on. It is the kind of answer that people could have given in the Middle Ages, before the rise of modern science. It talks of the feeling of pain in one's toe, exactly where the pain is felt and whether or not it is throbbing, of a desire that the feeling cease, of one's tendency to nurse one's toe, and so on. Let's call it, the folk answer or account of what happens. It is the answer we can give simply by virtue of having sometimes stubbed our toe and having suitable words in a natural language, English as we will suppose. No recourse to anything we learn when we study one or another of the physical sciences is needed. Another kind of answer draws on what we learn from those sciences. It talks of how the brain responds to bodily damage in one's toe, of how certain nerve pathways enable this response and the electrical and chemical processes that go on in these pathways, of how the brain's response causes movements that lead to limb withdrawal, and so on. Let's call this answer, the physical answer or account of what happens. In much the same way, we can contrast the folk answer to what happens when we look at ripe lemons with the physical answer. The first will talk of the distinctive look that ripe lemons have that differentiates them from, for example, ripe tomatoes and the sky, how seeing something as yellow is different from seeing it as green or as red, how something's looking yellow makes it stand out from dark surroundings, and so on. The physical answer will talk about wavelengths of reflected light, the way these wavelengths are processed by our visual systems, and, in turn, our brains, of the differences between the wavelengths of the light reflected from ripe lemons as opposed to ripe tomatoes, and so on.

I insist—and here I am in full agreement with Kind and Stoljar—that both answers are correct. The issue on the table is whether or not the physical answer, when filled out in suitable detail and modified in the light of advances in the physical sciences—what's above is simply a sketch to remind the reader of the kind of answer we are talking about—in some sense subsumes the folk answer, as physicalists (materialists) maintain. Of course, the two answers are framed in different terms or vocabularies, but maybe the different terms in the physical answer are different ways of talking about the very same properties and states that figure in the folk answer. For we know that this kind of thing can happen. One answer about the nature of a gas is framed in terms of temperature, pressure, and volume. This is the kind of answer we are familiar with from weather forecasts and what happens when we pump up a bike tire, for example. Another kind of answer is framed in terms of the motion properties of the atoms and molecules that make up the gas. This is the answer that explains temperature, for example, in terms of mean molecular (or atomic) kinetic energy. The famous reduction of the thermodynamic theory of gases (the theory framed in terms of temperature, pressure, and volume) to the molecular kinetic theory (the theory framed in terms of the motion properties of the molecules that make up a gas and their causal powers) means that the latter subsumes the former. The view of those philosophers of mind who embrace physicalism is that the relation between the folk account of what happens when we stub our toes or look at ripe lemons and the physical account is another example where an account in one set of terms subsumes the account in a different set of terms. In particular, the properties and states that appear in the folk account of mental states like pain and having something look yellow are one and the same as those that appear in the account offered by the physical sciences. Physicalists of course allow, as they must, that there are many details in the physical account that need further investigation, but when that has happened, we will, they urge, have two different ways of talking about the very same phenomena. Despite their differences, Kind and Stoljar agree that this would be the wrong way to think of the relationship between the folk and the physical accounts. They agree that the physical account does not subsume the folk answer, but they think this for very different reasons.

Some of the mental states that figure in the folk answer—examples are being in pain, something's looking yellow to one, hearing the rumble of approaching thunder, and feeling a spider crawling up one's leg—have a distinctive phenomenology. They are among the states that philosophers often refer to as those for which there is something it is like to be in them. The contrast is with believing that it rained some time in the past, a mental state we are all in but one which lacks a distinctive feel. Kind holds that certain properties of the "what it is like" mental states, namely, the properties that give them their distinctive feel or phenomenology, are absent from the physical account. She is influenced by many considerations in holding this, but two are prominent: one modal and one epistemic. The modal consideration is that a person's physical nature—everything about them that appears in the physical answer—does not necessitate that they are conscious in the sense of having states with a phenomenology, that they itch, feel pain, have things look yellow to them, and so on. For it is possible for a creature to be exactly like me in all physical respects and yet feel nothing, that he be, as philosophers often put it, a zombie. But this means that my physical nature is distinct from my phenomenal conscious nature: I share the first with the zombie but not the second. Here the example of the reduction of the thermodynamic theory of gases to the molecular kinetic theory is instructive. Two gases being exactly alike in molecular kinetic terms and their attendant causal roles necessitate their being exactly alike in thermodynamic terms. It is not possible for two gases to be alike in molecular kinetic terms and their attendant roles and for one to be a "zombie" gas, a gas that has, for example, no temperature.

The epistemic consideration is that full knowledge of physical nature, including the physical nature of surroundings, does not enable one to deduce the nature of conscious, "what it is like" mental states. Someone—often called "Mary"—confined from birth to a black-and-white room, dressed in black-and-white clothes, with skin painted black and white, and so on, might, as a result of a wonderful library of black-and-white books in her room and lectures on the black-and-white television in her room, know everything there is to know about the physical nature of each of us and of the world we occupy. In particular, she might know which wavelengths trigger the word "green" in the mouths of those English speakers she observes on her black-and-white television, and the processes in their brains that are involved. Nevertheless, she would not know, it seems, what it is like to have something look green. Or consider people who are profoundly deaf. They might be—for all I know, some in fact are—experts on hearing in the sense that they know everything there is to know about how the brains of people who are not deaf process the physical nature of incoming sound waves and use that nature to, for example, turn their heads toward the source of a sound or utter a sentence like "That's middle C." All the same, it seems that these profoundly deaf people will not know what it is like to hear middle C or to hear thunder approaching. The phenomenological side of hearing is hidden from them. Again, the example of the reduction of the thermodynamic theory of gases to the molecular kinetic theory is instructive. It is plausible that enough information about the energy and motion properties of the atoms and molecules that make up a gas allows one to deduce its temperature, volume, and pressure.

Physicalists, of course, resist these arguments. Some deny the modal and epistemic claims the arguments use as premises. They may grant (as they should) the intuitive appeal of the claim that a zombie physical duplicate of me is possible, but insist that, when one looks at the matter more closely, one can see that a zombie physical duplicate of me is not in fact possible. Any physical duplicate of me *must* feel pain when they stub their toe, have things look green to them on occasion, and so on. Likewise, they insist that Mary can know what it is like to see something as being green and that the profoundly deaf experts on neuroscience can know what it is like to hear thunder approaching, despite granting the intuitive appeal of the claim that she and they cannot. Others grant the modal and epistemic claims—the validity of the intuitions—but deny that they support anti-physicalist conclusions. Kind tells us why she is unmoved by these replies.

Stoljar's reason for holding that the physical answer does not subsume the folk answer is, as I said, very different from Kind's. We talk above of the physical account as drawing on what we learn from physics, chemistry, biology, and so on, but maybe, suggests Stoljar (in much good company), what we learn from these sciences is seriously incomplete, not merely incomplete in one or another detail (something we can all agree about). One reason—there are others—for holding this draws on the fact that the account of what we and our world are like that comes from the physical sciences goes back, in one way or another, to interactions between the world and various measuring devices. Now it is reasonable to think that these interactions tell us a lot. We are not flirting with skepticism. But it is also reasonable to think that there might be a lot that they do not tell us and accordingly that there are many more properties than appear in the accounts these sciences give of what our world is like. This is what Stoljar holds. We might reasonably call these properties "physical." This is because the reason for believing in them does not come from considerations special to the topic of consciousness. The reason just sketched for believing in these extra properties made no mention of what it is like to feel pain or to hear thunder approaching, and the same is true for many of the other reasons that have been given for holding that the picture the physical sciences give of what our world is like is seriously incomplete. Now we have a pressing question: What happens to the debate over consciousness when we factor in the idea that there exist the extra properties that Stoljar, and others, believe in, the properties that are left out of the accounts of what our world is like that we find in the physical sciences, but are physical properties in the sense of not being special to conscious mental states, the mental states with a phenomenology?

Stoljar's thesis is that the debate over consciousness gets transformed in ways that allow one to avoid the problems he finds in the kind of dualism Kind favors and to be a sort of physicalist, a non-traditional sort. He points out, for example, that the modal argument against physicalism sketched earlier rests on the intuition that a physical duplicate of me that lacks consciousness, a zombie me, is possible. That intuition is, however, one about a physical duplicate of me in the sense of physical tied to the physical sciences. It is accordingly arguably irrelevant to the question of whether or not consciousness can be accounted for in physical terms in the wider sense of physical. Likewise, the epistemic argument against physicalism sketched earlier rests on the intuition that Mary's full physical knowledge does not allow her to infer what it is like to see something as green. But that intuition is one about what she can infer from full knowledge of the physical in the sense of physical tied to the physical sciences. It is accordingly arguably irrelevant to whether or not consciousness can be accounted for in physical terms in the wider sense of physical. We could make the same point about the example of profoundly deaf experts in neuroscience, who do not know what it is like to hear thunder approaching. Their expertise is in physical properties in the narrow sense tied to the physical sciences.

What then do Kind and Stoljar disagree about? Many things, obviously, and it would be foolish of me to offer a summary of their differences when you have, in the pages that follow, chapter and verse. But I hope I have said enough to allow us to identify one key difference. Kind can, and I take it she does, agree with Stoljar that considerations that have nothing especially to do with consciousness tell us that there are more properties than those that figure in the physical sciences. A key difference between them is over whether or not these additional properties can give an account of consciousness. If you think that they can, you can be a physicalist about consciousness—a non-traditional, Stoljar kind. If you think that they cannot, that the properties we need to explain consciousness are ones tied to consciousness as such, you are in Kind's camp.

Enough from me; you have a treat in store.

Frank Jackson
21 January 2022
Australian National University
frank.jackson@anu.edu.au

Opening Statements

Chapter 1

The Mind-Body Problem
Dualism Rebooted

Amy Kind

Contents

Introduction	3	3.2. The Color Scientist	25
1. The Mind-Body Problem	5	3.3. The Zombie	30
1.1. Dualism	7	4. Theories of Consciousness	35
1.2. Physicalism	11	4.1. Representationalism	36
2. The Consciousness Problem	13	4.2. Higher-Order Theory	42
		4.3. Russellian Monism	45
2.1. Phenomenal Consciousness	14	5. Dualism Rebooted	52
		5.1. The Irreducibility of the Phenomenal	53
2.2. The Problem	18		
3. Why Consciousness Escapes the Physicalist Net	23	5.2. What Science Does (and Doesn't) Tell Us	58
3.1. The Bat	23	5.3. The Way Ahead	61

Introduction

At the heart of philosophy of mind is the mind-body problem: a question about the nature of mind: What is the mind, and what is its relationship to brain and body (and, more generally, to the physical world)? And at the heart of the mind-body problem is the consciousness problem: a question about the nature of consciousness: What is consciousness, and what is its relationship to the brain and body (and, more generally, to the physical world)? This latter problem is a notoriously thorny one, as accounting for consciousness has proved a particularly difficult challenge for philosophers attempting to account for the nature of mind.

In this volume, Daniel Stoljar and I take up the consciousness problem and defend competing answers to this question. While he argues that consciousness should be understood as a physical phenomenon,

DOI: 10.4324/9780429324017-2

I argue that a physicalist framework cannot adequately capture the full reality of our conscious experience. Our every waking moment is infused with these experiences—with vivid sensations of color, tantalizing whiffs of odors, buzzing noises, melodious chimes, sharp pains, irritating itches, momentary bursts of joy, and pangs of agonizing disappointment. Consider the experience of seeing a field of wildflowers, of hearing the radar ringtone on your iPhone, of getting a papercut on your index finger, of bubbling with laughter after hearing the unexpected punchline of a joke, or of being suddenly overtaken by all-consuming anxiety. What kind of explanatory story could science possibly tell us about these? No matter how much we learn about a given neural process, for example, it seems that we still won't have explained how the process gives rise to *this* particular conscious experience—or why it gives rise to any conscious experience at all.

In this opening statement, I start by tackling several preliminaries. In Section 1, I provide a quick overview of the mind-body problem and discuss some of the answers that have been proposed. Though the discussion of this section is meant primarily to provide some important background to the debate being conducted in this book, it is not entirely even-handed (this is a debate, after all!). Rather, since dualism is the response to the mind-body problem that provides the basic framework for the account of consciousness I will be defending, it's this theory that gets the lion's share of my attention.

Having laid out the basics of the mind-body problem in Section 1, I turn in Section 2 to the problem of consciousness itself. Explicating this problem requires us to attend more closely to consciousness and what philosophers typically mean when they refer to this phenomenon. With these preliminaries covered, I turn in Section 3 to arguments that aim to show that consciousness cannot be captured within a physicalist framework. Importantly, these arguments focus on the qualitative nature of consciousness and what it is like to undergo conscious experience. It's largely because of this qualitative nature that physicalist accounts seem inadequate.

In Section 4, I take a closer look at some of the specific physicalist accounts of consciousness on offer. In particular, I look at two different theories: representationalism and the higher-order theory. As I suggest, both of the theories are inadequate. At the end of the section, I look at a different theory—Russellian monism—that aims to offer a new approach to accounting for consciousness, in particular, an approach that transcends the traditional dualism-physicalism divide. In diagnosing why it is unable to do so, we are led to a closer understanding of this divide and of what it means to reject the physicalist framework.

This last issue occupies my attention in the final section of this opening statement. Many philosophers have worried that rejecting the physicalist framework with respect to consciousness commits one to an anti-scientific stance. On their view, rejecting physicalism is tantamount to believing in ghosts, or fairy dust, or magic. As I will suggest, however, the claim that consciousness is not a physical thing does not commit one to the existence of spooky stuff. Rather, it should be seen as perfectly consistent with an adoption of a broadly naturalistic conception of the world and our place in it. I will thus lay out a rebooted version of dualism, what I call dualism 2.0, in an effort to show what it looks like to adopt this kind of view from the vantage point of the 21st century.

I. The Mind-Body Problem

Although philosophers have worried about the nature of the mind since at least the time of Plato, the French philosopher Rene Descartes is generally credited with bringing the mind-body problem to prominence in Western philosophy. In his 17th-century work, *Meditations on First Philosophy*, Descartes famously adopts a method of doubt in an effort to find his way to the truth. Having come to discover that much of what he took himself to know was actually false, Descartes concludes that he needs to set aside all of his previous beliefs—that he must "demolish everything completely and start again right from the foundations"—if he ever is going to be able to achieve secure and stable knowledge. To carry out this demolition project, he supposes that he is being deceived by an all-powerful Evil Demon, one that can fool him into thinking that external things exist. He thus falls into a deep chasm of doubt in which he can no longer be certain of the existence of external things—neither the fire that he seems to be sitting beside nor the chair that he seems to be sitting on. Indeed, he cannot even be certain of the existence of his own body. But just as he begins to worry that there is absolutely nothing that he can know with certainly, that perhaps he cannot even know that he himself exists, he hits upon a way to end the doubt. For even if there were an evil demon who was deliberately and constantly deceiving him, the fact that he is being deceived shows that he must exist. The very act of doubting his existence is an act of thinking, and in order for one to think, one must exist. This famous line of reasoning is often put as "I think, therefore I am" (or in Latin, as *cogito ergo sum*).

Of course, this does not show us anything about what the "I" is who is doing the thinking. But because the existence of the body can be called into doubt, while the existence of the "I" cannot be called into doubt, Descartes takes seriously the possibility that the "I" must be distinct from the body. As he goes on to argue, it is the nature of the body to be extended in space, while that does not seem to be the nature of the "I"—the nature of the "I," or what we can think of as the mind, is to think. Moreover, since Descartes believes that we can clearly and distinctly conceive of the mind as separate from the body, and as existing independently of it, he concludes that the mind and the body are different things. This view—that the mind and body are distinct substances—has come to be known as dualism (or Cartesian dualism, where "Cartesian" is the adjectival form of "Descartes"). In subsection 1.1, we will explore dualism in more detail. Having done so, we will turn in subsection 1.2 to physicalism, the main competitor to dualism as an answer to the mind-body problem.

The Mind-Body Problem: A Taxonomy

Theories offered in an attempt to solve the mind-body problem fall into two broad classes: **dualism** and **monism**. Dualism claims that there are two fundamentally different kinds of things in the world, those that are physical and those that are mental. In contrast, monism claims that there is only one fundamental kind of thing in the world. Monism thus comes in several varieties. According to **idealism**, everything that exists is immaterial/nonphysical. This position is often associated with George Berkeley, an 18th-century philosopher. It has largely fallen out of favor in the 20th and 21st centuries. According to the position once known as **materialism** but now more commonly known as **physicalism**, everything that exists is physical. A third kind of monism, **neutral monism**, claims that everything that exists arises from fundamental properties that are best characterized as neither physical nor nonphysical but rather as neutral between the two. Neutral monism is often associated with Bertrand Russell and is hence often referred to as Russellian monism.

1.1. Dualism

Above we ran through a quick overview of the reasoning that leads Descartes to the dualist view. But people often find Descartes' line of reasoning puzzling when they first encounter it. As it is a style of reasoning that will reappear when we turn to the issue of consciousness, it will be worth taking a more careful look. Doing so will also help us to better understand what exactly the dualist view amounts to.

Though Descartes begins the Meditations in a chasm of doubt, he is gradually able to restore many of his previous beliefs. By the Sixth Meditation, Descartes takes himself not only to be able to know with certainty that he exists but also to be able to know with certainty that God exists. Thus, when Descartes himself presents his primary argument for dualism in the Sixth Meditation, an argument that I'll call *the conceivability argument for dualism*, he takes himself to be entitled to rely on the existence of God in defense of some of the premises. As a general matter, however, it is best to avoid relying on controversial premises whenever one can help it. For this reason, we'll try to simplify things a bit and consider a secularized version of the argument. Though this version does not rely on the existence of God, it is otherwise very much in the spirit of Descartes' own argument. Proceeding this way also underscores the important point that a commitment to dualism does not require any particular religious or spiritual commitment. Dualism is completely compatible with both atheism and agnosticism, for example, and the arguments for it need not depend on any theological considerations.

Descartes' basic reasoning, once secularized, can be put in standard argument form as follows:

The Conceivability Argument for Dualism

1. Whatever is clearly and distinctly conceivable is possible.
2. I can clearly and distinctly conceive the mind existing without the body.
3. Thus, it is possible for the mind to exist without the body. [From 1,2]
4. If it is possible for A to exist without B, then A and B are distinct entities.
5. Thus, the mind and the body are distinct entities; that is, dualism is true. [From 3,4]

> **Philosophical Argumentation**
>
> An **argument** is a set of claims—called **premises**—put forth in defense of a further claim—called the **conclusion**. Sometimes an argument will draw sub-conclusions along the way toward establishing the main conclusion. When the argument is put in standard form, it is presented as a numbered list of claims. Arguments can be either **deductive** or **inductive**. Deductive arguments aim to guarantee the truth of the conclusion. Inductive arguments aim to make probable the truth of the conclusion. The arguments in standard form that we will consider in this statement are all deductive arguments.

Let's start with premise 1, a premise that plays a particularly significant role in the argument. Perhaps what's most important is to clarify the notion of *possibility* that's in play and to do that, we need to distinguish **physical possibility** from **logical possibility**. For something to be physically possible, it has to be compatible with the laws of physics. Right now I am sitting at my desk, but it would be physically possible for me to be sitting on the couch instead, or standing up, or lying down. One thing not physically possible would be for me to be floating, unaided, three feet above the ground. Even though the floating scenario would be physically impossible, there is nothing conceptually incoherent about it. It is logically possible. Now consider some other scenarios: a ball that is at once entirely green and entirely red, for example, or a bachelor who is married. These scenarios, unlike the floating scenario, are conceptually incoherent and thus logically impossible. When Descartes claims that scenarios that can be clearly and distinctly conceived are possible, he is making a claim about logical possibility, not physical possibility. We might reasonably worry that not just every stray thought that pops into our head should be enough for us to conclude that the scenario depicted by the thought is logically possible. Perhaps someone confused could think they're conceiving of a married bachelor or of a hexagon that has seven sides. But here's where the notions of clarity and distinctness come in. Premise 1 does not say that just any old thought is enough. Rather it has to be a conceiving that's *clear and distinct*. To draw on some apparatus developed by Brie Gertler in the course of offering a similar conceivability argument for dualism (see Gertler 2007), we might think of a clear and distinct conceiving as one that relies upon concepts that are *sufficiently comprehensive* so as to rule out confusion or misunderstanding.

What about premise 2? Can we clearly and distinctly conceive of the mind existing without the body? Certainly, there are lots and lots of fictional depictions of this scenario. Consider movies like *Transcendence*, in which the scientist Will Caster uploads his mind to the internet after he's been fatally poisoned. Or consider books like *Ready Player Two*, in which computer genius James Halliday develops software that enables users of the Oasis, a virtual reality system, to upload their minds to the system and leave their bodies behind. When we engage with these works of fiction, we do seem to be conceiving of the mind apart from the body, and, given the level of engagement that many readers and viewers have with these works, it seems reasonable to count these conceivings as clear and distinct.

With sub-conclusion 3 following directly from 1 and 2, this leaves us with only premise 4 to consider. This premise often strikes people as puzzling when they confront it for the first time. Why should the mere possibility of separate existence be enough to show that two entities are distinct? And of course, we can't as a general matter move from the claim that a given scenario is possible to the claim that it is actualized. The fact that it's possible for me to be floating three feet above the ground does not show that I'm actually floating three feet above the ground. What's important to note, however, is that the claim being made in premise 4 is slightly more subtle than that. Though it would be a mistake to move from a claim about how a thing possibly is to the claim that it's that very way in actuality, there are nonetheless certain facts about possibility that allow us to conclude certain other facts about how things are in actuality. For example, the fact that it's possible for a given material to stretch without breaking shows that the material actually has the property of elasticity, even if the material is not currently being stretched. In fact, this is really just a definitional matter. That's what it means for something to have the property of elasticity. Likewise, the fact that it's possible for two objects to exist apart shows that they are actually distinct items, even if the two items do not currently exist apart. This too is really just a definitional matter. It's what it means for two items to be distinct entities. Despite first appearances, then, premise 4 of the argument turns out to be an uncontroversial one.

Though our discussion of the Conceivability Argument should help to make it more plausible than it might have initially appeared, it's important to note that the argument can be subjected to criticism. Perhaps most importantly, the murkiness inherent in the notion of "clear and distinct conception" poses a deep threat to the argument's success (see Kind 2020, 26–31, for discussion). Fortunately, for our purposes here it's not necessary that we settle definitively on whether or not the argument works to establish dualism. Rather, I have spent time discussing it for two main reasons. First, as we move forward, it will be helpful for us to have before us at least a rough sense of what kinds of considerations might be used to motivate a dualist view of the mind. And second, it will also be helpful for us to have a sense of how considerations of conceivability play a role in philosophical debates. We will return to these kinds of considerations in Section 2.

In offering the Conceivability Argument, Descartes aimed to show that mind and body are distinct substances—entities capable of independent existence even if, in actuality, they exist together. (For this reason, his view is often referred to as substance dualism.) Moreover, he takes these two substances to have radically different natures: While the body is a material thing, extended in space, the mind is not. Importantly, however, many philosophers embrace dualism without embracing substance dualism. Rather, they offer a different form of dualism often referred to as property dualism. According to property dualists, while the only kinds of substances that exist are physical ones, some physical substances have non-physical, mental properties over and above their physical properties. For example, a human brain has many physical properties: it weighs approximately 1,200 grams; it contains approximately 86 billion neurons, it has two distinct hemispheres connected by a bundle of nerve fibers known as the corpus callosum, and so on. But a human brain also has many non-physical properties: it has beliefs, intentions, emotions, and so on. And, importantly, these non-physical properties cannot be reduced to physical properties; rather, they exist over and above the physical properties.

It's in virtue of this last claim that dualism can be best distinguished from its primary competing theory on the mind-body problem, namely, physicalism. In the following subsection, we will consider the basic principles underlying physicalism as well as some more specific versions of the view.

1.2. Physicalism

Though physicalists typically accept the existence of mental states like beliefs, intentions, emotions, and so on, they think these mental states are nothing over and above the physical.[1] Consider the version of physicalism known as the identity theory. On this theory, mental states are simply to be identified with brain states—so a mental state like happiness might be identified with the activation of a certain kind of nerve fiber while a mental state like pain might be identified with the activation of a different kind of nerve fiber. The problems with the identity theory have been much discussed. In particular, identity theorists cannot account for the possibility of mentality in beings with physical constitutions very different from ours, be they animals with very different kinds of brains, humans with inorganic neural implants, artificially intelligent systems, or even aliens.[2] But even physicalists who don't accept the claim of identification nonetheless think that mental states can be explained entirely in physical terms. One way to put this point is in terms of technical notion of supervenience. According to physicalists, mental states supervene on physical states; that is, there can be no mental difference without a corresponding physical difference.

Though I won't here review the arguments given in defense of physicalism, it's worth mentioning three different kinds of considerations that tend to get raised. First, physicalism is thought to gain support from considerations of simplicity. Other things equal, and when we have two theories that explain a certain phenomenon equally well, it seems that the simpler theory should be preferred. Given that dualism posits the existence of two fundamentally different kinds of things (or two fundamentally different kinds of properties) while physicalism posits the existence of only one fundamental

---

1. Not all physicalists accept the existence of mental states like beliefs, intentions, and so on. In particular, the version of physicalism known as eliminative materialism claims that once we develop a mature scientific theory of mind, we will see that notions such as belief prove to be outdated posits of an immature "folk" theory of mind. Just as we discarded many of the theoretical posits of other folk theories such as folk physics or folk biology once more mature versions of the theories were developed, so too should we discard the theoretical posits of folk psychology. As such, this theory aims not to reduce mental states to physical states but to eliminate them altogether. For development of eliminative materialism, see P.S. Churchland (1986) and P.M. Churchland (1981).
2. For an overview of the problems with the identity theory, see Kind (2018).

kind of thing, then even if both theories have equivalent explanatory adequacy, physicalism is often taken to win on grounds of simplicity. Second, physicalism is thought to gain support from considerations of the explanatory power of science and its past record of success. Often throughout our history we have encountered phenomena that appear so mysterious as to defy physical explanation. But time and time again, science has eventually provided such an explanation. Why, then, would we have any reason to believe that the mind would be the one exception? And third, physicalism is thought to gain support from considerations of causation. Mental states seem to cause all sorts of physical states—as when my intention to wave to a friend causes my arm to go up. But given that our scientific theories suggest that we can give a complete causal explanation of any physical event in completely physical terms, there seems to be no room for mental causes. The only way for them not to be entirely superfluous would be if they were the very same things as the physical causes, that is, if physicalism were true.

As traditionally construed, physicalism attempts to explain mental states in terms of facts about the physical structure of brain states. In the second half of the 20th century, a different approach became popular. Inspired by developments in computing and artificial intelligence, many philosophers began to advance a theory known as **functionalism**. On this view, mental states are not explicated in terms of their physical nature but rather in terms of their functional nature. In particular, a mental state is defined in terms of the functional role that it plays in the overall system, that is, in terms of its causal relationships to inputs, outputs, and other mental states. One of the key benefits of this sort of definition is that it allows the functionalist to embrace the **multiple realizability** of mental states. To understand multiple realizability, an analogy to computing systems proves helpful: Just as a software program can be instantiated by many different kinds of hardware, so too can the mind be instantiated by many different kinds of physical systems. If mental states are identified with particular kinds of neural structures, then aliens and artificial intelligences who don't have those neural structures can't have mental states. But if mental states are characterized functionally, then any system with the appropriate functional organization can be seen as having a mind. In this way, functionalism can avoid one of the key problems facing the identity theory.

Strictly speaking, functionalism is compatible with both dualism and physicalism. When states are functionally specified, the specifications do not make reference to any particular physical instantiations. Thus, it's at least possible that non-physical entities could exhibit the right type of functional organization necessary for mentality. That said, however, functionalists tend to be physicalists, and functionalism is often classified as a physicalist view rather than as an alternative to it. I will here follow this general practice. In particular, when I talk about the "physicalist framework" (or the "physicalist net") I mean to be including functionalism within that.

Many have thought that functionalism seems especially plausible for mental states like beliefs and desires, states that are often referred to as propositional attitudes (since they involve taking a particular attitude toward a given proposition). What is it to have a belief other than to respond in a certain way to certain inputs? But functionalism has seemed considerably less plausible when it comes to other kinds of mental states and, in particular, the ones that have a qualitative character, that are conscious. Experiencing the emotion of happiness or a pain in your toe seems to involve something more than just inputs and outputs. In particular, it seems to involve a certain *feel*. This brings us directly to the problem of consciousness, to which I will now turn.

> In this section, I discussed the mind-body problem. This problem, which concerns the nature of the mind and its relation to brain and body, is at the center of philosophy of mind. I then turned to the two main theories offered in attempts to solve this problem: dualism and physicalism. The discussion of dualism outlined its key claims. I also laid out the theory's historical origins in Descartes and discussed some of the reasons that he offered in support of the view. The discussion of physicalism outlined its key claims and distinguished several different versions of the theories. I also briefly discussed some of the reasons usually offered to support physicalism. With this background framework in place, in the next section, I turn directly to the problem of consciousness that will occupy our attention in this debate.

2. The Consciousness Problem

Before we can talk about why consciousness might be thought to raise a special problem in accounting for the nature of mind, we need to get clear on the phenomenon we mean to be picking out by the term "consciousness." As Ned Block has put it, the concept of consciousness is a "mongrel" one (Block 1995, 227); unfortunately, the term is used to pick out several different aspects of mentality. Even worse, because these aspects are often connected to one another in various ways, it turns out to be surprisingly tricky to home in on the sense of consciousness that raises the problem of interest to us in this debate. Doing so will be the principal task of Section 2.1. Once we have pinpointed the notion of consciousness that is the subject of this debate, we will be better positioned to take up the problem of consciousness. This will be the principal task of Section 2.2.

2.1. Phenomenal Consciousness

Let's start by clearing away the senses that will not be relevant to us. Sometimes we use the terms "conscious" and "unconscious" in connection with wakefulness. When someone is in a coma, they are said to be unconscious, and when they emerge from their coma, they are said to return to consciousness. We often talk this way about sleep as well as about comas, particularly when someone is deeply asleep (or "dead to the world"). In contrast, sometimes we use the terms "conscious" and "unconscious" in connection with awareness. When someone is aware of something, they are said to be conscious of it; when it is outside of their awareness, it's something of which they are not conscious. When the 1960s feminists engaged in consciousness raising, for example, they were trying to bring awareness to their cause. Talk of the unconscious mind—or the Freudian unconsciousness—seems also to relate to the awareness sense of consciousness. Yet another sense of consciousness is that which Block has called *access consciousness*. When something is conscious in this sense, it is available for use in reasoning and in guiding action. Finally, we also often talk of self-consciousness, the sense that one has of oneself and the related ability to reflect on one's self.[3]

There are various ways in which these different senses of consciousness seem to be related to one another. Consider the wakefulness and awareness senses of consciousness, for example. When you're in a coma (and thus unconscious in the wakeful sense), you're

---

3. For related discussion of different senses of consciousness, see Chalmers (1996, 26–27).

largely unaware of your surroundings (and thus unconscious in the awareness sense). That said, there are many times when you're not in a coma and fully awake (so conscious in the wakeful sense) and yet there are things to which you're oblivious (so not conscious in the awareness sense)—as when you fail to notice that you have spinach stuck in your teeth or that you've accidentally put on one blue sock and one black sock. So while these two senses are related to one another, they are nonetheless different senses of consciousness. Likewise, access consciousness also seems different from either of these other two senses. For example, there may be mental items that escape our awareness but yet are still poised for use in reasoning or guiding action, that is, that are access conscious despite being unconscious in the awareness sense. Although the nature of implicit bias is not yet fully understood, it seems plausible that some of our implicit biases may fall into this category. Consider George Yancy's "elevator example," in which a white woman clutches her purse nearer to her when he, a black man, enters the elevator—even though he is wearing a suit (Yancy 2008, 846). The woman may not be aware that she harbors a fear of black men, yet it still seems to guide her behavior.

None of the senses of consciousness thus far identified picks out the sense of consciousness that is relevant for our discussion here. Following David Chalmers, one might group all these senses of consciousness together as forms of psychological consciousness (Chalmers 1996, 26). All of these senses are functional notions, notions that are specifiable in terms of the overall organization of a system, its relationship to environmental stimuli, and behavioral outputs. In contrast, we will be focusing on what philosophers often refer to as phenomenal consciousness. In this sense, a state is conscious when there is something that it is like to experience it. Consider the experience you have when you take a bite of chocolate souffle and you taste that rich chocolatey gooeyness in the center. Or consider the experience you have when your most hated rival wins an award that you had been competing for and you are overcome by an intense pang of jealousy. There is something that it is like to taste that chocolate, and there is something that it is like to be overcome by jealousy. It might be hard, perhaps even impossible, to articulate exactly what it's like. But when a mental state has this kind of distinctive feel, this qualitative aspect, it's said to be phenomenally conscious. Philosophers often refer to these qualitative aspects as *qualia*. The problem of consciousness that we're interested in might also be thought of as the problem of qualia.

> **Qualia**
>
> The term "**qualia**" was first used in its contemporary sense by C.I. Lewis in the early 20th century. "Qualia" is a plural term; the singular form is "quale" (pronounced "kwol-ay"). As Lewis used the term, qualia were claimed to be properties of sense-data, mind-dependent objects that we are aware of when having a perceptual experience. For example, when you see a Gala apple, the sense-data theorist would say that you have an image of the Gala apple, and this image is the sense-datum. Among the sense-datum's qualia are its properties of redness and roundness. On sense-data theory, we have direct experience of our sense-data and only indirect experience of worldly objects like apples. This theory has largely fallen out of favor; almost no one in the 21st century accepts the existence of sense-data. However, the notion of "qualia" has been retained, and, in contemporary usage, it has been broadened to refer more generally to properties of experience—so, for example, it refers to the redness you experience when you see a Gala apple. Traditionally, qualia have been characterized as intrinsic features of experience that are available to introspection. They are often also characterized as ineffable or, at least, nearly ineffable; it is thought to be impossible (or nearly impossible) to fully capture a particular quale via a verbal description.

Many different kinds of mental states are phenomenally conscious. Just as there is something it is like to taste the chocolate souffle, there is also something it is like to smell a skunk's spray, to see a beautiful sunset, or to hear the shrill blaring of your alarm. As this suggests, perceptions are phenomenally conscious states. This claim, however, requires one important clarification: While *perceptions* are phenomenally conscious, we shouldn't conclude that all of the states involved in perceptual processing are phenomenally conscious. Consider vision, for example. In recent years, based largely on work by vision scientists Melvyn Goodale and David Milner, it has become common in neuroscientific discussions to distinguish two different streams of visual processing: the ventral stream, which is often referred to as *vision for perception*, and the dorsal stream, which is often referred to as *vision for action* (Goodale and Miler 1992). As Goodale notes, the processing in the ventral stream accounts for "the rich and detailed visual representations of the world that allow us to identify objects and events, attach meaning and significance to them and establish their causal relations" (Goodale 2014, 2). In contrast, the processing in the dorsal stream accounts for "the real-time control of action, transforming moment-to-moment information about the location and disposition of objects into the coordinate frames of the effectors being used to perform the action" (Goodale 2014, 2). Unlike ventral stream processing, much of the dorsal stream processing does not rise to the level of conscious awareness and is not phenomenally conscious. However, as Goodale notes, dorsal stream processing "does not generate visual percepts; it generates skilled actions" (Goodale 2014, 2). It's these *percepts*, or what I above called *perceptions*, that philosophers mean to be pointing to as phenomenally conscious states.

In addition to perceptions, bodily sensations provide another obvious example of phenomenally conscious states. There is something it is like to have a pain in your left toe or to have an itch between your shoulder blades that remains just out of reach. Other paradigmatic examples of phenomenally conscious states include emotions (as suggested by the above example of jealousy), hallucinations, dreams, and imaginings. The fact that dreams are phenomenally conscious also helps to underscore the difference between phenomenal consciousness and consciousness in the sense of wakefulness. One might be asleep, and thus unconscious in the wakefulness sense, and yet still be in a phenomenally conscious state in virtue of the fact that one is dreaming.

At this point, however, one might wonder whether *all* mental states are phenomenally conscious. Traditionally philosophers have treated phenomenally conscious states as a subset of mental states more broadly. Consider belief, as when someone believes that Sacramento is the capital of California. Is there something that it is like to have this belief? Does that state have a characteristic feel? Here I suspect there's a strong temptation to answer these questions in the negative. With respect to phenomenal consciousness, having a belief seems to be very different from having an itch or feeling a pang of jealousy.

Not everyone agrees. In recent years some philosophers have suggested that there is a distinctive kind of phenomenal feel—what they call *cognitive phenomenology*—that's possessed by states such as beliefs (or thoughts more generally). Though I'm personally not convinced by this claim, for our purposes here we need not settle the issue. If it turns out that more mental states are phenomenally conscious than has been traditionally thought, then that will just make the problem of consciousness even more pressing.

2.2. The Problem

So what is that problem? Having clarified the relevant notion of consciousness, we are now ready to tackle this question directly. As I noted at the start, the mind-body problem concerns the nature of mind. It is a broad question about our ability to account for mentality. The consciousness problem is considerably more specific, as it focuses on the nature of consciousness in particular. As such, it is a narrower question about our ability to account for consciousness. That said, many philosophers have taken this narrower issue to be at the heart of the broader one. As Thomas Nagel famously said, "Consciousness is what makes the mind-body problem really intractable" (Nagel 1974, 435).

To start to get a sense of the intractability of this problem, let's think a little bit about the brain. The brain is an incredibly complex organ. As we've noted, a typical brain is composed of 86 billion neurons with hundreds of billions of neural pathways connecting them. Yet even in light of this immense complexity, it is hard to see how it would manage to produce consciousness. After all, we see incredible intricacy and complexity all throughout nature. Spiderwebs have amazingly intricate designs, and the silk material of which they are made has been found to be stronger than Kevlar. We see incredibly complex fractal patterns in leaf capillaries and watershed tributaries. Spiky coccolithophores, algae that are only a few microns in diameter, construct limestone shells for themselves that are among the most elaborate structures found in nature. None of this immense complexity produces consciousness. What's so special about the brain? Why should this particular hunk of matter have anything to do with consciousness?

With each passing day, we gain more and more understanding of the brain. But even so, the prospects of answering this question seem dim. Scientists have long been trying to discover what is often referred to as the *neural correlates of consciousness*, "the minimum neural mechanisms sufficient for any one specific conscious percept"

(Koch et al. 2016). Some neuroscientists think these correlates can be found in the fronto-parietal network of the brain; others think they're in a posterior area of the brain. There is still considerable disagreement on the matter. But let's now suppose that one particular team of neuroscientists has a significant breakthrough. After years of searching for the neural correlates of consciousness, this particular team declares success, having identified a particular set of neural activations—call them N—as being sufficient for consciousness. On their proposal, whenever we have N, we have consciousness. The problem, however, is that it's hard to see exactly what we are to make of this discovery, that is, whether and how this discovery genuinely explains anything.

Interestingly, the very fact that the enterprise has been put in terms of finding neural *correlates* of consciousness helps to underscore the point. As a general matter, identifying a correlation can help us make important progress, but questions will nonetheless remain about how to explain the correlation.[4] Couldn't it be an accidental correlation? Couldn't it be due to a common cause? These same questions arise in the specific case of the correlation between consciousness and N. Identifying this neutral correlate would be important progress, but it doesn't succeed in answering the basic question before us: the question about the nature of phenomenal consciousness. N itself doesn't tell us that, and it can't itself provide an explanation for its correlation with phenomenal consciousness. Why couldn't N have occurred with a different kind of conscious experience, or perhaps even absent any conscious experience whatsoever? Whatever N is—whatever kind of neural activation it describes—it is hard to see why that particular kind of brain activity (or any brain activity, for that matter) would have to be correlated with the rich kind of phenomenal experience that we have.

It might help to consider this basic point in the context of a specific example of a phenomenally conscious experience, a color experience say. In fact, this is one area of neuroscience where there's already been great progress, and neuroscientists have already developed a fairly sophisticated understanding of the way that our brains process color. Suppose you're looking at an American goldfinch and have a yellow experience. When light hits an object such as the plumage of the goldfinch, some of that is reflected. It enters the

---

4. I will return to these points in Section 5.1.

optic system through the cornea, then impinges upon the retina where the photoreceptors (rods and cones) are activated, and a signal is sent along the optic nerve to the visual cortex of the brain. This signal is processed by the brain and then, depending on the strength of the signal and the information that it transmits about which photoreceptors were activated, the brain will interpret the experience as of a given color, in this case, as yellow. As impressive as this story sounds, however, it still seems to leave the basic question unanswered. And that would be true even if we were to take the whole process, or perhaps one isolated part of it, as the neural correlate of the phenomenal experience of yellow. Why, as a result of all this optic and neural processing, should there be the kind of rich and vibrant yellow experience that there is? Why not a red experience? Or perhaps even no experience at all?

The problem that we've been discussing is sometimes put by saying that, when it comes to consciousness, there is an *explanatory gap* (Levine 1983). The sophisticated story about vision that we get from neuroscience is one involving the functions of the optic and neural system. It is a story about information processing. The information processing story can get more and more sophisticated, but no matter how detailed it gets, it doesn't seem that it will be able to provide the kind of story that we are looking for, a story about phenomenal consciousness. It appears that there will always be a gap between these two types of stories.

More recently, Chalmers has captured this point by distinguishing two different kinds of problems about consciousness: easy and hard. Easy problems relate to psychological consciousness—problems such as providing accounts of attention or awareness. Granted, as Chalmers himself admits, "easy" may be something of a misnomer. Providing such accounts may be extremely difficult. Solving them may take decades, even centuries, of focused empirical investigation. But no matter how difficult they are, they still pale in comparison when it comes to the task of explaining phenomenal consciousness, that is, the hard problem of consciousness. With the easy problems, though we don't yet have an answer, we at least have a clear idea about how the path we might take to get to one. But with respect to the hard problem, we don't even have this. Chalmers' own description of the problem is as follows:

> It is undeniable that some organisms are subjects of experience. But the question of how it is that these systems are subjects of experience is perplexing. Why is it that when our cognitive systems

engage in visual and auditory information-processing, we have visual or auditory experience: the quality of deep blue, the sensation of middle C? How can we explain why there is something it is like to entertain a mental image, or to experience an emotion? It is widely agreed that experience arises from a physical basis, but we have no good explanation of why and how it so arises. Why should physical processing give rise to a rich inner life at all? It seems objectively unreasonable that it should, and yet it does.

(Chalmers 1995b, 201)

In a sense, acceptance of the hard problem amounts to an indictment of neuroscientific attempts to explain consciousness—and, more generally, to an indictment of physicalism. It's thus unsurprising that many physicalists have denied that there is any such problem. Patricia Churchland, a philosopher whose website has as its tagline "To understand the mind, we must understand the brain," has been a particularly vocal critic of the hard problem.[5] In her view, this problem is really a pseudo-problem; we only see it as a problem because we've been "hornswoggled" (her paper on the topic is called "The Hornswoggle Problem"). Philosophers such as Chalmers start with the fact that, at this point in time, we don't really understand much about consciousness. With this much Churchland agrees. But, she says, it is a mistake to move from that starting point to the conclusion that nothing science might do would ever deepen our understanding of consciousness or to the conclusion that consciousness can never be explained. As she argues,

> the mysteriousness of a problem is not a fact about the problem, it is not a metaphysical feature of the universe—it is an epistemological fact about us. It is about where we are in current science, it is about what we can and cannot understand, it is about what, given the rest of our understanding, we can and cannot imagine. It is not a property of the problem itself.
>
> (Churchland 1996, 406)

At the conclusion of her paper, she offers a helpful summary of her basic response: "when not much is known about a topic, don't take

---

5. Or at least, this was its tagline as of early 2022. See https://patriciachurchland.com/. Note also that *Neurophilosophy* (1986), the book in which she sets out her own account of mentality, has as its subtitle "Towards a Unified Science of the MindBrain."

terribly seriously someone else's heartfelt conviction about what problems are scientifically tractable. Learn the science, do the science, and see what happens" (Churchland 1996, 408). Her prediction? Given the progress that neuroscience has already made on a great variety of very challenging problems, we can reasonably expect it to make progress on the so-called "hard" problem as well.

On the one hand, Churchland seems to be onto something. At this point in time, neuroscience is still in a fairly early stage of development. So rather than making pronouncements now about the inadequacy of neuroscience, why wouldn't we simply wait until the neuroscientists do their work? But, on the other hand, the argument that Chalmers is making does not seem to require a wait-and-see approach. When you need to bring a cup of flour to a neighbor and I see that you're planning to transport it in a bag that has a gaping hole in the bottom, I don't need to wait to see whether your efforts will be successful. I can know in advance that they won't be. Likewise, if we can see that the apparatus that neuroscience is using to try to explain consciousness has a gaping hole in it, we don't need to wait to see whether its efforts will be successful.

In the next section, we will turn to various arguments that aim to show that this is indeed the kind of situation we're in with respect to neuroscience. When it comes to the problem of phenomenal consciousness, we have reason to believe that neuroscientific work cannot be successful, and we can reach that conclusion now, even before that work is completed. As these arguments aim to show, we have good reason to believe that phenomenal consciousness is not the kind of phenomenon that can be accounted for within a physicalist framework. Learning the science and doing the science won't be able to change that.

> This section took up the problem that frames the debate of this book: the problem of consciousness. I started by clarifying the kind of consciousness in question—what's known as *phenomenal consciousness*—and distinguishing it from other kinds of consciousness like awareness and awakeness. I also discussed which kinds of mental states are phenomenally conscious and which kinds are not. I then turned to clarifying what is meant by the problem of consciousness. To my mind, this is best understood as what David Chalmers has called *the hard problem*. I also began to discuss why this problem seems so hard, that is why it looks so difficult to give an adequate account of consciousness in physical terms. Developing this point will be the main task of the next section.

3. Why Consciousness Escapes the Physicalist Net

In what follows, we will focus on three different sets of considerations that have been offered in support of the claim that consciousness escapes the physicalist net. The first, which comes from Thomas Nagel, was developed in his 1974 paper, "What Is It Like to Be a Bat?" The second, a thought experiment developed by Frank Jackson, was first presented in his 1982 paper "Epiphenomenal Qualia." Finally, the third owes primarily to the work of David Chalmers (though similar ideas appeared earlier in the work of others) and was developed in detail in his 1996 book, *The Conscious Mind*.

3.1. The Bat

Each of us knows about our own consciousness from the inside—we can each tell that we're undergoing phenomenally conscious experiences by way of introspection. We can't know about each other's consciousness that way. To judge that a human being other than oneself is conscious, one typically relies on evidence of a different sort: first, the fact that they're of a similar physical constitution to oneself, and second, that they're exhibiting relevant and sophisticated behavior. Unless we're in the grips of deeply skeptical worries, this tends to be enough to go on. When I accidentally step on your toe, and you react by exclaiming "ouch," grimacing, and rubbing your toe, that's typically enough for me to judge that you're experiencing the phenomenally conscious state of pain.

Things are likewise when it comes to judgments about the consciousness of non-humans. In cases where a non-human creature seems to have a physical constitution at least somewhat similar to our own, and in cases where they exhibit relevantly sophisticated behavior, we can reasonably judge that a non-human animal is in a phenomenally conscious state. When I accidentally step on my dog's paw, for example, and she reacts by pulling the paw away, whining, licking it, and so on, that's typically enough for me to judge that she's in pain. Perhaps we can make these judgments when we see the creature produce relevantly sophisticated behavior even when their physical constitution is pretty different from our own—an octopus, say, or a raven. (Presumably this is all that an alien species would have to go on in making judgments about us, were such a species to encounter human beings.) Of course, there might be cases in which we simply don't know what to say. Is a shrimp phenomenally conscious? What about a snake? But certainly when the creature has a physical constitution that's particularly close to ours in virtue of their being a mammal, it seems immensely plausible to consider them to be phenomenally conscious creatures.

So now consider one particular non-human animal: the bat. Bats are mammals, and as such, it seems plausible that they're phenomenally conscious. There is something it is like to be a bat. But, interestingly, the way that bats navigate the world is very different from the way that humans navigate the world. While we use sight, they use echolocation. And in fact, echolocatory experience is entirely foreign to us. According to Nagel, we can't experience anything like it, and we can't even imagine anything like it: "Bat sonar, though clearly a form of perception, is not similar in operation to any sense that we possess, and there is no reason to suppose that it is subjectively like anything that we can experience or imagine" (Nagel 1974, 168). Thus, even though it seems clear that bats have phenomenally conscious experience, we can't understand what that experience is like. In short, we can't know what it is like to be a bat.

These reflections on bats lead Nagel to draw a conclusion about the inadequacy of the physicalist framework when it comes to phenomenal consciousness. Consciousness is a subjective phenomenon. It can only be understood from within a subjective framework. Physicalism, like all scientific theories, employs an objective framework. As such, consciousness seems to escape the physicalist net.

We can formalize this reasoning roughly as follows:

The Bat Argument

1. There is something that it is like to be a bat engaging in echolocation.
2. We cannot experience or imagine what it is like to be a bat engaging in echolocation.
3. If we cannot experience or imagine the bat's experience, that experience must be essentially subjective.
4. Thus, the bat experience is essentially subjective.
5. There is nothing special about the bat experience.
6. Thus, experiences in general are essentially subjective.
7. Physicalism takes the objective point of view.
8. One cannot capture subjective facts from the objective point of view.
9. Thus, there are some facts about experience that cannot be captured by physicalism.

In offering his argument, Nagel leaves open the possibility that we might one day develop a vocabulary that allows us to bridge the gap between objective and the subjective perspectives (a gap that should seem reminiscent of the explanatory gap we discussed in the previous section). But he seems skeptical that this can be done. There seems to be good reason to be skeptical in this regard. Many philosophers have found the sorts of considerations raised by Nagel's discussion of the bat to be extremely compelling and thereby to pose a significant challenge to attempts to account for consciousness in physical terms.

Perhaps there are some reasons to worry about Nagel's particular choice of example here. In particular, we might worry that echolocation is not as alien to human experience as he would have us believe. People who are blind often draw upon capacities that seem remarkably like echolocation to make their way in the world, and via training, they can become quite good at it. Furthermore, the advent of virtual reality systems opens up all sorts of possibilities for humans to have batlike experiences. But even though these worries have some bite, they don't really undermine Nagel's basic point; that is, they do nothing to challenge the claim that experience is essentially subjective. In fact, insofar as they seem to presuppose that one can only understand an experience by having it one's self, these worries might even be said to add further support for this claim. So even if it turns out that Nagel was mistaken to think that humans could not know what it is like to be a bat, there is no reason to think that he was mistaken about the fact that experience is fundamentally subjective in nature. The considerations raised by Nagel thus offer us a persuasive reason to worry about physicalism.

3.2. The Color Scientist

The second set of considerations is based on a thought experiment developed by Frank Jackson (1982). In order to conduct a thought experiment, one doesn't need any beakers or Bunsen burners and one doesn't need a laboratory. It's the kind of experiment that one can conduct from one's armchair simply by exercising one's imagination. In essence, a thought experiment proceeds by describing a hypothetical scenario, the contemplation of which yields some important insight into a philosophical matter under consideration. Sometimes it provides a counterexample to a theory that we're considering or shows us that the theory has a hidden inconsistency.

Sometimes it reveals something we hadn't previously realized about a phenomenon under consideration, or perhaps it reveals a constraint on any acceptable theory offered to explain the phenomenon. The use of thought experiments is common not only in philosophy of mind but also in philosophy more generally. As we'll see, the third set of considerations we will consider in this section, those developed by Chalmers, will also involve a thought experiment.

Jackson's thought experiment revolves around a character he calls Mary, a color scientist who lives and works at some point in the future when neuroscience and color science have developed significantly; in fact, they've developed to the point of completion. But Mary is in a very special situation. Since birth, she's been kept in a black-and-white room, and she's never had any experiences of color. To ensure this, not only is everything in the room black and white but she's also always worn black-and-white clothing (including gloves), and she's never been permitted to catch sight of herself in a mirror or any reflective surface. Nonetheless, Mary has been provided with textbooks and a computer (with black-and-white monitor) while in the room, and by way of careful and diligent study, she has learned everything that science has to say about color and color experience. She knows about rods and cones and about how color experience is processed in the brain, she knows about color's reflectance properties, she knows about the relative similarities and differences among the colors, and so on. We can describe her knowledge by saying that she knows the totality of physical facts about color and color experience.

We're then asked to imagine the following: One day, Mary is let out of the black-and-white room and sees a ripe tomato for the first time. How will Mary react? When considering this scenario, most people conclude that she will have a kind of "Eureka!" moment. Though she knows all of the physical facts about the color red, it nonetheless seems obvious to most people considering the thought experiment that she learns something upon seeing red for the first time. "Aha!," she might say. "So that's what it's like to see red!" In this way, the thought experiment suggests that the physical story about color experience is incomplete. Color experience, and phenomenally conscious experience more generally, cannot be fully explicated in physical terms.

It should be immediately apparent that Jackson's argument—often referred to as the *Knowledge Argument*—bears a lot of similarity to Nagel's argument. But the reasoning proceeds slightly differently, as becomes clear once we look at the argument in standard form.

The Knowledge Argument

1. While in the room, Mary has acquired all the physical facts, there are about color sensations, including the sensation of seeing red.
2. When Mary exits the room and sees a ripe red tomato, she learns a new fact about the sensation of seeing red, namely what seeing red it is like.
3. Therefore, there are non-physical facts about color sensations. [From 1,2]
4. If there are non-physical facts about color sensations, then color sensations are non-physical events.
5. Therefore, color sensations are non-physical events. [From 3,4]
6. If color sensations are non-physical events, then physicalism is false.
7. Therefore, physicalism is false. [From 5,6]

Interestingly, most philosophers—even most physicalists—agree with Jackson that Mary has a Eureka moment upon exiting the room and seeing color for the first time (for a notable exception, see Dennett 1991). It seems hard to deny that she learns something new. But there are still several avenues of response available to the physicalist. Perhaps the most common responses try to deny that what Mary learns when she exits the room is a new fact, thereby rejecting premise 2. This kind of denial takes several different forms. I'll here briefly mention three of them.

First, some physicalists offer what's known as the *ability hypothesis*. On this hypothesis, associated primarily with David Lewis (1988) and Laurence Nemirow (1990), though Mary learns something when she leaves the room, her new knowledge does not consist in factual knowledge but rather in the acquisition of a new ability. Factual knowledge can be thought of as knowledge-that. Were Mary to come to have new factual knowledge, she would come to know that such and such is the case. But ability knowledge is best understood as know-how. Moreover, know-how need not consist entirely in facts. Just as knowing how to juggle amounts to more than just knowing a collection of facts, proponents of the ability hypothesis argue that knowing what a color is like amounts to more than just knowing a collection of facts. Rather it involves various abilities, such as the ability to imagine what the color is like, to remember what the color is like, or to recognize what the color is like.

Initially, it may seem that the ability hypothesis is successful in refuting Jackson's argument. After all, it does seem true, perhaps even obviously so, that knowledge of what an experience is like goes hand in hand with the abilities just listed. The problem, however, is that we can easily come up with cases in which these two things do not go hand in hand. Consider someone with a rare neurological condition that renders them incapable of forming new memories. Though they do not have the ability to remember what seeing red is like, it still seems plausible that they can know what seeing red is like. Certainly in the very moment of seeing red, at least, they have this knowledge. We can make a similar point about someone with a recognitional deficit or a deficit of imagination. Thus, even if knowledge of what's it like normally goes hand in hand with these abilities, the fact that we can have this knowledge without having these abilities shows that we cannot analyze the former in terms of the latter. The ability hypothesis fails.

So let's turn to the second kind of response often offered to the knowledge argument, what's known as the *acquaintance hypothesis* (see, for example, Conee 1985). Like proponents of the ability hypothesis, proponents of this hypothesis also deny premise 2. But while they agree that Mary's new knowledge is non-factual in nature, they deny that it consists in the acquisition of new abilities; rather, they suggest that it can best be understood as coming to be acquainted with something. Just as you might know all the facts there are about Catalina Island in virtue of having read guidebooks and seen pictures and maps, it's only when you go to Catalina Island for the first time that you become acquainted with it. Likewise, it's only when Mary sees red for the first time that she becomes acquainted with it.

Intuitively speaking, there's something very plausible about the acquaintance hypothesis. In particular, it seems to pinpoint exactly what changes for Mary when she exits the room. The problem, however, is that it's not clear why this kind of change should matter in the way that it needs to in order to rebut the Knowledge Argument. If Mary really did have all the facts about the experience of seeing red even before leaving the room, it's not clear why becoming acquainted with the color would provide her with the kind of "Eureka" moment that she seems to have. Armed with the entirety of facts about something, there's no reason to think that adding in the experience of becoming acquainted with it should be particularly enlightening. Insofar that we think that acquaintance adds something or teaches us something, then it seems that we are back to where we started: There are some facts about the experience of seeing red that Mary did not have while she was in the room, facts that she can gain only upon exiting it.

That brings us to the third response to the Knowledge Argument, what's often referred to as *the old fact/new guise hypothesis* (see, for example, Horgan 1984). Though proponents of this hypothesis also reject premise 2 of the above argument, they do so for a different reason than proponents of the other two hypotheses we have considered. In particular, proponents of the old fact/new guise hypothesis do not deny that Mary's knowledge of what red is like is factual knowledge. Instead, they deny that this knowledge consists in learning a *new* fact. According to this hypothesis, what happens when Mary sees red for the first time is that she comes to appreciate an old fact in a new way. Consider these two claims: "The roly-poly has seven sets of legs" and "The *Armadillidium vulgare* has seven sets of legs." Since "roly-poly" and "*Armadillidium vulgare*" are different names for the same creature, these claims both express the same fact, that a certain type of animal has seven sets of legs, though they express that fact in two different ways. If you already knew that the roly-poly has seven sets of legs then were you to learn that the *Armadillidium vulgare* has seven sets of legs, you wouldn't be learning a new fact. You would simply come to have a new way to apprehend a fact about this terrestrial crustacean that you already knew. Likewise, proponents of the old fact/new guise hypothesis say that when Mary comes to know that seeing red is like *this*, she simply comes to have a new way of apprehending a fact about red that she already knew.

This hypothesis too seems unsuccessful. We can bring out the problem by way of a simple dilemma: Either the guise in question was available to Mary inside the room or it was not. If it was, then that means that it was part of the physical story about color. But then that means that we initially weren't really imagining what we were really being asked to imagine, that is, that Mary knew the entire physical story about color before leaving the room. We should then reconsider the case and specifically imagine that Mary accesses this guise before leaving the room. Once we do so, there should be no "Aha" moment. Unsurprisingly, this seems as implausible as it did initially. Whatever Mary can have while she's in the room, including the guise in question, does not seem to be enough. That suggests that we should take the other horn of the dilemma and deny that the guise in question is not available to Mary while she was in the room. What that means, however, is that the guise in question is not part of the full physical story about color. Perhaps it's not quite right to call it a fact, but it still amounts to an important way in which the physical story of color is incomplete. The Mary case thus still seems to pose an important problem for physicalism.

Though each of these three hypotheses has some initial plausibility, I do not think that any of them are ultimately successful in defending physicalism against Jackson's critique. As with the Bat Argument, the Knowledge Argument presents us with a compelling reason to think that physicalism cannot adequately account for consciousness.

3.3. The Zombie

The third set of considerations often raised to show that consciousness escapes the physicalist net also relies on a thought experiment. In this case, what we're asked to imagine is a zombie. But unlike the zombies of horror movies, this zombie is not out to eat your flesh. Rather, it is exactly like an ordinary human being, with one exception: it lacks phenomenal consciousness altogether.

To get a handle on this, it may help to consider your zombie twin. Zombie-You is physically identical to you, all the way down to the molecular level, and behaviorally identical to you as well. Just like you'll say "yum" when you bit into a peach, so too will Zombie-You. But while you'll be having a sweet-juicy-peach gustatorial experience, Zombie-You won't be. They won't be having any gustatorial experience. And just like you'll exclaim "ouch" when you step on a stray Lego left on the floor, so too will Zombie-You. But while you'll be having a painful sensation in your foot, Zombie-You won't be. They won't be having any sensations. Zombie-You lacks phenomenal experience altogether. We can put this metaphorically by noting that for Zombie-You, it's all dark inside.

Is the zombie scenario coherent? Can you imagine it as specified? If so, then we have a further reason to reject physicalism. We can summarize the reasoning in standard form as follows:

The Zombie Argument

1. Zombies, creatures that are microphysically identical to conscious beings but that lack consciousness entirely, are conceivable.

2. If zombies are conceivable then they are possible.
3. Therefore, zombies are possible. [From 1,2]
4. If zombies are possible, then consciousness is non-physical.
5. Therefore, consciousness is non-physical. [From 3,4]

Although as stated the Zombie Argument comes from the work of David Chalmers (see especially 1996, 94–99), similar considerations have also been raised by other philosophers. To give just one example, Ned Block raises a related scenario often referred to as *the homunculi-headed robot* in the context of arguing against functionalism (Block 1978). This species of argument, in which we're presented with two systems that are identical functionally and/or physically but where one has phenomenal consciousness and the other does not, can be characterized more generally as an Absent Qualia argument. Arguments have also been developed in which we're presented with two systems that are identical functionally and/or physically, but where one system's phenomenal consciousness is inverted relative to the other's; for example, one system has a red experience in the situation where the other system has a green experience. This kind of argument, which seems to be found as early as the 17th century in the work of John Locke (1689), is usually referred to as the Inverted Qualia argument. To keep things simple, however, we will here confine our attention to the Zombie Argument.

Structurally speaking, the Zombie Argument has a lot in common with the Conceivability Argument that we considered in Section 2. The Zombie Argument takes the conceivability of a certain scenario to show the possibility of that scenario, and then it takes that possibility to show us something about the nature of consciousness. As was the case with the Conceivability Argument, the relevant sense of possibility here is logical possibility. It might be that zombies are not possible given the laws of physics; the argument does not take a stance on that question. Rather, in claiming that zombies are possible, the argument affirms simply that there is no logical contradiction or conceptual incoherence inherent in the notion.

Most of the action of the argument takes place in the very first premise. But before we turn to the issue of whether zombies are really conceivable, it's worth pausing for a moment to discuss why their possibility would entail that consciousness is non-physical. Why is this mere possibility enough? To answer this question, it may be helpful to consider an analogy. Consider two line segments.

The line segments do not intersect. But is it possible for them to intersect? If they were each extended, would they intersect? Suppose the answer to these questions is yes. From this fact, from this possibility of intersection, we can conclude that the line segments are not parallel. We don't need actual intersection to draw this conclusion; the mere possibility is enough. Something similar applies in the debate about consciousness. We don't need to show that anyone is actually a zombie. The mere possibility is enough.

We can now focus our attention on the first premise. Are zombies conceivable? Someone inclined to reject the first premise will probably grant that many people think they are conceiving of zombies, but such people have misidentified what they are really conceiving. To put the point in the terms used by Descartes, our conceiving may not be clear and distinct, as our concept of zombie is not a sufficiently comprehensive one. So perhaps someone who thinks they are conceiving their zombie twin is not really conceiving of something that is microphysically identical to them. Rather, what they've conceived is a creature who is simply extremely physically similar to them. In offering this diagnosis of what's gone wrong with the conceiving, the opponent of the Zombie Argument might point to the fact that our conceiving is a very broad-based one that doesn't go into the microphysical details with any specificity. When someone claims to conceive of their zombie twin, for example, they certainly haven't clearly conceived each of the 86 billion or so neurons in the zombie's brain.

This gives just one reason the opponent might offer to discount the first premise of the Zombie Argument. But one might think of various other ways that the situation that we claim to be conceiving has been misdescribed. Daniel Dennett, a staunch opponent of the zombie argument, summarizes this basic line of criticism as follows:

> Supposing that by an act of stipulative imagination you can remove consciousness while leaving all cognitive systems intact—a quite standard but entirely bogus feat of imagination—is like supposing that by an act of stipulative imagination, you can remove health while leaving all bodily functions and powers intact. If you think you can imagine this, it's only because you are confusedly imagining some health-module that might or might not be present in a body. Health isn't that sort of thing, and neither is consciousness.
>
> (Dennett 1995, 325)

In addressing these criticisms, we might note that the opponent of the Zombie Argument has not done enough to establish their claims. If someone wants to deny that zombies are conceivable, it doesn't seem to be enough for them simply to note that there might be a hidden conceptual confusion lurking somewhere in the background. Rather, it seems that they owe us some sense of what the conceptual confusion is.

But even if this response fails, there are things that one can do to show how and why zombies are conceivable. For example, one might try to show how one can conceive of the zombie scenario by building up from simpler scenarios—in the way that we might show that a mile-high unicycle is possible by first considering a 10-foot-tall unicycle, and then a 20-foot-tall unicycle, and so on (see Chalmers 1996, 96–97). Let's try to spell out how this might go in the zombie scenario. One source of resistance to the conceivability of this scenario might lie in worries about how a non-conscious creature is able to produce the sort of complex and subtle behavior produced by conscious humans. To address this concern, one might recommend proceeding in the following stepwise fashion: First, try to conceive of a human who is fully phenomenally conscious but who is an excellent actor. So they can behave exactly like they are having a phenomenal conscious experience of pain even when they are in a completely pain-free state. Now suppose that we somehow take away their ability to feel pain (they can still experience other phenomenally conscious states, but not pain). In taking away their ability to feel pain, we haven't affected their acting ability, so they are still able to behave exactly like they're in pain. We now have a partial zombie (a zombie with respect to pain). Now let's go through the same steps with respect to tickles and then with itches. And so on. With each step, the creature becomes more and more zombified, and eventually we get to a creature who is a full-on zombie. Insofar as each step seems relatively unproblematic, it's hard to see where a lack of conceivability would creep in.

In a sense, this strategy works by providing a sort of instruction manual, a how-to guide to conceiving zombies. This is not the only how-to guide that we could adopt. One might instead try to counter the resistance to premise 1 by providing an analogy to sophisticated robots. Many people find it relatively easy to conceive of human-like robots that are wholly mechanical rather than organic. Certainly there are many such robots depicted in science fiction—from Andrew, the artificial life form depicted in Isaac Asimov's novella *Bicentennial Man*, to the Life-Model Decoys of *Agents of S.H.I.E.L.D.*, to the hosts of *Westworld*. Many people also find it easy to conceive of such robots as engaging in complex and subtle behavior—behavior that is so complex and subtle that we may even be fooled into thinking that the robot was human. But such people often have trouble conceiving of the mechanical robot as having phenomenal consciousness. Sure, the robot can behave as if it is in pain, but it doesn't really feel the ouchiness; sure, it can behave as if it is in love, but it doesn't really feel the pull on its mechanical heartstrings. If complex and subtle behavior can come apart from phenomenal consciousness in the robot case, then it helps to show that it could come apart from phenomenal consciousness in the zombie case. Just as there isn't any conceptual incoherence in the robot case, there shouldn't be any conceptual incoherence in the zombie case.

> This section focused on three different sets of considerations that aim to show why it does not seem possible to explain phenomenal consciousness in physical terms. The first set of considerations concerned Nagel's bat case. The fact that it does not seem possible for a human to know what it is like for a bat shows that facts about consciousness are subjective ones. Given that physicalism is cast entirely in objective terms, it does not seem capable of capturing these facts. The second set of considerations concerned Jackson's case of the color scientist. Since someone might know all the physical facts of color without knowing what color sensations are like, it looks like the physical story about color sensations (and hence about phenomenal consciousness more generally) is incomplete. The third set of considerations concerned Chalmers' case of the zombie, a creature who is physically indistinguishable from a human being but who lacks phenomenal consciousness altogether. If you and your zombie twin are physically identical but are not the same with respect to phenomenal consciousness, then phenomenal consciousness cannot be reductively explained in physical terms. In taking up these three sets of considerations, we also discussed various objections that have been posed to them. Ultimately, however, none of the objections seems decisive. The case that phenomenal consciousness cannot be explained in physical terms is a very strong one.

4. Theories of Consciousness

The arguments discussed in Section 3 suggest that physicalist theories of consciousness are inadequate. Physicalism is unable to capture the phenomenal nature of mental states; that is, it is unable to solve the consciousness problem. The inadequacy is perhaps especially clear when considering the kinds of theories we briefly considered earlier, where mental states are identified with or directly reduced to physical or functional states. One might naturally wonder whether more sophisticated physicalist theories could be more successful. As compelling as the arguments of Section 3 may be, the sense may still remain that the physicalist must have some way out, some way to capture consciousness within a physicalist framework. Moreover, insofar as the theories mentioned earlier were meant to be theories of mentality in general, as opposed to theories of consciousness in particular, one might reasonably expect that a philosophical theory would have more success in addressing the phenomenological considerations raised in Section 3 if it were to focus specifically on consciousness. In fact, several such theories have emerged over the last several decades. It will thus prove instructive to consider a couple of the most prominent of such theories. In Section 4.1, I will take up representationalism, and in Section 4.2, I will take up the higher-order theory. By showing their inadequacy, we will reinforce the moral of Section 3 that consciousness cannot be explained in physical terms. Finally, in Section 4.3, I will turn to a different theory that has become popular in recent years: Russellian monism. Unlike the other two theories considered, this theory is not a physicalist one: Rather, Russellian monism aims to offer an importantly new approach to accounting for consciousness and touts itself as transcending the traditional dualism-physicalism divide. As I will suggest, it is unable to do so. Importantly, however, our discussion of Russellian monism's attempt to transcend the dualist-physicalist divide leads us to a closer understanding of this divide and, correspondingly, of what it means to reject the physicalist framework. We will thus be in a good position to take up this issue directly in Section 5, the final section of this opening statement, where I aim to lay out how, from the vantage point of the early 21st century, one might think about consciousness from a dualist perspective.

> **Three Theories of Consciousness**
>
> In addition to the physicalist theories that we previously discussed, all of which were general theories of mentality, several theories have been offered to explain consciousness in particular. Among such theories, three of the most prominent include representationalism, higher-order theory, and Russellian monism. According to *representationalism*, we can explain why a given mental state has the phenomenal character that it does wholly in terms of the representational content of the state. According to *higher-order theory*, we can explain why a given mental state is conscious wholly in terms of the existence of an appropriate higher-order representation about that state. According to *Russellian monism*, we can explain why a given mental state is conscious wholly in terms of the existence of a class of fundamental properties; such properties are analogous to mass and charge but lie outside the domain of physics.

4.1. Representationalism

Our focus in this chapter has been on the phenomenal character of mental states. But in order to understand representationalism, we need to talk about another important feature of mental states, namely, their intentional content. Confusingly, the notion of intentionality has two very different senses when it comes to mentality. In the sense that matters for intentional content, the notion of intentionality doesn't have anything to do with intentions, with an action's being done on purpose. Rather, when philosophers speak of intentional content, we mean something like *representational content*. Intentionality in this sense is often characterized in terms of "aboutness" or "directedness." When a mental state has intentionality it is about, or directed at, a state of affairs. Consider, for example, my belief that the can of Diet Coke on the desk in front of me is empty. This belief is about a particular thing, a particular can of Diet Coke and, more specifically, about the particular state of affairs of that can being empty. Importantly, beliefs can have intentionality even when the thing they are about does not exist. For example, I might believe that there is a can of Raspberry Diet

Coke on the desk in front of me, even though there is no such thing as Raspberry Diet Coke (and thankfully so—though who knows what the marketing geniuses at Coca-Cola will come up with next). Also importantly, beliefs are not the only kind of mental state that has intentionality. My desire for a can of Diet Coke, my hope that there are more cans of Diet Cokes in the refrigerator, and my happiness that my son just brought one to me even without my asking him to, are also all intentional states.

As these examples suggest, some states have intentional content even though they don't have phenomenal character (as in the case of beliefs and desires), while some states have both intentional content and phenomenal character (as in the case of emotions like happiness). Are there also states that have phenomenal character but do not have intentional content? Most representationalists think not.[6] For example, perceptual states are representational in nature, and so too are dreams and hallucinations. (Remember that a state can have intentional content even if it is not about an actually existing thing, so a hallucination of a double-headed snake is about or directed at a double-headed snake even if no such creature exists.) Moreover, not only do representationalists think that intentional content and phenomenal character go hand in hand but they also think that we can offer an account of the latter in terms of the former. On their view, what it is for a mental state to have phenomenal character is just for it to have a certain kind of intentional content.[7] Phenomenal consciousness, that is, can be wholly explained in terms of intentionality. (For this reason, representationalism is often also referred to as intentionalism.)

In support of their theory, representationalists often invoke considerations of simplicity. If it's true that phenomenal character and

---

6. Some representationalists restrict their theory so that it applies only to a subset of phenomenal states. In my view, however, the only way that representationalism can be seen to offer a theory of phenomenal character is for it to be unrestricted, that is, for it to be applied to all phenomenally conscious states. For further discussion, see Kind (2007).
7. Two different versions of representationalism are often distinguished: strong representationalism and weak representationalism. While both theories claim that the phenomenal character of our phenomenal mental states supervenes on the intentional content of such states, only strong representationalists claim that the phenomenal character of our phenomenal mental states *consists in* the intentional content of such states. My discussion of representationalism in this chapter should thus be seen as a discussion of strong representationalism.

intentional content go hand in hand, that all states with phenomenal character have intentional content, then we might wonder what accounts for this correlation. As Michael Tye asks, in defending representationalism, is the correlation "a brute fact, admitting of no further explanation? Surely not. The *simplest* explanation is that the phenomenal character of a state is itself intentional" (Tye 1995, 134).

Another consideration raised concerns what's often called the *transparency of experience*. Experience is said to be transparent in the sense that we "see" right through it to the object of that experience, analogously to the way we see through a pane of glass to whatever is on the other side of it. Although the ideas date back at least to the early 20th-century writing of G.E. Moore (see, e.g., 1903, 25), they were introduced to the contemporary debate by Gilbert Harman:

> When Eloise sees a tree before her, the colors she experiences are all experienced as features of the tree and its surroundings. None of them are experienced as intrinsic features of her experience. Nor does she experience any features of anything as intrinsic features of her experiences. And that is true of you too. There is nothing special about Eloise's visual experience. When you see a tree, you do not experience any features as intrinsic features of your experience. Look at a tree and try to turn your attention to intrinsic features of your visual experience. I predict you will find that the only features there to turn your attention to will be features of the presented tree.
> (Harman 1990, 667; see also Tye 1995, 2000)

According to representationalists, the fact that we cannot attend to such features of experience is best explained by the fact that the phenomenal character of one's experience is wholly constituted by its intentional content, that is, that representationalism is true.[8]

Different representationalists have different ways of specifying the kind of intentional content in which phenomenal character is supposed to consist. To give just one example, Tye has offered what he calls the PANIC theory (Tye 1995; see especially 137–144). PANIC abbreviates "poised, abstract, nonconceptual intentional

---

8. Elsewhere I have argued that this transparency argument does not succeed; see Kind (2003).

content," and it's this kind of intentional content that Tye takes to give rise to phenomenal character. To say that content is poised means that it's available to interact with a person's belief/desire system. To say that content is abstract means that no particular object need enter into it, and to say that its nonconceptual means that the person need not possess concepts that match the general features involved in it. This last aspect helps to account for the fact that we can discriminate different phenomenal states that are closely related to one another, even when we don't have concepts specifically relating to such states—as is the case with shades of color, for example. It also helps to account for the fact that unsophisticated creatures like squirrels or possums, creatures that likely lack much of a conceptual repertoire, can still have phenomenally conscious states

Earlier we noted that phenomenal consciousness seemed to be what makes the mind-body problem *a problem*. Intentionality, in contrast, has been thought to be a much more tractable aspect of mental states. Though we don't yet have a fully satisfactory account of it, and though developing one does not look to be particularly easy, it seems likely that it's a phenomenon that can be analyzed functionally. Granted, some philosophers have questioned this (see, e.g., Searle 1980). But, on the assumption that intentionality can be handled within a physicalist framework, if we could reduce phenomenal consciousness to intentionality, then phenomenal consciousness could be handled within a physicalist framework. This is the basic hope underlying the representationalist project.

Let's suppose we just grant this assumption. We won't question whether intentionality can be accommodated within a physicalist framework. Even so, there is good reason to think that representationalism does not offer us an adequate account of phenomenal consciousness. The basic problem is twofold. First, there seem to be clear counterexamples to the representationalist thesis—examples of states that clearly have phenomenal character but yet also seem clearly to lack intentional content. Second, even in states that do have both phenomenal character and intentional content, there are reasons to doubt that the former is exhausted by the latter.

One strand of counterexample comes from consideration of moods. Moods and emotions are often grouped together under the heading of affective states. These two kinds of states are remarkably similar to one another, and in fact, we might think that every example of a mood can be paired with a corresponding emotion. On the one hand, for example, one might feel a stab of anxiety when called upon to take a penalty kick with the soccer game on the line; on the other hand, one might be in an anxious mood during the whole game. One might feel a surge of joy when one's favorite soccer team wins the World Cup final, or one might simply be in a happy mood while watching the entirety of the match. As these examples suggest, however, there are some important differences between emotions and moods, perhaps most notably that emotions tend to be of relatively short duration, while moods tend to last for a more extended period of time. Another difference pointed to by the examples is one relating to intentional content. It's relatively plausible that emotions have such content, at least as a general matter. One's emotional experience of anxiety is about having to take the penalty kick, and one's emotional experience of joy is about the outcome of the World Cup final. In contrast, however, it seems considerably less plausible that moods are intentional. One can be in an anxious mood without one's anxiety being directed at or about anything, and one can be in an elated mood without one's elation being directed at or about anything.

Confronted with this counterexample, the representationalist typically suggests that we need to think more broadly about intentional content when it comes to moods. When you're in an anxious mood, your anxiety might not be directed at something *in particular*, but that doesn't mean it's not directed at anything. Rather, it's directed at the whole world. In fact, this way of characterizing moods occurs in philosophical treatments of moods entirely outside the context of representationalism, as evidenced by the following passage from Robert Solomon:

> Euphoria, melancholy, and depression are not about anything in particular (though some particular incident might well set them off); they are about the whole of our world, or indiscriminately about anything that comes our way, casting happy glows or somber shadows on every object and incident of our experience.
> (Solomon 1976, 173)

Though there seems to be something importantly right about a description of moods as generalized or diffuse, to my mind it's not clear that this aspect of moods is best understood as a point related to their intentional content. Yes, someone's anxious mood affects everything that they encounter and do, but that's a different thing from saying that someone's anxious mood is *about* everything that they encounter and do. For example, as I sit at my desk looking at the various objects in front of me, is my anxious mood really about, or even directed at, my computer monitor, keyboard, and webcam? This strikes me as deeply implausible.

That said, even if we were to accept that moods have this kind of generalized intentional content, that will not be enough to save representationalism. For now there's a further problem: Whatever intentional content moods may have, that content does not seem able to adequately account for the phenomenology. As William Lycan has put the point, when it comes to mental states like moods, the intentional content "does not loom very large in the overall phenomenal character of the mental state in question" (Lycan 2019).

We see a similar dialectic when it comes to bodily sensations like itches and pains. Many philosophers have taken these states to present another counterexample to representationalism, as it is hard to see what an itch or pain could be about. In response, the representationalist typically tries to find some intentional content for the state to have. Pains are said to be about tissue damage, for example, while itches are said to be about a different kind of disturbance in the body, perhaps a certain condition of the skin (see, e.g., Tye 1995, 113–117). This claim can be called into question by the existence of pains and itches that are medically inexplicable, that is, entirely disconnected from any bodily disturbance. But again, even if we were to accept that bodily sensations like pain and itches have intentional content, the representationalist still has to convince us that this intentional content is sufficient to account for the phenomenal character of the experience. And this seems like a very difficult task to accomplish. Maybe the claim is plausible for a subclass of pains and itches. Maybe. But the plausibility of the claim goes down pretty dramatically when we consider instances of these states where the phenomenal character of such states is particularly impressive. Consider an especially painful toothache, a case where the throbbing keeps you up at night and won't subside. The toothache is presumably caused by some kind of decay or infection. But does the throbbingness of the pain consist wholly in the representation of that decay or infection? Having had some memorable experiences with toothaches, I'm inclined to think not. For example, in one particularly dreadful case, I was in intense pain emanating from the lower right side of my mouth. Despite the pain, however, I wasn't even sure which particular tooth was the problem. Even when I probed each tooth with my tongue or my finger, I couldn't definitively narrow things down. The pain throbbed on, horrible but diffuse. Eventually, the dentist pinpointed the problem spot by whacking the decaying tooth with a dental instrument (I sincerely hope that you never have to have your dentist do this). Is it plausible that the phenomenal character of this intense pain consisted in a representation of some particular tooth decay, even when I myself could not identify the relevant tooth, let alone the decay itself? How could a phenomenal experience be that intensely available to me when the intentional content was so completely unavailable to me?

As we noted earlier, representationalism has some initial plausibility, especially when we focus on perceptual states. But there are too many other cases in which it seems like a non-starter. Ultimately, representationalism does not seem well positioned to provide an adequate theory of phenomenal consciousness.

4.2. Higher-Order Theory

The theory that we've just considered, representationalism, aims to reduce the phenomenal character of a conscious state to the intentional content of that same state. As such, it is often referred to as a *first-order* theory—or first-order representationalism. The higher-order theory that we'll now be considering is also a sort of representationalist theory, but it is not a first-order theory. Instead, the higher-order theory operates at a higher order of mental states, typically the second order. A second-order state is a state about another state. Consider someone who not only has a desire to help out at the local homeless shelter this weekend but also desires that they have this desire. They like being the kind of person who does charitable acts, and so they want to have the kind of charitable-oriented desires that they do. Their desire about the desire is a second-order desire. We have not only second-order desires but also second-order beliefs, hopes, and so on. According to the higher-order theory of consciousness, we can explain why a given state is conscious in terms of the existence of a higher-order representation about that state. When, and only when, there is the relevant kind of higher-order representation will the lower-order state be conscious.

Higher-order theorists differ about what the relevant kind of higher-order state must be. Some claim that there needs to be a higher-order thought—call this the *HOT theory* (see, e.g., Rosenthal 2005). Some claim that there needs to be a higher-order perception—call this the *HOP theory* (see, e.g., Armstrong 1968).

For our purposes, these differences won't matter. We'll focus on a generalized form of the theory in terms of higher-order representation, where we won't specify precisely what kind of state the representation must be.

To see the motivation for the higher-order theory, we might consider an example owing to David Armstrong (1968) of the distracted driver. If you've ever driven a car, you are probably familiar with the experience of "coming to" all of a sudden, perhaps when you reach your destination, to realize you had been completely zoned out for the entirety of the trip. Maybe you were daydreaming or thinking intently about something. But as for the driving itself, it's as if you were on auto-pilot. Now presumably during the drive itself you had various perceptual experiences. After all, given that you reached your destination safely, you presumably came to an appropriate stop at the relevant intersections when the light was red, and then resumed driving when the light turned green. So you presumably saw the red light and then saw the green light. You didn't crash into the car in front of you, so you presumably saw that as well. Given that you were zoned out, however, these perceptual experiences must have been unconscious—you saw the red light but weren't consciously seeing it. What explains the difference between a case in which you consciously see the red light and a case in which you see it unconsciously? Higher-order theorists claim that what makes a state conscious is that we are aware of it, and this awareness consists in the existence of a higher-order representation about it. Importantly, this higher-order representation need not itself be a state of which you are aware. But the presence of such a higher-order state is what makes the first-order state a conscious one.

In thinking about the plausibility of the higher-order theory, some of the objections that have been offered target only HOP theory while others target only HOT theory. Here we will focus on two objections that seem to apply across the board, whatever version of higher-order theory is on offer. First, one might wonder why being the target of a higher-order state would be able to make something phenomenally conscious. Suppose that someone is in a mental state that isn't currently phenomenally conscious, perhaps an unconscious perception. If they now come to think about or otherwise represent that state, how would this representation enable it to acquire phenomenal properties that it did not previously have? As Alvin Goldman notes: "A rock does not become conscious when someone has a belief about it. Why should a first-order psychological state become conscious simply by having a belief about it" (Goldman 1993, 366).

Second, the higher-order theory seems to have implausible implications about animal consciousness. In requiring that a being have higher-order representations in order for it to have phenomenally conscious states, higher-order theory seems to imply that creatures that are cognitively unsophisticated cannot be phenomenally unconscious. While it seems immensely plausible that a dog or cat has phenomenally conscious states, it seems implausible that these animals have higher-order representation. It's even questionable whether more sophisticated mammals such as chimpanzees have this capability, but it seems unquestionable that a chimpanzee can feel pain. Depending on exactly how the higher-order theory is specified, this implication might even extend to young infants. If the higher-order theory has to deny that a young infant can have phenomenally conscious states—if they have to deny that infants can feel pain or having phenomenally conscious perceptions—that seems like a very good reason to reject the theory.

Unsurprisingly, the higher-order theorist has various responses to these objections (see e.g., Lycan 1996; Gennaro 2004, 2005). But even if these responses succeed, there is a deeper problem threatening the theory. To see this problem, it helps to remind ourselves why the higher-order theory might have seemed intuitively plausible in the first place, namely, that when we think about the difference between being conscious of state and not being conscious of it, or about the question of how a mental state that we're not conscious of could become one that we are conscious of, the fact that the state is the subject of another state, a higher-order state, does seem relevant. It's the higher-order representation that accounts for one's consciousness of the first-order state. If this is what accounts for the plausibility of the higher-order theory, then an important issue question arises. In order to flesh out the intuitive plausibility of higher-order theory, I had to switch from talking of *a state's being conscious* to talking of *someone's being conscious of a state*. Is being *conscious of* a state the same thing as a state's being *phenomenally conscious*? As we saw in Section 2, there are many different senses of consciousness in play, both in ordinary discourse and in philosophical discussion. Our focus in this debate is on consciousness in the phenomenal sense. It's phenomenal consciousness that seems to present a special problem for physicalism. Is that what the higher-order theorists are focused on as well? One might worry that the account of consciousness offered by the higher-order theory addresses consciousness in the awareness sense, not consciousness in the phenomenal sense.

Consider again the distracted driver. When the driver stopped at the red light, the driver presumably was having a phenomenal experience of red. After all, if they weren't, they wouldn't have stopped. So it looks like they were having a phenomenal experience of which they were not aware—an experience that was conscious in the phenomenal sense even though it was not conscious in the awareness sense. When they come to have a higher-order thought about the experience, the higher-order thought brings that experience to conscious awareness. This suggests that the presence of a higher-order thought explains what makes us consciously aware of a state, not what makes that state phenomenally conscious. We might also pursue this kind of worry by a variant of the conceivability arguments we saw earlier. Can't we conceive of beings that have the relevant higher-order representations, representations that stand in the postulated relation to first-order states but that aren't phenomenally conscious of those states? In fact, doesn't the zombie scenario allow for exactly this kind of situation? As this suggests, insofar as the higher-order theory has provided us with an adequate theory of consciousness, it has done so by changing the subject.

4.3. Russellian Monism

Having looked in some detail at two physicalist theories of consciousness, we will now look at a theory of a different sort. In recent years, a growing dissatisfaction with both dualism and physicalism has led a number of philosophers to look for some kind of different alternative or some kind of middle path between the two. The basic line of thought might be summed up roughly as follows: Dualism respects what seems to be a basic fact about our existence as humans, namely that we are phenomenally conscious. But in doing so, it seems to fly in the face of science. In contrast, physicalism accords nicely with our scientific understanding of the world. But in doing so, it seems unable to accommodate phenomenal consciousness in any robust way. Isn't there some way that we can take science seriously while also taking consciousness seriously? Russellian monism claims to be able to do precisely this.

Named after 20th-century philosopher Bertrand Russell, Russellian monism takes its inspiration from some of his remarks in *The Analysis of Matter*:

> Physics, in itself, is exceedingly abstract, and reveals only certain mathematical characteristics of the material with which it deals. It does not tell us anything as to the intrinsic character of this material.
>
> (Russell 1927/1954, 10)

Here Russell seems to be pointing to the fact that physics defines its basic entities only in structural or relational terms. Chalmers provides a useful elaboration of this point:

> Basic particles, for instance, are largely characterized in terms of their propensity to interact with other particles. Their mass and charge is specified, to be sure, but all that a specification of mass ultimately comes to is a propensity to be accelerated by certain forces, and so on. Each entity is characterized by its relation to other entities, and so on forever.
>
> (Chalmers 1996, 153)

What underlies all of these structural and relational facts? It seems that there must be some underlying intrinsic or categorical properties to ground them. Because it's impossible to analyze or even scrutinize these properties via the lens of physics, they are sometimes referred to as inscrutables (see Montero 2010). The Russellian monists claim that all of the inscrutables are the same fundamental kind of property. (That's what makes the view monistic.) Moreover, in their view, these underlying properties are what give rise to consciousness.

Different versions of Russellian monism characterize these underlying properties in different ways. Sometimes the inscrutables are taken to be phenomenal properties. Proponents of this version of Russellian monism, often called phenomenal monism, seem committed to panpsychism, the view that (roughly speaking) everything that exists has a mind. At least on first hearing, such a view strikes most people as counterintuitive. We're strongly disinclined to attribute mentality even to simplistic organisms like bacteria and protozoa, let alone to non-organisms like quarks and atoms.

In defense of their view, panpsychists will typically deny that things like quarks and atoms have mentality in exactly the same way that we humans have mentality. As a general matter, we're typically inclined to think of conscious experience on a spectrum from the very simple to the very complex. Compare the experience you have when you're at a crowded party, where you're bombarded with sights and sounds and smells, with the experience you have when you're waiting for the doctor in a quiet examination room. The latter experience is considerably simpler than the former, and the phenomenal monist suggests that the experiences of a quark or an atom will be even simpler than this. In trying to flesh out what this might be like, Gregg Rosenberg (2004) claims that the interactions between atoms might be thought of analogously to phenomenal fireflies flickering in the night. The experiences would just be momentary flashes of extraordinarily simple feeling.

In further defense of their view, the panpsychist notes that we should not be misled by our inability to imagine what such simple feelings would be like. Even if we cannot imagine what it is like to be a bat, we're not inclined to deny that there is something that it is like to be a bat. Likewise the fact that we cannot imagine what it is like to be an atom should not incline us to deny that there is something that it is like to be an atom.

Four Versions of Russellian Monism

Russellian monism posits that consciousness can be explained by fundamental intrinsic properties that underlie all of reality. On their view, these intrinsic properties are entirely outside the domain of physics. Indeed, they think it's impossible to analyze or even scrutinize these properties via the lens of physics. For this reason, the properties are often referred to as inscrutables. Different versions of Russellian Monism give different accounts of the inscrutables.

Phenomenal monism: The inscrutables are phenomenal in nature.
Protophenomenal monism: The inscrutables are not themselves phenomenal in nature but they are a precursor to phenomenal properties.
Physical monism: The inscrutables are physical in nature, though they are outside the domain of physics.
Neutral monism: The inscrutables are neither phenomenal nor physical but rather have a nature that is neutral between the two.

A different version of Russellian monism, what we might call protophenomenal monism, denies that the inscrutables are phenomenal. Rather, they are a precursor to phenomenal properties, what we might think of as *protophenomenal*. When a sufficiently high degree of structural complexity has been achieved, these protophenomenal properties give rise to consciousness. Because protophenomenal monism does not take the inscrutables to be phenomenal, they can avoid attributing consciousness to entities like quarks or atoms, thereby avoiding the unintuitive implications of panpsychism.

In order for protophenomenal monism to be at all plausible, its proponent needs to provide us with some kind of substantive account of what a protophenomenal property is. Obviously it's not enough for them to characterize these properties negatively as nonphenomenal; we need some kind of positive characterization of them. In his discussion of this version of monism, Chalmers classifies the protophenomenal inscrutables as having some sort of especially close connection to phenomenal properties.

A third version of Russellian monism claims that the inscrutables should be understood to be physical properties. For this reason, the view is typically called physical monism. Physical monism shares much in common with physicalism, but whether physical monism counts as a version of physicalism will depend on exactly how the physicalist characterizes the nature of the physical. In positing the existence of inscrutables, the physical monist accepts the existence of properties that lie outside the domain of physics as its currently understood (and maybe even outside the domain of ideal physics). But since the inscrutables are the categorical or intrinsic bases for ordinary physical properties, the physical monist claims that they should still be understood as properties that are physical in some sense. We might think of them as physical properties of a special sort.

Here it might help to draw on a distinction that Daniel Stoljar, my opponent in this debate, has drawn in his previous work between two different ways of understanding the notion of the physical and, correspondingly, two different ways to understand the physicalist view (Stoljar 2001). On the one hand, we might take a theory-based conception of the physical. On this conception, physical properties are those that physical theory tells us about plus those that supervene on the sort of properties that physical theory tells us about. Following Stoljar, we can call these the t-physical properties. On the other hand, we might take an object-based conception of the physical. On this conception, physical properties are those required by a complete account of the intrinsic nature of paradigmatic physical objects and their constituents plus those that supervene on the sort of property required by such an account. Again, following Stoljar, we can call these the o-physical properties.

As traditionally understood, physicalism seems to operate with something like the theory-based conception of the physical. In contrast, physical monism operates with the object-based conception of the physical. By definition, inscrutables are not t-physical properties; they are outside the realm of physical theory. But, since inscrutable properties are required by a complete account of the intrinsic nature of physical objects, they clearly count as o-physical properties. If we understood physicalism in terms of the object-based conception rather than the theory-based conception, then physical monism would count as a version of physicalism.

The last version of Russellian monism, and the one that is usually taken to be Russell's own position, denies that the inscrutables are either phenomenal or physical but instead treats them as neutral between the two. For this reason it's often referred to as **neutral monism**. As Russell puts it in *The Analysis of Mind*:

> The stuff of which the world of our experience is composed is, in my belief, neither mind nor matter, but something more primitive than either. Both mind and matter seem to be composite, and the stuff of which they are compounded lies in a sense between the two, in a sense above them both, like a common ancestor.
>
> (Russell 1921, 10–11)

In elaborating this position, the neutral monist faces a problem that's similar to the one that faces the protophenomenal monist. Just as the protophenomenal monist owes us a substantive characterization of protophenomenality, the neutral monist owes us a substantive characterization of neutrality. The passage from Russell suggests that we should understand the relevant sense of neutrality as simply "neither mental nor physical," or perhaps, as "neither *intrinsically* mental nor physical." Given that the dichotomy between the mental and the physical is often understood to be exhaustive, however, it's not clear that there is any room for neutral entities of this sort.

Alternatively, the neutral monist might try to understand the notion of neutrality in terms of causal laws. Normally we understand the mental as subject to distinctively psychological laws and the physical as subject to distinctively physical laws. But the neutral monist predicts that in our ultimate scientific account of the world, the causal laws will not be stated in terms of matter; rather, they will be stated in such a way as to apply equally to both psychology and physics. The existence of a single set of laws governing the inscrutables would suggest that they were not properly understood as either mental or physical but rather as neutral between the two.

These four different versions of Russellian monism face different problems. As we've already seen, both neutral and physical monism face problems specifying how exactly we are to understand the inscrutables consistent with the kind of theory they want to put forth. Is there really a robust sense of neutrality such that the inscrutables can be understood as neutral? Is there really a robust sense of physicality such that the inscrutables can be understood as physical? Absent answers to these questions, these monistic views seem at best underdeveloped (and at worst, incoherent). Even if such answers were to be developed, however, one might wonder whether these versions of the view succeed in taking consciousness more seriously than the traditional physicalist views. That said, I have a strong suspicion that we will be hearing more about physical monism in Daniel Stoljar's opening statement, so I will postpone further discussion of this theory for later in this debate when I give my response to him.

Perhaps the biggest problem for both phenomenal monism and protophenomenal monism is what's known as the combination problem. Even once we assume that there are little bits of consciousness (or protoconsciousness) everywhere, we still need some explanation as to how they combine to produce the sort of unified consciousness that we experience. Such an explanation is not easily forthcoming. The problem was put especially vividly by William James (1890) in his *Principles of Psychology*. Suppose we have 100 different feelings and we now bundle them together. No matter how tight the bundle is, there is no way for the feelings to intermix with one another. As James puts it, each individual feeling still remains "the same feeling it always was, shut in its own skin, windowless, ignorant of what the other feelings are and mean" (1890, 160). The combination problem often seems particularly forceful when we consider it in terms of subjecthood or point of view. Each individual phenomenal inscrutable has its own point of view, and it seems impossible that these could combine into an overarching point of view.

Over and above these specific problems, to my mind there is a bigger, more general problem for Russellian monism. I began the discussion of this theory by noting that it is motivated in part by the desire to offer an interestingly different alternative to dualist and physicalist views. But one might wonder whether it really succeeds in doing so. Some versions of Russellian monism, like panpsychism, seem to share a lot in common with dualist theories. Other versions of Russellian monism, like physical monism, seem to share a lot in common with physicalism. Ultimately, in explicating the nature of the inscrutables, all versions of Russellian monism have to take a stance on a basic question: Is mentality part of the fundamental nature of reality, or not? Since answering this question tracks pretty closely with the traditional divide between dualism and physicalism, it's not clear that Russellian monism can really successfully transcend this divide. The various versions of the theory collapse either into versions of dualism or into versions of physicalism, and we thus haven't found a new and different way of accounting for the robustness of consciousness while still respecting the dictates of science.[9]

That said, consideration of Russellian monism proves instructive, for I think both the physicalist and dualist can learn something from the monist position about how best to craft their own theories. As we turn to a development of dualism in the final section of this chapter, that's what I will aim to do. In particular, I will aim to show how we can develop a dualist treatment of consciousness that's viable in light of our 21st-century naturalistic understanding of the world around us.

> Section 4 took a closer look at some particular physicalist theories of consciousness in an attempt to show why they cannot adequately account for phenomenal consciousness. Three theories were considered: representationalism, higher-order theory, and Russellian Monism. Though the problems that beset these theories are different, there are compelling reasons to reject them all. In conjunction with the big-picture worries that we encountered in Section 3, it looks like the case against physicalism is a strong one. To provide an adequate account of consciousness, we must adopt a dualist theory.

---

9. See Kind (2016) for a more detailed development of this worry.

5. Dualism Rebooted

No matter how compelling the objections to specific versions of physicalism are, and no matter how compelling the general arguments against physicalism are, there may still be a latent sense that dualism is simply an untenable position to take in the 21st century. Journalist Christopher Beha, in a recent article in *Harper's* magazine, notes that if we were still as ignorant about the workings of the brain as we were in Descartes' time, then we might be able to share his dualist inclinations, but given the vast scientific progress that's been made in the almost four centuries since, there is no longer any reason to resist the claim that "the mind *is* the physical brain, or at least a function of it, and that no additional mental substance or thinking thing exists." As examples of the stunning scientific progress that we have made, he notes that we now understand which parts of the brain are responsible for a variety of things ranging from basic life functions to speech, spatiotemporal coordination, and higher-order reasoning. We also have developed a sophisticated understanding of perception, memory formation, and memory retrieval. Given all of these neuroscientific advances, Beha questions how anyone in the 21st century could still hold on to what appears to be a wildly outdated view. Perhaps one can understand why Descartes, stuck as he was with the limited 17th-century understanding of the workings of the brain, would adopt dualism, but why would anyone do so today?

Interestingly, people do still hold to this view. Dualism is by no means a dead position among the general populace. In a 2004 piece for the *New York Times*, psychologist Paul Bloom notes that most of us are "common-sense dualists."[10] One finds expressions of the dualist perspective in a diverse variety of contemporary sources. The recent Pixar movie *Soul* rests on the assumption that each of us has a non-material essence that exists apart from our flesh-and-blood bodies. In the cardio videos put out by Team Body Project on YouTube, instructor Daniel Bartlett constantly exhorts his viewers that exercise is all about the mind, not the body.

Nor is dualism a dead position among philosophers. In a 2009 survey of more than 3,000 professional philosophers, while approximately 54% of respondents indicated that they accept or lean toward physicalism, approximately 29% of the respondents

---

10. See www.nytimes.com/2004/09/10/opinion/the-duel-between-body-and-soul.html.

indicated that they accept or lean non-physicalism. (The remaining respondents were mostly undecided or indicated that they held some other view.) When it comes to the general populace, one might be able to explain the common-sense dualism in terms of underlying religious or spiritual tendencies, but this suggestion does not wholly account for philosophers' inclinations toward dualism; in the same survey, only approximately 15% of respondents indicated that they accept or lean toward theism, and there was not a particularly high correlation between these two positions.[11]

In fact, many (perhaps even most) contemporary dualists fully embrace science and have a naturalistic worldview. But what does a scientifically respectable 21st-century dualism look like? Sketching the contours of such a position is the goal of this final section of my opening statement. Insofar as the very term "dualism" carries unsavory connotations and vestiges of an outdated outlook, we need to have a reboot. The dualism of today has come a long way from its 17th-century roots. To keep this fact front and center, to keep us focused on the fact that we're working with a new and improved version of the view, I'll refer to the view as *dualism 2.0* going forward.

5.1. The Irreducibility of the Phenomenal

At the heart of dualism 2.0 is a simple claim: Just as physical states, events, and processes are an irreducibly real part of the world, so too are phenomenal states, events, and processes an irreducibly real part of the world. For simplicity, let's jointly refer to states, events, and processes as "activity." In virtue of its recognition of the existence of both phenomenal activity and physical activity, and further, in virtue of its claim that these two kinds of activity cannot be reduced to one another, the view is appropriately characterized as dualistic. Importantly, however, this duality need not be thought of in terms of mental substances. We can have duality of activity without duality of entities.

In talking of these phenomenal events and processes as irreducibly real, dualism 2.0 distinguishes itself from physicalism. It also distinguishes itself from Russellian monism. Recall that the

---

11. See https://philpapers.org/surveys/results.pl for the survey results. Note that the survey question about physicalism was focused on "mind" not "consciousness."

Russellian monists claim that phenomenality (or protophenomenality) can be found at the fundamental level of reality, that is, that it is a property like mass and charge. This claim is consistent with dualism 2.0, but it is not required by it. Because dualism 2.0 treats phenomenality as irreducibily real, there's a sense in which it might be said it treats phenomenality as a fundamental part of reality. But it's important not to interpret this as the claim that phenomenality exists at the fundamental *level* of reality. Dualism 2.0 need not take mass and charge to be the appropriate model for phenomenality. Unlike Russellian monism, then, dualism 2.0 does not commit itself to the ubiquity of phenomenality.

Perhaps most importantly, in saying that phenomenality is irreducibly real, dualism 2.0 need not be seen as committing itself to anything spooky. The fact that something cannot be reduced to the physical does not mean that it is magical or mystical. Take mathematics, for example. Mathematicians are committed to the existences of numbers, like the number 2 or 17 or 24. Indeed, it's not only mathematicians who are committed to the existence of numbers; so too are the rest of us. But while numbers can be represented physically with a numerical inscription, numbers themselves don't seem to be physical things. I can have 17 peas on my plate, for example, but I can't have the number 17 on my plate. And mathematics commits us not only to rational numbers like 2 or 17 but also to mathematical constants like π and *e* (known as Euler's number), irrational numbers, and even imaginary numbers. Some of these mathematical entities may be strange, but their strangeness doesn't get characterized as spooky—as in some way magical or mystical.

It's not only in the realm of mathematics that we commit ourselves to entities that are non-physical. Consider political ideals, such as the ideal of justice. Justice doesn't seem to be a physical thing, but in striving to achieve it, we aren't engaged in a spooky enterprise. Consider aesthetic ideals, such as the ideal of beauty. Although many physical things are beautiful, beauty itself doesn't seem to be a physical thing. Yet beauty, like justice, is not something spooky.

One reason that mathematics doesn't seem spooky is that numbers are part of a well-ordered system. The fact that numbers are governed by various mathematical laws makes mathematics seem akin to science, where physical entities are governed by various physical laws. It's undoubtedly at least partly in virtue of the apparent absence of any such laws regarding phenomenology that phenomenal consciousness seems spooky in a way that numbers do not. Importantly, however, dualism 2.0 is fully consistent with the existence of laws governing phenomenal consciousness. Some of these laws will lay down principles about the relations between different kinds of phenomenal activity, and some of these laws will lay down principles about the relations between phenomenal activity and physical activity. Even though dualism 2.0 denies that consciousness reduces to the physical, that's not to say that there are no connections between phenomenal activity and physical activity. Indeed, we have every reason to believe that phenomenal activity, at least in our case, arises from physical activity. Specifying the phenomenal laws will be no easy task, and very little progress has thus far been made on this front. But when we consider the lack of progress that the physicalists have had in giving precise physical or functional specifications of phenomenally conscious states, we see that dualism 2.0 is not here in any worse shape than its competitors. As Chalmers notes, in offering his own version of naturalistic dualism, at this stage, we have no idea what a comprehensive phenomenal theory and its laws will look like, "but we have every reason to believe that such a theory exists" (Chalmers 1996, 127). We also have some sense—at least at the meta-level—of what such laws will look like: "The case of physics tells us that fundamental laws are typically simple and elegant; we should expect the same of the fundamental laws in a theory of consciousness" (Chalmers 1996, 127).

Another difficult task lies in tackling the issue of mental causation. Currently, our understanding of causation makes it hard to see how there could be causation between the mental and the physical. Also problematic is the fact that physical events seem to be fully explicable in terms of physical causes, thus seeming to leave no room for mental causes. Indeed, as we mentioned briefly in Section 2, considerations of this sort often serve as a driving motivation for the physicalist view.

In an effort to address this issue, many contemporary dualists embrace epiphenomenalism: the view that there is no mental-physical causation. Phenomenal consciousness, on this view, would be merely an epiphenomenon with no causal force. Perhaps this will end up being the best option for dualism 2.0, despite its being counterintuitive—after all, it certainly seems to us that our phenomenally conscious states causally matter. But any view on the problem of consciousness is likely going to have to embrace some counterintuitive result at some point. It's unlikely that all of our pre-theoretic intuitions can be wholly accommodated.

To my mind, however, dualism 2.0 might do better by holding out hope that, in the course of specifying the psychophysical laws, we will be able to come to a better and broader understanding of the nature of causation that enables us to accommodate mental causes and thus affirm the causal efficacy of the phenomenal. At this point, dualism 2.0 cannot do much better than issue a promissory note in this regard. But when we think about the enterprise underlying dualism 2.0, we can see why it is reasonable to hope that this promissory note can be filled: As our understanding of phenomenal consciousness develops in such a way so that we can understand it in a non-spooky way, we are likely to be able to give an account of how it can enter it causal relations without those seeming either mysterious or spooky.

At this point, however, an important question arises. For the more work we do to show that phenomenality is not spooky, the more it might seem that it can simply be incorporated into the physical framework. There are all sorts of entities accepted as part of the physical framework of the early 21st century that have only recently been discovered and thus were not part of the physical framework of the early 20th century, let alone the physical framework of the 17th century. For example, prior to the 1960s, scientists did not recognize the existence of gluons; now they are an uncontroversial part of the standard model of particle physics. Interestingly, gluons are massless properties—something that would have seemed impossible in Descartes' time. As our physical theory changed and expanded in order to include them, we had to accept that there could be physical entities without mass, thus giving us a different conception of the physical. Likewise, there is now a consensus among physicists that the standard model with which they are operating is inadequate in various respects and thus likely to one day be superseded by a new model, one that goes beyond the standard model. As this new model is developed, our physical theory will again change and expand in order to include any new entities that are posited. These new entities may be very different in various respects from the physical entities we already accept. In short, what counts as physical is not fixed. As physical theory changes, our concept of the physical adapts. Why, then, couldn't it adapt to incorporate the phenomenal?

Addressing this question requires us to think seriously about exactly what claim the physicalist is making. We've seen that the physicalist claims that everything (and hence, the phenomenal) is physical. But in making this claim, the physicalist owes us an explanation of what is meant by this notion. Typically, the explanation makes reference to physics. A property is physical if it falls into the domain of theories of physics. Granted, when the explanation is put this simply, obvious counterexamples immediately arise. *Being a diamond* seems to be a paradigmatic physical property, but theories of physics don't themselves tell us about this property. To get around these kinds of obvious counterexamples, we might say that a property is physical if it falls into the domain of a theory of physics or can be wholly explained by properties that fall into that domain. While *having charge* is a property of the first sort, *being a diamond* is a property of the second sort.

As this discussion suggests, physical theory changes over time. The physicalist thus faces a dilemma. This problem is often referred to as Hempel's Dilemma, so-called because it was given a particularly forceful explication by the 20th-century German philosopher Carl Hempel. In short, the problem concerns how the physicalist defines the notion of "physical" on which their theory rests. Do they define it in terms of the currently accepted physical theory, or in terms of an ideal, future physical theory? Suppose they take the first option and define physicalism in terms of the physical theory that is currently accepted. On this definition, physicalism will almost certainly be false, since we have very strong reason to believe that our current physical theory is still incomplete. So it might seem that the physicalist would be better off taking the other option and defining physicalism in terms of some future, ideal physics. On this definition, physicalism will be true. The problem is that it will also be trivial, since exactly what's covered by a future physics cannot be predicted, and it might even include properties that, on our current understanding at least, are the sorts of things that we now think of as purely phenomenal.

To see more clearly the force of the second horn of the dilemma, it may help to consider the property *being made of fairy dust*. Suppose that 22nd-century science finds strong evidence for the existence of mysterious and magical entities, and they are unable to explain any of this evidence in terms of any already accepted physical properties such as having mass, having charge, and so on. As a result, they add the property *being made of fairy dust* to their physical theory and explain the mysterious and magical entities in terms of it. Intuitively speaking, one would think that the existence of entities made of fairy dust would serve as a counterexample to physicalism. But once we define physicalism in terms of a future physics, we don't get this result. Being made of fairy dust will be just as physical a property as being made of atoms. Physicalism thus becomes trivial. If every time we come across something that can't be explained in terms of accepted physical theory, we simply add it as a new primitive element of that physical theory, then the notion of physical is emptied of any real content.

I won't try to solve this problem for the physicalist; that's on them. But insofar as dualism 2.0 (like any version of dualism) is defined partly in terms of the notion of the physical, this problem is relevant for our theory as well: In saying that phenomenal consciousness is irreducibly real, we're saying that it can't be reduced to the physical, thus relying on the same notion that the physicalists do. Here's how I propose that we proceed. However physicalism is to be defined—whether it's in terms of current physics of future physics, or some other way entirely—we should see the theory as committed to an important constraint: Physicalism can be true only if the phenomenality is not a primitive aspect of the world. This constraint is sometimes referred to as the "no fundamental mentality" constraint (see, e.g., Wilson 2006). What counts as physical may adapt as physical theory evolves, but the notion cannot adapt so far as to include primitive phenomenality within it. The divide between dualism and physicalism can thus be best case as a disagreement on exactly this issue, that is, on whether phenomenality is primitive to our world.

5.2. What Science Does (and Doesn't) Tell Us

By fleshing out dualism 2.0 and countering the charge of spookiness, the discussion of the previous section should help to support the view. But we now encounter a different stumbling block. Throughout this opening statement, I have called upon many thought experiments in making the case against physicalism—thought experiments involving color scientists, inverted qualia, and zombies. As I noted, the philosophers putting forth these scenarios do not mean to claim that they are physically possible. Rather, the mere logical possibility of these scenarios is enough to count against physicalism. But sometimes readers confronted with these thought experiments get impatient with them. Such readers find it frustrating that we are focused on outlandish scenarios that couldn't possibly occur (though remember, this claim has to be understood in the sense of physical possibility—it's only in the sense of physical possibility that these scenarios could not occur). By relying on these kinds of thought experiments to make the case against physicalism and for dualism 2.0, we seem to be committed to the claim that the question of consciousness is not an empirical one.

A similar frustration may arise from my earlier discussion of the neural correlates of consciousness (Section 2.2). As I noted there, the neuroscientific exploration of consciousness aims to identify the states or processes of the brain that are correlated with consciousness. Although science might discover this correlation, additional questions remain. First is the question about whether the correlation is a necessary one. (The various thought experiments that we have considered would deny that it is.) But even if the correlation is indeed necessary, a second question arises about how this correlation is best explained. One explanation, of course, is that consciousness should be identified with the relevant brain states or processes. But there are other explanations possible. Perhaps there is a causal relationship between these brain processes and consciousness. Perhaps these brain processes and consciousness share a common cause. Determining the nature of the correlation and determining which of these explanations is the best one are matters that extend beyond brain science itself. These are not wholly empirical matters. And this brings us back to the impatience and frustration I just mentioned. For some readers, perhaps for many readers, the claim that the question of consciousness is a non-empirical matter seems tantamount to a repudiation of science, and thus serves as a reductio of the dualist position, that is, as a demonstration that the dualist position is an untenable one—even our rebooted version, dualism 2.0.

Importantly, this line of thinking is mistaken, and making clear why is a crucial further step in our defense of dualism 2.0. In short, not every question is an empirical one. We routinely and uncontroversially accept the importance of many issues that we recognize to be non-empirical (or, at least, not wholly empirical). Much of mathematics is not an empirical matter, but we don't think of mathematicians as engaged in an enterprise that is tantamount to a repudiation of science. Likewise, many matters of legal interpretation are not empirical ones. Consider, for example, questions about the meaning of a particular statute. But even though these legal questions are not empirical questions, we don't take that to imply that the US Supreme Court justices—or all of the justices in the US state and federal systems—are engaged in an enterprise that is tantamount to a repudiation of science. Finally, many matters of public policy are not empirical ones. Consider, in particular, questions about the fairness of a given policy. Even once the relative impacts of two competing policies have been empirically determined, a further question remains about which of the impacts achieves a fairer outcome. But again, we don't think that public policy experts are, in principle, engaged in an anti-scientific enterprise. So why should it be any different when it comes to philosophers who are committed to a particular view about consciousness?

In fact, once we reflect further on this, we can see that there are even questions that fall *within the scientific domain* that are not wholly empirical in nature. During the coronavirus pandemic of 2020 (a pandemic that remains ongoing as I am writing this), various statistics are reported about fatalities. Some of these statistics report deaths from the virus. Others report deaths "due to" the pandemic. Of course, empirical data underlie the second statistic just as much as the first; one needs a count of fatalities, a determination of cause of death for each fatality, and so on. But even once these empirical matters are settled, further questions arise. When we talk about the deaths that are due to the pandemic, do we include fatalities where the death is attributable to complications that developed subsequent to recovery of the virus but seem at least indirectly linked to it? Do we include the deaths of people who died from conditions that could have been better treated had people not been delaying medical treatment during stay-at-home orders? How exactly we are to understand what deaths "due to the pandemic" means is not a determination that can be made empirically.[12]

One way to make this point more generally is to reflect on how research is conducted in both science and social science. Emphasis is often put on the process of operationalization. As defined by Earl Babbie in his influential textbook *The Practice of Social Research*, operationalization is "the development of specific research procedures (operations) that will result in empirical observations representing those concepts in the real world" (Babbie 1975/2020, 138). Operationalization goes hand in hand with conceptualization, a process of refinement whereby abstract notions are made more specific and precise. Scientific refinement of the concepts requires a

---

12. For discussion of some of these issues, see Zylke and Bauchner (2020).

particular kind of specification and precision, namely an attempt to produce a definition that allows for measurement, that is, an operational definition (Babbie 1975/2020, 133). But the process of conceptualization must begin with an attempt to understand a concept, to figure out the real essence of a concept. It's only when there is an adequate understanding that we will be led to an operational definition that measures what we really want it to be measuring. (When we ask, have we arrived at a good operational definition, we mean not only: "Is this measurable?" but also: "Is what we'll be measuring really going to give us insight into the phenomenon we meant to be investigating?") Thus, the interrelated process of conceptualization and operationalization, a process that's central to the pursuit of empirical research, relies on a certain background that is not itself an empirical one.

Of course, we want our legal decisions and public policy to be evidence-based. We want our justices and our public policy experts to take scientific findings into account when issuing their judicial decisions and their policy recommendations. We want our medical statistics to be reported in light of the empirical evidence. But saying all of this does not amount to a dismissal of the importance of non-empirical matters. Likewise, the best contemporary philosophy of mind and philosophy of consciousness is informed by empirical evidence—in particular, by neuroscientific findings. These findings constrain our theories and they constrain what theories remain possible. But they are not the end of the story. We can accept all of this while still insisting that the question of consciousness is not wholly an empirical matter.

5.3. The Way Ahead

There is hard work ahead in developing dualism 2.0. But, as I have tried to show in this opening statement, doing so is our best hope for achieving an adequate theory of phenomenal consciousness. The case that consciousness cannot be accommodated within a physicalist framework is a very strong one, and we have seen good reasons to dismiss any lingering worries that one cannot develop a scientifically respectable theory outside of this framework.

Phenomenal consciousness is at the core of our very existence. The difference between having it and not having it is like the difference between Dorothy's experience of Oz and her previously drab existence in Kansas. When we think of our lives as being lived in technicolor, in stereo, this is all because we are phenomenally conscious beings. From the agony to the ecstasy, from hope to despair, phenomenal consciousness is what it's all about it. Ultimately, as I have tried to show throughout this opening statement, dualism 2.0 is our only real hope for recognizing any of this. If we want to take phenomenal consciousness seriously, then we should put our philosophical energies into the further development of this theory.

> This section aimed to provide a development and defense of the dualist view I am defending, what I'm calling dualism 2.0. This dualism is importantly different from the dualism defended by Descartes, and the discussion of this section aimed to show how it is entirely compatible with our contemporary 21st-century naturalist outlook. At the core of the dualist view is the claim that the phenomenal is irreducible. But this need not imply anything spooky or mysterious. Moreover, as also discussed in this section, we should not be troubled by the implication that the problem of consciousness is not a wholly empirical matter and cannot be wholly settled by science. Many other questions that we consider important are also outside the domain of science and cannot be wholly settled by empirical means. As I have argued throughout this opening statement, if we want to take phenomenal consciousness seriously, a dualist view is our only option.

Chapter 2

Non-standard Physicalism
The Epistemic Approach to the Problem of Consciousness

Daniel Stoljar

Contents

Introduction	63	2.4. Features of This View	103
1. What Consciousness Is	68	2.5. Objections to This View	107
1.1. Phenomenal Consciousness	68	3. The Metaphysics of the Science of Consciousness	114
1.2. Complications	70	3.1. Case Study: Aaronson Versus Tononi	115
1.3. Higher-Order Consciousness	78	3.2. The Laws of Consciousness Thesis	118
1.4. Access Consciousness	83	3.3. Are There Laws of Consciousness?	123
1.5. Relations Among These Notions	87	3.4. Consciousness Science Without the Laws?	128
2. Consciousness and the World	91	3.5. Consciousness Science After Ignorance	130
2.1. The Conceivability Argument	92		
2.2. The Epistemic View	94		
2.3. Alternatives to This View	99		

Note to Reader: I have marked with an asterisk (*), sections that are more difficult; you can easily skip them and retain a sense of the whole.

Introduction

Sometimes the solutions to philosophical problems are right under your nose and yet you can't see them. You go over and over the problem, looking for an answer. It must be somewhere, but where? And then it turns out you knew the solution all along. It is just that you didn't recognize it as the solution.

It's like one of those Scandinavian crime series on Netflix. The killer is introduced in the first scene, but because he doesn't look much like what you imagine, you miss it. You know the perpetrator, but you don't know that he is the perpetrator. Likewise, in philosophy, you sometimes know the solution but you don't know that it is the solution.

That's what's the case in what is variously called "the problem of consciousness," "the mind-body problem," "the hard problem of consciousness" or more briefly "the hard problem."

Actually, names like this are misleading. There is no such thing as "the" problem of consciousness, at least if that means some unique problem. There is no unique problem, not in philosophy and not in the sciences. There are in fact many problems, and only a co-ordinated effort by many researchers in different fields will allow us to move forward.

Still, when people talk about consciousness, especially in philosophy, and when they use labels like "the mind-body problem" or "the hard problem," they often have a specific problem in mind, one that seems to attract more attention than anything else.

That problem is about whether two big ideas can both be true together. The first is the existence of consciousness. The second is a worldview (a picture of everything that exists) that many people think you must believe if you hold a vaguely scientific or rational approach to the world, namely, physicalism. It's this *compatibility problem*, as I will call it, that I think has a solution right under our nose.

The solution to the compatibility problem—brace yourself!—is that we are missing something. What we are missing is a type of physical fact or property relevant to consciousness. More than this, we are profoundly ignorant of the nature of the physical world, and ignoring this ignorance is what generates the problem.

I call the idea that we are ignorant of a type of fact or property that is relevant to consciousness *the ignorance hypothesis*, and I call the idea that the ignorance hypothesis solves the compatibility problem *the epistemic view*.

Most people, when they first hear suggestions like this, do not disagree so much as do not even recognize them as a solution—just like those killers on Netflix. Yes we are ignorant of something, they say, but repeating that obvious point is no sort of solution to the problem.

Some people go on to suggest that I don't really mean what I seem to mean. Don't you mean you are just not interested in the problem? Don't you mean there must be a solution but you don't know what it is?

Some go further, insisting I have missed some important philosophical point. I've even been told that the position is unanswerable, which is a strange thing to say since you might have thought it was good in a philosophical view to be unanswerable.

But I do mean what I say, and I haven't missed any point. Whether something is a solution to a problem depends on what that problem is. And most people who talk about "the" problem of consciousness don't spend enough time saying what "it" is, or better what the several problems mistakenly called "the" problem are.

When I say that the fact that we are ignorant of the physical world solves the problem, I mean it solves this quite specific problem: the compatibility problem, i.e., the problem of whether physicalism and claim that consciousness exists can both be correct. But I also mean it solves it in a specific way, namely, by showing that the arguments that apparently support incompatibility fail, and for a single reason. These arguments all presuppose that we have complete knowledge of the physical facts relevant to consciousness. According to the epistemic view, that presupposition is false, so the arguments don't work.

I don't mean that getting past this presupposition is easy. On the contrary, the idea that "all the relevant facts are in" has a powerful grip on our philosophical imagination. It has deep origins in various religious approaches to philosophy on which God created the world in such a way that it is intelligible to us. But it is also explicitly presupposed in some of the dominant non-religious traditions in meta-philosophy in the 20th century and after. To solve the problem in the way suggested by the epistemic view, therefore, means rethinking what counts as a solution to a philosophical problem.

"Ah," people sometimes say, "but even if what you say is right, that would at most show that various arguments for incompatibility fail. It doesn't show positively that physicalism is true."

That's correct, but it's not as important as it sounds. If physicalism is true, it is an empirical truth. We can't argue a priori that it's true. But what we can do, and this is what drives the compatibility problem, is to argue here and now that it is incompatible with the existence of consciousness. If we make the further assumption that consciousness exists, we may immediately conclude that physicalism is false. If that were so, all theorizing about consciousness, and indeed about everything else, would need to accommodate that fact. What the epistemic view says is that this isn't so: there is no persuasive "here and now" argument for incompatibility.

But what about all the other problems, problems distinct from the compatibility problem but which often also go under the label "hard problem"? Does the epistemic view solve them too?

What are these problems? Here are some of them:

- What in general terms is consciousness; what is it to be a conscious subject or a conscious psychological state?
- What precisely is the relation between conscious states and other psychological phenomena, such as perception, emotion, belief, knowledge, memory, and so on?
- How do we come to know that we ourselves are in conscious states (when we are) and is this interestingly different from the way in which we come to know other things?
- Can we imaginatively identify with the conscious states of people in the deep past or in other cultures and what role does this play in understanding such people?
- How did consciousness evolve? Is it an adaptation or is it a by-product of other features of conscious individuals?
- Does it exist or take an alternative form in different creatures such as non-human mammals, birds, insects, and so on?
- Can it come about in artificial systems? Corporate systems?
- How is it realized in, or correlated with, physical systems, such as the brains of conscious individuals?
- Does it come in degrees? Can you be more conscious than someone else? Is there such a thing as an amount or level of consciousness?

I don't think solutions to these problems are lying under our noses. How could they? Saying we are ignorant of some part of the physical world has no bearing on them whatsoever!

However, while the epistemic view doesn't solve these problems, it does help us think about them in a clearer way than people usually do. These problems are routinely entangled with the compatibility problem. In thinking about them, people often have one eye on the compatibility problem, and reject potential answers because they don't solve that problem.

Take the first question: what in general consciousness is. In philosophy, one historically important way to approach this issue is to offer a reductive definition of consciousness, an account that analyses it entirely in physical terms. A proposal of this sort, if correct, would answer two questions at once: It would say what consciousness is, but also that it is compatible with physicalism. But there is no law that says you must answer two questions at once. On the contrary, all the problems on the list above can fruitfully be addressed in the absence either of a reductive definition or of a precise account of how the building blocks of nature, whatever they might be, add up to consciousness.

When you think about it, this is the normal situation. The project of rational inquiry, whether in philosophy, the natural or social sciences, or elsewhere, is the project of trying to understand various aspects of the huge system of existence of which we are a part. We may carry out that project, and often do so successfully, even when we don't have a full theory of what that system amounts to. Why should consciousness be any different?

*

So these are the main points in my contribution to this debate on the nature of consciousness: that the ignorance hypothesis is true, that we can appeal to this hypothesis to solve the compatibility problem, that solving the problem in this way is better than any alternative, and that this epistemic view puts us in a much better position to deal with further problems about consciousness, not because it solves them directly but because it detaches them from the compatibility problem with which they have been historically associated.

In Section 1, we will look at what is meant by "consciousness" in contexts like this. The basic message here is *pluralism*: there are various different things we talk about when we talk about consciousness, and there is no point debating which of these is "really" consciousness.

In Section 2, we will look at the compatibility problem, and the epistemic response to that problem. The basic message here is that the epistemic view is better than other approaches, by which I mean dualist (including panpsychist) views, eliminativist or illusionist approaches, and what I call *standard* physicalist responses, by which I mean versions of physicalism that make no theoretical use of the ignorance hypothesis.

In Section 3, we will examine what consciousness science might look like after the epistemic view is adopted. Partly my focus here is on a central idea about the shape of such a science, namely, that there are empirical laws between each conscious state and some physical system, and that the science of consciousness is the attempt to provide systematic knowledge of such laws. I think this idea is implausible on its own terms; it is preferable to understand the science in a more modest way. But I am also concerned to demonstrate that it is perfectly possible to construct a science of consciousness even if we accept that we do not and may never have a complete theory of the world.

1. What Consciousness Is

1.1. Phenomenal Consciousness

When I was in my 20s, I discovered I had gout. My father had it so it's not surprising I got it too, even though my older brother escaped it. I remember my father hobbling about in the hallway in the house where I grew up. As children we thought it was a bit comical. We suspected he was putting it on, maybe because of the weird cultural association of gout and braininess. The truth is we didn't imagine the excruciating agony that goes along with an attack of gout.

Let me tell you about one of the ways it is excruciating. It turns out that when you are walking around normally, your feet are slightly bigger than they would otherwise be because they have more blood in them. When you go to sleep the blood settles into other parts of your body and so your feet contract slowly in size. This data point interacts in a particularly devilish way with gout. You drag yourself around during the day, your bum foot behind you. When you get home, you pass out from exhaustion. But then at some point during the night your feet contract and your skin puts pressure on the joint of your big toe. You are woken up by . . . well, I will let you imagine it for yourself.

When people talk about consciousness in philosophy, they often have episodes like this in mind. I felt the most intense pain in the joint of my big toe. In feeling that way, I was conscious. At any rate, I was conscious in a particular way, the way that philosophers call "phenomenal consciousness." I was phenomenally conscious because I felt that way in my toe.

1.1.1. The Phenomenal Account

We have just introduced phenomenal consciousness with an example, but we need to talk generally, not limited to this case—how to do this?

Perhaps the simplest way is to think of phenomenal consciousness as a generalization of the notion of feeling. I was conscious because I felt a particular way in the joint of my big toe. The same thing would be true if I felt a tingle in the elbow, or butterflies in the stomach, or any other sort of feeling. And the same is true of you too. In general, people are phenomenally conscious when they feel some way or other.

This certainly is a simple way to put it, but it will help to frame matters a little bit more technically as well.

In philosophy, when people want to talk generally, they often appeal to what they call *properties* (also known as features or attributes or characteristics). All of us have (or instantiate) many properties, in fact a potential infinity of properties. I am of a certain weight and height; I have certain social and economic features; I am located in a particular place in space and time. Similar things apply to you and other people, and to non-people too.

When I felt the way that I did in my toe, I had or instantiated a property, namely, the property of feeling that way in my toe. If you felt that way, you would have that property also. Likewise, if you felt some other way, you would instantiate some other related property. Suppose we refer to such properties as *phenomenal properties*. To a first approximation, phenomenal properties are the properties you have when you feel a certain way; if you like, think of "phenomenal" as being spelt with an "f" for feeling.

Now we can formulate the first of several accounts of consciousness we will discuss. Here it is:

The Phenomenal Account:

> A subject is conscious if and only if the subject instantiates some phenomenal property or other.

This account provides necessary and sufficient conditions for consciousness, or, more accurately, for a subject to be conscious. The phrase "if and only if," which will occur a lot in what follows, is the standard way in philosophy of expressing this. It means that it is necessary ("only if") and sufficient ("if") for a subject to be conscious that they have or instantiate a phenomenal property. In what follows, when I speak of phenomenal consciousness I mean consciousness according to this account.

1.2. Complications

We have made our first moves in thinking about consciousness, but even these can be confusing. So let me make a number of comments designed to forestall possible misapprehensions.

1.2.1. Terminology

As it occurs in the phenomenal account, "conscious" is an adjective that applies, when it does, to a particular subject, such as me. In that usage, it is like "Californian" or "six-feet tall." But the word appears in various other guises (see the box on pages 77–8) and the account says nothing about them. In particular, it says nothing about the construction "is conscious of," which as we will see is prominent in other accounts of consciousness.

Even as it occurs as an adjective like this, "conscious" in the phenomenal account departs from ordinary usage. To say you are conscious without further qualification usually means you are awake or alert. That is not what it means in the context of phenomenal consciousness. When you are awake or alert, it may be that you feel some way, but the phenomenal account says nothing about this one way or the other.

Here we may notice something that may well have occurred to you already: phenomenal consciousness is not very well served by the English word "conscious." As we will see later, other notions of consciousness integrate better with linguistic practice. If we are looking for an ordinary language counterpart of this notion of consciousness, it would be "feeling" and related expressions such as "how it feels," "the way you feel," and so on. That's why we started off by saying that phenomenal consciousness is a generalization of the notion of feeling.

There are three further bits of vocabulary here to mention.

First, "what it's like." This phrase has had a major impact on the development of consciousness studies; see the box on pages 82–3. But for our purposes we can think of it as equivalent to "what it feels like." Hence using it doesn't add to what we already have.

Second, "experience." Sometimes "experience" is used to record the fact that you feel a certain way; if so it doesn't add to what we already have either. But "experience," like "consciousness," has other uses too. Sometimes it occurs as a verb, as when we say "we experience something"; the phenomenal account says nothing about that. And often "experience" denotes an event, like a birthday party or a funeral, which in some hard-to-explain way is striking in the life of someone. But if I am phenomenally conscious, this need not involve any event that is striking; it may on the contrary be extremely boring and mundane. Perhaps, for example, all of us have a constant level of background feeling, at least when we are awake.

Finally, Latinisms, such as "qualia," which is a phrase sometimes used for phenomenal properties, but is also used for related properties of a special sort. I'm going to try to keep Latinisms on the index of prohibited words, which is a fancy way of saying we won't use them. So I won't employ the word "qualia" in what follows. But keeping Latinisms out of philosophy entirely is a tall order and one or two will creep in, and in fact already have crept in; why don't you see if you can spot them?

1.2.2. Conscious Subjects

The phenomenal account says that a subject is conscious if and only if there is a phenomenal property they have, or, more colloquially, they feel a certain way. But what *is* a subject exactly?

For our purposes, subjects are in the category that philosophers call *particulars*, that is, any existing thing at all that is (a) capable of instantiating properties but (b) is not itself a property. There are many such particulars: my left hand, Alice B. Toklas, the Milky Way, the number two, the arc of the moral universe, and so on.

What distinguishes subjects among particulars is that they are particulars capable of instantiating psychological properties. I am a subject because I can believe things, want things, imagine things, remember things, and feel things. Alice B. Toklas is (or was) a subject for the same reason. The Milky Way on the other hand is a particular but not a subject, since it has no psychological properties at all.

1.2.3. Conscious States

While "conscious" is often used to characterize subjects, it is also used to characterize things that aren't subjects. Alice may be conscious, for example, but perhaps her desire for revenge is conscious also.

But what is this thing, Alice's desire for revenge, that we are here describing as conscious? Answer: it is a psychological state or condition that she is in. So in this case a state of a subject is conscious in addition to the subject herself.

What are states of subjects? Whenever I have a property, I am in the corresponding state. I weigh n kilos; therefore, I am in the state of weighing n kilos. I instantiate various psychological properties; I believe, imagine, feel various things; therefore, I am in the state of believing, imagining, feeling various things. What we have just noticed, from this point of view, is that "conscious" applies to psychological states of subjects, in addition to subjects themselves. (It may also apply to events or processes subjects participate in, or acts they perform; I will set that aside.)

As we formulated it, the phenomenal account applies only to subjects. But we may adapt the basic idea so that it applies to psychological states too.

To do so, notice that phenomenal states—states you are in when you have a phenomenal property—are themselves a kind of psychological state, states you are in when you have a psychological property; nevertheless, not all psychological states are phenomenal. A person who is in a coma, for example, may be truly said to want or know various things, and so be in various psychological states, but they may nevertheless feel nothing at all and so be in no phenomenal states.

Notice also that some psychological states, while not themselves phenomenal, are nevertheless necessarily connected to phenomenal states in this sense: it is impossible for you to be in the psychological state without also being in a phenomenal state. When you remember a painful episode of your past, for example, that state seems necessarily to involve a phenomenal state, but it also necessarily involves something more, e.g., you representing the past in a certain sort of way.

These comments about the relation between psychological and phenomenal states permit a version of the phenomenal account that applies to states rather than subjects:

Phenomenal Account (State Version):

> A psychological state of a subject is conscious if and only if the state either is a phenomenal state or is necessarily connected to a phenomenal state.

From this point of view, my feeling a certain way may count as a conscious state immediately. But any other psychological state will count as conscious if it is necessarily connected to my feeling in some way.

The distinction I have just drawn, between "conscious" as it applies to subjects and as it applies to states of subjects, is sometimes described as the distinction between *creature* and *state* consciousness, and moreover as being an important divide in different kinds of consciousness (Rosenthal 2005). However, while we can certainly draw this distinction, it is not as momentous as it is sometimes presented as being. Whenever I am conscious, there is a psychological state I am in which is conscious, and vice versa. In what follows, therefore, I will move back and forth between the version of the phenomenal account that applies to subjects and the version that applies to states.

1.2.4. Membership of the Class of Phenomenal Properties

Phenomenal properties are a kind of psychological property; what kind exactly?

As we have seen, the most obvious candidates are bodily sensations, similar to the one I had when I had my attack of gout.

Another typical candidate for being in the class of phenomenal properties is properties associated with emotions. You feel anger, embarrassment, or annoyance. All of these are emotions, and when you feel them, you instantiate a phenomenal property in the sense we have in mind.

One thing that brings these together is the English word "feeling." Both bodily sensations and emotions are characteristic examples of feelings. But it is often unappreciated how wide the category of feeling is for English speakers. Consider the acronym "TFW," that is, that feeling when, often used on social media. Here are some examples:

> "TFW you walk into the bathroom with dry socks but the floor is wet."
> "TFW you have just bought a new car and you realize all you want is your old car back again."
> "TFW you are sitting quietly in the sunshine and nothing much is going on."

Notice that the sentence that completes the expression "TFW..." can be any sentence at all no matter how long or complicated. Nevertheless, all of these expressions are associated with a phenomenal property, though perhaps a very complex one. When you have that feeling when you walk into the bathroom with dry socks but the floor is wet you have a phenomenal property. It is a property you have when you feel a certain way. Since there are potentially infinite sentences of the form "TFW . . .," there are potentially infinite phenomenal properties. In fact, there are even more phenomenal properties than this, since it is very plausible that there are more phenomenal properties than there are linguistic expressions of this sort.

1.2.5. Perception

There is one member of the class of phenomenal properties that deserves special consideration: perception. Right now, I can perceive a coffee cup out of the corner of my eye. There it is on the desk. It is a Beatles-themed cup, orange and red with superimposed images from various phases of the fab four's glorious career. To what extent is this a case of my having a phenomenal property?

When thinking about this question, it is helpful to divide things into three sub-questions.

Sub-question #1: Is there any associated feeling at all when I perceive the coffee cup? Is there a feeling I get when I look at the cup? Or, to borrow a phrase from a considerably more limited British band, is there a feeling I get when I look to the west?

Sub-question #2: Is this associated feeling, assuming there is one, of a kind distinct from other more familiar kinds of feeling, that is, ones associated with bodily sensations or emotions? If so, then in our terminology we have found a phenomenal property different from, but related to, these more familiar kinds.

Sub-question #3: What is the relation between this associated distinct feeling (assuming there is one) and the perceptual state I am in when I perceive the mug? There are a number of different possibilities here. One is that the feeling and the perception are identical in the logical sense, that is, one and the same. Another is that the feeling and the perception are empirically correlated, but not identical; that is, they may go together in any circumstance we are liable to encounter but are not literally one and the same. A third possibility is that the feeling and the perception are neither identical nor merely empirically correlated, but are necessarily connected. From this point of view, if someone perceives the mug, or at any rate perceives it in the way that I do, they must also feel a particular way.

A very typical position in philosophy answers these sub-questions in the following way. First, yes, there is a feeling associated with perceptual states of the kind we are talking about; we can talk perfectly correctly, in other words, about TFW you look at a Beatles-themed coffee mug. Second, this feeling is distinct from other sorts of feeling; hence it is a feeling special to perception, or at least to this case of perception. And third, the feeling is not identical to the perceptual state I am in, but is also not merely empirically correlated with it; rather it is necessarily connected to it.

These claims are open to question. For some people, for example, it stretches the concept of feeling out of all recognition to say that there is a distinctive sort of feeling necessarily connected to perception.

I am not so sure; as we have seen, the concept of feeling is very broad. But in any case, I will set aside criticisms like this here, for three reasons.

First, questions of this sort concern the extent of the class of feelings, but most of the issues we will be concerned with arise no matter how precisely the class is to be extended.

Second, I said just now that a "very typical" position in philosophy is one according to which there is a distinctive feeling associated with perception, but that is to understate it. Perception is usually thought of in philosophy as a central case of phenomenal consciousness, certainly as central as bodily sensations or emotions—so much so in fact that these latter phenomena are often understood as varieties of perception themselves: sensation is perception of one's own body, and emotions such as fear are perceptions of properties like danger. Whatever is true in ordinary thought or language, therefore, in philosophy there is a widespread view that these cases are deeply similar to each other. So, to assume perception is not included in the class of phenomenal properties would be to distort the issues we are discussing.

Finally, it is possible to adjust what we have said to accommodate the person who resists saying that perceiving something feels a certain sort of way: by distinguishing a narrower and a broader notion of feeling, or equivalently, a narrower and a broader class of phenomenal properties. In the narrow sense, a feeling is something strongly associated with certain paradigms such as bodily sensations or emotions. In a broader sense, a feeling is something that *either* is strongly associated with these paradigms *or* is very similar to things associated with these paradigms. It may be true that the concept of feeling we normally use is a narrow one, but for all that there is no problem with introducing a broader one, if it is theoretically advantageous to do so.

1.2.6. Metaphysical Structure*

We have been considering the membership of the class of phenomenal properties. A different issue is what philosophers sometimes call the *metaphysical structure* of properties in that class.

The history of philosophy has thrown up several different answers to the latter question. Probably the most notorious of these is what is called *the sense-datum theory*. On this theory, when you instantiate a phenomenal property—for example, when you feel a pain in your toe—what is in fact going on is that you bear a certain sort of relation to a mental particular. Likewise, when you perceive a blue object, and so instantiate a different phenomenal property, you bear a relation to a different mental particular. It might also be that there are physical objects as well in your environment or your body that cause you to go into various states, but these are separate from the phenomenal properties themselves on the sense-datum theory.

In contemporary philosophy, the sense-datum theory is widely rejected, but the literature is divided over which of two main positions should take its place—perhaps a hybrid of both should do so.

The first, often called *relationalism*, says that when you instantiate a phenomenal property, you bear a relation to a physical object of some kind. This view is logically like the sense-datum theory, but it does not say that you are related to a mental particular. It says instead that you are related to ordinary physical objects and their properties.

The second position, often called *representationalism* (sometimes also representationism or intentionalism), says that when you instantiate a phenomenal property you are in a certain kind of representational state, that is, a state of representing things to be thus and so, for example, that a physical object is in your local environment. Since you can represent that a physical object is in your local environment without that being the case, representationalism is a distinct position from relationalism.

It won't matter for our purposes how to resolve these issues, though the notion of a representational state, and representationalism more broadly, will come up several times as we proceed, particularly, in Section 3, and in the box on pages 121–3.

The Word "Conscious"

The root word "conscious" can appear in different forms. Sometimes it appears as an abstract noun; that's how it appears in the title of this book. In fact, this is a rather strange occurrence; according to the linguist Anna Wierzbicka, it has no counterpart in other languages (Wierzbicka 2010). We might think of it like "art" or "religion," a word that denotes a huge area of academic study.

But "consciousness" can also appear in a less academic way, as the name for a state or condition a person can be in. That's how it appears when we say, for example, that Bernice has regained consciousness after being in a coma. Bernice has in some sense come back into a state, consciousness, which she was in before but has not been in in the recent past.

Sometimes it appears as an adjective, applying (as we noted in the text) either to subjects or to states or conditions that subjects are in. Bernice might be conscious again after being in a coma, but her knowledge of the syntactic rules of her language may remain unconscious, even when she herself is conscious.

There is an important distinction between the two uses of the adjective "conscious." Sometimes it requires *complementation* by some other phrase or clause, sometimes not. Suppose Bernice is conscious of movement in the nearby undergrowth. She is in that case conscious of something, namely movement. Here the prepositional phrase "of movement" complements "conscious." Similarly, suppose she is conscious that the day is nearing its end. In that case, she is conscious that such and such, just as she may believe or know that such and such. Here the clause "that the day is nearing its end" complements "conscious."

Both of these uses of "conscious" are to be contrasted with uses that do not require complementation. When we say that Bernice is conscious after not being so or that some state of hers is conscious, we are using the adjective in a way that does not require complementation. In neither case must we go on to ask "conscious of what?" Indeed, in the case in which we are speaking of a state of Bernice, rather than Bernice herself, this question is out of place.

It is common in philosophy to contrast transitive uses of "conscious" with intransitive ones. Norman Malcolm, for example, says that there is a "grammatical distinction" between a use of "conscious" in which it requires an object (he includes both "conscious of" and "conscious that") and a use of "conscious" in which it does not (Armstrong and Malcolm 1984).

Malcolm is right there is a distinction here, but he mischaracterizes it. What he has in mind is the distinction between the use of "conscious" on which it requires complementation and the use on which it does not. Calling it a distinction between transitive and intransitive is misleading since that distinction applies typically to verbs or verb phrases. On his usage, for example, the phrase "is conscious that" is both transitive and not.

The word "conscious" appears not only as a noun and an adjective but also as an adverb. Bernice might consciously perceive something, where this means that she perceived it in a certain way. In fact, any psychological verb can be modified in this way. You can consciously know, imagine, perceive, or remember something.

What is the way you perceive something when you do it consciously? A natural thing is to explain the adverb in terms of the adjective. To perceive something consciously is to be in a state of perception that is conscious. Of course, that only gets us so far since there are several things it means to say that psychological states are conscious.

1.3. Higher-Order Consciousness

Phenomenal consciousness is central for us, but it is nevertheless just one of the things operating under the label "consciousness."

Actually, it is a typical feature of philosophy that people come to realize that different things are called by the same name. Some philosophers work on probability, the general idea that some events or states of affairs are probable or likely, more likely than others, more likely than not, and so on. If you talk to such philosophers, they are bound to tell you that there are different notions of probability that need to be kept apart—they often speak of "objective" versus "subjective" probability, for example. Such philosophers are *pluralists* about probability because they think there is more than one thing that reasonably goes by the name.

Much the same is true for consciousness. Phenomenal consciousness is a reasonable notion but it is only one thing going by the name. What are the others? The most obvious is what I will call *higher-order consciousness*, the topic of this section.

1.3.1. The Higher-Order Account

Suppose I notice that my neighbor has put out his bins early (as he tends to do) and therefore come to believe that it is garbage night. This is for me to have a certain sort of psychological property, namely, the property of believing that it is garbage night. I am therefore in a psychological state, the state of believing that it is garbage night. What is it for this state to be a conscious state?

On the phenomenal account, as we have seen, it must either be or be necessarily connected to a phenomenal state. The higher-order account gives a different answer. It says that this state is conscious because the subject of the state, namely me, bears a certain relation to it; in particular, this state is conscious if and only if I am conscious of believing that it is garbage night.

To express this more generally, the higher-order account says this:

Higher-Order Account:

> A psychological state of a subject is conscious if and only if the subject of the state is conscious of being in the state.

It is easy to get confused here. Isn't the higher-order account trivial? Doesn't it say that a psychological state is conscious if and only if . . . well . . . it is conscious? No; look again. The word "conscious" appears here in two different guises. It is one thing to say that a psychological *state* is conscious; it is quite another to say that a *subject* is conscious *of* something; see the box on pages 77–8. What the higher-order account does is explain the first of these in terms of the second, and that is not a trivial thing to do.

Since it explains the first in terms of the second, the higher-order account is concerned in the first instance with what it is for a psychological state to be conscious, not a subject. But we could modify the underlying idea so that it applies to subjects too. We might say for example, that a subject is conscious, on the higher-order account, if and only if they are in at least one psychological state that is higher-order conscious. As before, we may move back and forth between these two formulations, though it turns out that the one in terms of psychological states is easier to work with.

1.3.2. Being Conscious Of

Like the phenomenal account, the higher-order account uses "conscious" as an adjective for psychological states, but unlike the phenomenal account, it explicitly invokes "is conscious of." It entails that when you are in a conscious state, you are conscious of something.

But what is it to be conscious of something? At this point we encounter one of the most common ideas in the philosophical literature on consciousness: that "conscious of" is synonymous with "aware of" (Armstrong and Malcolm 1984; Dretske 2000).

I think this idea is mistaken. They are certainly closely related, but they are not synonymous. We can speak of being consciously aware of something, but we can't speak (except perhaps as a joke) of being consciously conscious of something.

This suggests that while being conscious of something entails being aware of it, the reverse does not hold. In particular, to be conscious of something is to be aware of it, not as such, but in a certain way: being aware of something does not entail that you are conscious of it, but being aware of something *in a certain way* does entail this.

Factoring this into the higher-order account, we arrive at this version of the view: A psychological state is conscious if and only if the subject of the state is *aware of* being in the state *in a certain way*. It follows that anybody who defends the higher-order account must say something about what "aware of" means, and what "in a certain way" means.

On the issue of "aware of," the most common suggestion in the literature interprets it as similar to belief (Armstrong 1981; Rosenthal 2005); roughly, to be aware of something is to believe something, to be aware of your having a pain is to believe that you have a pain. On this approach, what the higher-order account entails is that a psychological state of yours is conscious *only if* you believe that you are in it. (The version of the higher-order account that treats "aware of" as akin to belief is sometimes called the higher-order *thought* account, to distinguish it from accounts that understand "aware of" differently. I am going to set aside other such accounts here.)

Turning to "in a certain way," let's notice first that it is not plausible to say outright that a psychological state of yours is conscious *if and only if* (i.e. not merely only if) you believe you are in it. That's because you can come to believe that you are in various psychological states in any number of ways. You may believe it on the basis of inference, for example, from what a doctor or a friend tells you. You may even believe it on the basis of perception of your own behavior, for example, when you see yourself in a mirror and say, "Ah, that person must believe such and such," and only later realize you are that person. Coming to believe that you are in a psychological state in these ways does not make the state conscious. So the phrase "in a certain way" must mean something specific in the context of the higher-order account.

In philosophy, there is a famous name for the way in which you come to know or believe that you yourself are in psychological states that is neither inferential nor perceptual, at least as these are usually understood. That name is "introspection," though this label, like others we have used, departs from ordinary usage; see the box on pages 109–10. Adopting this terminology allows us to formulate the version of the higher-order account I will concentrate on, namely, that a psychological state is conscious if and only if the subject of the state believes that they are in the state by introspection. It is because of this connection to introspection that higher-order consciousness may also be called "introspective consciousness."

1.3.3. Higher-Order Versus Phenomenal*

So understood, higher-order consciousness is different from phenomenal consciousness.

First, as the name suggests, the higher-order account has consciousness involving a higher-order belief, that is, a belief about another psychological state, while the phenomenal account does not.

Second, the higher-order account, but not the phenomenal account, applies to psychological states of any kind, phenomenal or not. In principle, I can believe that it is garbage night and feel nothing whatsoever. Yet I may still believe by introspection that I believe that it is garbage night. If so, the state of believing that it is garbage night will be conscious in the higher-order sense, but not in the phenomenal sense. The same thing is true in the other direction.

I may feel a certain way, and yet not believe by introspection that I do so. If so the relevant state will be phenomenally conscious but not higher-order conscious.

In the literature on the higher-order account, a distinction is sometimes drawn between "ambitious" and "modest" versions of the view (Block 2011). On the modest version, the account articulates one notion of consciousness among many. That is how I have been interpreting it here.

On the ambitious version, the account is presented as a definition of phenomenal consciousness: You feel a certain way if and only if you believe that you are in some psychological state; that is, it is necessary and sufficient for you to feel a certain way that you believe something about yourself.

This ambitious version of the higher-order theory is in my view extremely implausible. Did I really feel the way I did in my big toe *because* I believed that I was in some state? No, the belief and the feeling can and do come apart. Indeed, on the ambitious interpretation, the higher-order account is so implausible that you might wonder whether it has been confused with something else, for example, an empirical claim about the states that are contingently associated with phenomenally conscious states. I will come back briefly later to this empirical interpretation of the higher-order account, but for the most part I will set it aside.

What It's Like

Sometimes a phrase so precisely captures something elusive that it changes our experience of the world.

This happened in the realm of academic philosophy, when Thomas Nagel published "What Is It Like to Be a Bat?" (Nagel 1974). This absolutely ordinary phrase, "what it's like," transformed the philosophy and science of consciousness.

Nowadays, whenever anybody writes a book or article about consciousness, whether for a popular or for a professional audience, they talk somewhere about what it's like. The phrase is a linguistic portal to what bothers us most about consciousness.

Nagel wasn't the first to use it. Ludwig Wittgenstein, perhaps the most famous philosopher of the 20th century, employed it some 25 years earlier (Wittgenstein 1980). Wittgenstein, who wrote in German but lived in Britain, deliberately used the English phrase "what it's like." For him it was a piece of English that mattered, not its German counterpart. But even Wittgenstein couldn't have anticipated what happened after Nagel's paper.

What explains the magic of the phrase? In Wittgenstein's native German, and in many other languages, the corresponding expression is unassuming. It just means "how is it?" or something similar. And in English too we sometimes use the phrase without any overt connection to consciousness. What would it have been like if the president were re-elected? What were cars like in the 1920s? What's it like from an economic point of view to have no dental insurance?

Nevertheless, while the phrase can be used in this way, English speakers stereotypically use it to mean something very close to "what it feels like." When the Bee Gees sang "you don't know what it's like to love someone," they meant you don't know how it feels, and in doing so they were using the phrase in a very ordinary way (Stoljar 2016).

Perhaps it's the very ordinariness of the phrase that makes it so powerful. Back in 1974, many people tended to think that what generates problems about consciousness is a technical, insider-y theory about consciousness, a theory expressed in the strange professional vocabulary of philosophy, in words like "qualia," "sense data," and so on.

If the issues were generated by a theory like that, the philosophy and science of consciousness would be much less interesting. You could solve the problems by rejecting the theory. But the power of "what it's like" is that it tells us this isn't true; it isn't what it's like. The problems aren't driven by an insider-y theory but by the ordinary world around us, and the ordinary ways that we think and talk about that world.

1.4. Access Consciousness

Phenomenal consciousness is distinct from higher-order consciousness, but when you think about the relation between these two notions, it is natural to suspect there must be a third notion in the background. The specifications of this third notion are as follows: like the phenomenal notion, it will not require a higher-order state of belief, but like the higher-order notion, it will apply, not only to phenomenal states but to psychological states of any sort.

This idea has come to be called *access consciousness*, and that is the terminology I will use here (Block 1995).

1.4.1. The Access Account

A good way into the notion of access consciousness is to start with a common idea in philosophy of mind: the *functional role* of psychological states.

In general, any psychological state, conscious or not, is associated with a functional role, a typical profile of psychological causes and effects. For example, if you perceive a red ball in front of you, you will in the normal case be disposed to reach for it if you want it, or avoid it if you want to, or form the belief there is a red ball in front of you. Some philosophers will say that these functional roles are exhaustive of the nature of psychological states, but we don't need to go that far to agree that for each psychological state, there is an associated functional role.

If we agree that psychological states are associated with functional roles, the key point about access consciousness is this: A state is access conscious just in case its functional role is enhanced in specific ways. There are at least three ways in which this enhancement might happen.

The *first possible way* is that the state will be more likely than it otherwise would be to produce the effects it is disposed to produce. When you perceive the red ball, there is some likelihood of your reaching for it if asked. When you *consciously* perceive the red ball, however, that likelihood increases. In Block's (Block 1995) terminology, you are not only disposed to reach for the ball, you are *poised* to do so. To be poised to do something in this context is to be more likely than you otherwise would be to do the thing in question.

The *second possible way* is that the state will have a wider functional role than it otherwise would have. When you perceive the red ball, there is some associated functional role, some profile of psychological causes and effects that the state has. When you *consciously* perceive the red ball, however, that profile is increased. In Dennett's (Dennett 1993) terminology, your state of perceiving the red ball has *cerebral celebrity*. For a state to be a cerebral celebrity is for it to have a wider profile of causes and effects than it otherwise would have.

The *final possible way* is that the state will be more likely than it otherwise would be to involve attention (see, e.g., Watzl 2017; Jennings 2020). When you perceive a red ball, it is usually possible that you also attend to the ball, or at least a visually related thing, by which I mean focus on it, concentrate on it, be concerned with it, and so on. When you *consciously* perceive the red ball, however, that level of attentional involvement increases: You will pay more attention than you otherwise would to the ball you perceive.

There are multiple issues here about how to understand these ways in which access consciousness affects the functional role of a psychological state. What exactly is the relation between poise and cerebral celebrity? What is the relation between both of these and attention? Is one thing here explanatorily basic or do we have three separate effects on functional role? Different writers give different answers to these questions, and sometimes the same writers give different answers at different times. When Block first introduced the notion of access consciousness, for example, he focused exclusively on poise, but in later work, he emphasizes the others in addition or instead (see, e.g., Stoljar 2019).

It is not necessary for us to go into these details. Instead it is sufficient to formulate the access account of consciousness as follows:

Access Account:

> A psychological state of a subject is conscious if and only if the standard functional role of the state is enhanced, for example, because the state exhibits poise, cerebral celebrity, or attentional involvement, or some combination of these.

As before, we may say that access consciousness is consciousness as defined by the access account.

1.4.2. Access Versus Higher-Order Versus Phenomenal*

So understood, the access account is different from both the phenomenal account and the higher-order account.

In contrast to the phenomenal account, it applies both to phenomenal states and to psychological states of other sorts, since both sorts of states may have an enhanced functional role in this way. In principle my belief that it is garbage night might be access conscious and yet I feel no way at all.

In contrast to the higher-order account, it does not require that, when you are in a conscious state, you form a higher-order belief: A psychological state may have an enhanced functional role in the ways we have been discussing without being accompanied by a higher-order belief.

One might object that the access account is unlike these other accounts in not describing a genuine notion of consciousness. Isn't calling a state "access conscious" merely to comment on its functional role rather than to attribute a sort of consciousness to it?

But there is a series of points a friend of the access account can make in response to this. First, they can say that there is a very general sense of "aware of" in which whenever you are in any psychological state at all, you are aware of something. In fact, this very general notion of "aware of" is closely related to the idea of representation that we considered briefly when distinguishing representationalist and relationalist approaches to perception; see 1.2.6.

When you believe that it is garbage night, for example, you represent a certain state of affairs, the state of affairs of its being garbage night. If that state of affairs obtains, your belief is true; if that state of affairs does not obtain, your belief is false. We may also say, to put the point in the language of awareness, that when you believe that it is garbage night, you are aware in a general sense of this state of affairs, and so you are aware of something. Likewise, when you perceive a red object in front of you, you represent the red object, and so are aware of it. Hence, when you perceive a red object, you are aware of something.

Second, they can say whenever you are in psychological state that is access conscious, you are not simply aware of something but aware of something *in a particular way*. As we just noticed, if you are in a psychological state there is a very general sense in which you are aware of something, and if the psychological state has an enhanced functional role, as it will if it is access conscious, then you are aware of something in a particular way, since the functional role of the state of awareness will be enhanced.

Finally, they can appeal to an idea we considered before in connection with the higher-order account: that to be conscious of something is to be aware of it not as such but in a certain way. Since, as we have just seen, the access account agrees that when you are in an access-conscious psychological state you are aware of something not as such but in a certain way, it follows that when you are in an access-conscious state, you are conscious of something. In fact, the only difference between the access account and the higher-order account is that, in the case of the higher-order account, you are aware of a psychological state itself, while in the case of the access account, you are conscious of the state of affairs that would obtain if your belief is true or the object that would be in front of you if your perception were veridical.

Putting these points together: The notion of consciousness described by the access account is a genuine notion, or at any rate as genuine as the one described by the higher-order account, since it too involves the view that when you are in a conscious state you are conscious of something.

1.5. Relations Among These Notions

I said in the introduction that the goal of this first section is to get clear on what "consciousness" amounts to. We've come a long way, as I'm sure you will agree.

We started, in particular, with the idea that it is subjects that are conscious, but we have ended up with three distinct theories about when a psychological state is conscious:

- The phenomenal account: A psychological state of a subject is conscious if and only if it is or is necessarily connected to the subject's having a phenomenal property.
- The higher-order account: A psychological state of a subject is conscious if and only if the subject is aware of being in the state in a certain sort of way.
- The access account: A psychological state of a subject is conscious if and only if the standard functional role of the state is enhanced in distinctive ways.

These theories are not in competition. They are instead theories of different things that might reasonably be called "consciousness." In that sense, the situation as regards consciousness is similar to the situation as regards probability.

Suppose we accept there are three different notions, then the natural question is: What relations hold among them?

There are two sorts of extreme positions here. One answer is that there is no meaningful relation at all. It may be true that we in our culture call them by the same name but that is of no interest from the point of view of the universe.

Another answer is that one of these notions is basic in the sense that the other two are to be explained in terms of it. At the limit, this position will deny the pluralism we have so far been defending.

But there is a different and more attractive line on the relation between these different notions. On this approach, while these notions of consciousness are distinct, they are nevertheless connected in principled ways. Articulating these principles is a major project, and we won't try to complete it here. Instead, I will end this section by conveying a sense of what such principles might look like.

1.5.1. The Connection Between Higher-Order and Access Consciousness*

A good way to think about the relation between higher-order and access consciousness is to note a problem for the higher-order account I didn't mention earlier.

On the higher-order account, as we developed it, a state is conscious if and only if you believe you are in it by introspection. A problem for this account is that, when you believe you are in a psychological state by introspection, the state must *already* be conscious in some sense or other.

Suppose I believe it is garbage night, and come to know by introspection that I believe this. In that case, my belief that it is garbage night must already have been conscious. If it were not, I could hardly have known I was in it by introspection. After all, that is what introspection is: the distinctive method whereby you come to know or believe that you are in various conscious states (see the box on pages 109–10).

There is a sense in which this problem doesn't threaten the truth of the higher-order account. It remains possible for a psychological state to be such that you believe you are in it by introspection; there is no reason why in that circumstance it might not deserve the label "conscious."

But what the problem brings to light is that, while higher-order consciousness is a reasonable notion, it is also a limited one, since it presupposes a different notion of consciousness. Whenever you are in a state that is conscious in the higher-order sense, that state must be conscious also in some other sense.

What could this other notion be? Given our discussion so far, it must be either phenomenal consciousness or access consciousness.

At this point, some people might plump for phenomenal consciousness and say that whenever a state is conscious in the higher-order sense, it must also be conscious in the phenomenal sense. But this is too restrictive. When you know by introspection that you are in some psychological state, the state may be phenomenally conscious. But not always; many psychological states are knowable by introspection, and yet are not phenomenal. I may know by introspection that I believe it is garbage night, and nevertheless feel nothing relevant whatsoever.

A better option appeals to access consciousness. On this approach, when you believe that you are in a state by introspection, and so that state is higher-order conscious, it is also access conscious. When I believed it was garbage night, for example, and that state was conscious in the higher order sense, it must also have exhibited the functional features associated with access consciousness. Notice that this does not stop you from coming to believe by introspection that you are in a phenomenal state too; it only means that such a state must be also access conscious if you are to do so.

Does the reverse entailment hold? No; the whole point of introducing the idea of access consciousness is to acknowledge the possibility of being in an access-conscious state, and yet not believe you are in it by introspection. Perhaps, for example, you are simply not interested in or capable of forming the higher-order belief. If you are an animal stalking its prey, for example, you may perceive the prey, and your perception may be access conscious, but you may well not believe by introspection that you are perceiving the prey. Or perhaps you are interested and capable of forming the higher-order belief but are not rational enough to form it. There is no requirement, after all, that subjects who are in access-conscious states are rational. If not, they may believe, or fail to believe, anything whatsoever.

These considerations show it is not true *in general* that if you are in an access-conscious state, you will believe by introspection that you are in the state, and so be in a higher-order conscious state. Still, it remains an option that something along these lines is true in a more restricted way. In particular, it may be true in the special case of rational subjects who meet certain psychological conditions, namely, rational subjects who are psychologically capable of forming the relevant introspective belief and are concerned with whether that belief is true.

This provides us with one plausible linking principle about access and higher-order consciousness: Among rational subjects who meet these conditions, a psychological state is access conscious if and only if it is higher-order conscious. Whether even this principle is ultimately correct is an interesting question, but we will not pursue it here.

1.5.2. The Connection Between Phenomenal and Access Consciousness*

Where does this leave phenomenal consciousness; how, in particular, is it related to access consciousness? There are two potential answers to this question, and it won't be necessary for us to decide between them.

The first answer is that, while phenomenal and access consciousness are distinct, they are also correlated from an empirical point of view—typically but not always phenomenally conscious states are access conscious.

The second answer imposes a further condition on phenomenal consciousness. The phenomenal account above says that a psychological state is phenomenally conscious if and only if it either is or is necessarily connected to a phenomenal state. But it is possible to articulate an alternative account, which builds an access condition into phenomenal consciousness:

Phenomenal Account (Access Version)

> A psychological state is (phenomenally) conscious if and only if (a) it either is a phenomenal state or is necessarily connected to a phenomenal state; and (b) it is access conscious or at least could easily become access conscious.

This variation on the phenomenal account has a number of interesting features. It does not imply, for example, that feeling in a particular way must be or easily be access conscious, only that it must if it is also phenomenally conscious. But it does imply that phenomenal and access-conscious states are not merely empirically correlated; rather, they stand to each other as species to genus.

Should we accept this alternative or should we stick with the original? As I say, let's leave it open.

The key points of this first section are as follows. Phenomenal consciousness is a generalization of the notion of feeling. We can express that notion in terms of the idea of a phenomenal property. The notion of a phenomenal property raises lots of further issues: its relation to our ordinary talk about "consciousness," the distinction between subjects and states, the extent of the class of phenomenal properties, and their metaphysical structure. Higher-order consciousness is a matter of belief or knowledge by introspection. It is distinct from phenomenal consciousness. Access consciousness is a matter of a psychological state having an enhanced functional role. It is distinct from both phenomenal and higher-order consciousness. It is plausible to think that higher order and access conscious are related to each other by the principle that, among subjects who are rational and who meet certain psychological conditions, a psychological state is access conscious if and only if it is higher-order conscious. Phenomenal and access consciousness are related by the fact that empirically they often come together. But it is also possible to adjust the definition of phenomenal consciousness to require phenomenally conscious states to be either access conscious or such that they could easily become access conscious.

2. Consciousness and the World

So much for what consciousness is; let's turn to the questions we may ask about it.

Actually, there are many such questions. This is in part because of pluralism; there is more than one thing here. But it is also because different questions could be asked about each of these things. Research in consciousness studies, like research quite generally, is often hobbled by not identifying clearly enough what question you are trying to answer.

As a philosopher, I am interested in philosophical questions about consciousness, rather than questions of a more obviously scientific character. But what are philosophical questions?

That's a big issue, but my own view is that philosophy is identified by its subject matter rather than its methodology. Philosophers tend to ask about the scope and limits of human knowledge, what the world or the entire system of existence is like in general, and the position of various items such as freedom, morality, rationality, and knowledge within that system. So philosophical questions about consciousness will be questions about consciousness that bear on these sorts of issues.

And consciousness *does* bear on these issues, in several ways. "Consciousness is what makes the mind-body problem really intractable," Thomas Nagel famously wrote. "Perhaps that is why current discussions of the problem give it little attention or get it obviously wrong" (Nagel 1974).

In speaking of "consciousness," Nagel is talking about phenomenal consciousness, that is, consciousness according to the phenomenal account. In saying people get it obviously wrong, I think he means that people confuse phenomenal consciousness with other notions, in particular the higher-order notion. One benefit of pluralism about consciousness is that we avoid squabbles about whether people get "it" wrong; there is no single "it" to get wrong. Be that as it may, there is no doubt that phenomenal consciousness is a legitimate thing to focus on.

What question is Nagel asking about that notion? When he says phenomenal consciousness makes the mind-body problem intractable, what he has in mind is not the science of consciousness but the more general idea that consciousness doesn't fit into a physicalist worldview. So for Nagel the label "mind-body problem" picks out the compatibility problem I mentioned in the introduction. That problem is the topic of this section.

2.1. The Conceivability Argument

Why is the existence of phenomenal consciousness thought to be incompatible with physicalism?

There are a number of distinct arguments designed to bring this out. Here we will focus on one, sometimes called the conceivability argument ("CA" for short). Strictly speaking, CA is an argument against the truth of physicalism. However, since it presupposes the existence of consciousness, it may be regarded also as an argument for the incompatibility of physicalism and the existence of consciousness.

CA is easiest to understand if we put it in premise-and-conclusion form, and then comment on the premises. Here it is:

The Conceivability Argument Against Physicalism:

> *Premise 1:* It is conceivable that there is a situation exactly like the actual situation in respect of all instantiated physical properties, but different from it in respect of some instantiated phenomenal property, that is, in some respect having to do with phenomenal consciousness.

Premise 2: If it is conceivable that there is a situation that meets the description in Premise 1, then it is possible that there is.
Premise 3: If it is possible that there is a situation that meets the description in Premise 1, then physicalism is false.
Conclusion: Physicalism is false.

This argument has a straightforward logical structure. It has the form "A, if A then B, if B then C, therefore C." So one thing we know about CA is that it is valid: If the premises are true, the conclusion must be true. Hence, the assessment of the argument turns on whether its premises are true. So what motivates them?

2.1.1. Motivating the Premises of CA

As regards premise 1, it is common to support this by appealing to very extreme cases: zombies, inverted spectra, and so on; see the box on page 98. But the premise can also be motivated with examples that are not so far-fetched.

Right now, for example, I am sitting out in the patio, a glass of pastis is on the table in front of me, the crickets are singing, and a podcast is playing on my phone. I feel a certain way, or at least I am in some overall system of feeling. But now imagine a situation which is exactly like this in terms of what physical properties are instantiated but is different in respect of some phenomenal property. In this situation my body and brain, their myriad constituents, my local and global environment, all have whatever physical properties they have, and yet there is some even very small phenomenal difference somewhere. Perhaps the pastis tastes just a bit more of liquorice than it usually does, or perhaps the podcast is a little more distinct. This situation, were it to exist, would be one which is the same as the actual one in all physical respects but different from the real situation in some phenomenal respect. To the extent that the situation is conceivable, premise 1 is true.

Turning to premise 2, this entails that if the pastis situation is conceivable, it is possible too. What does that mean?

That something is possible, in contexts like this, is intended to be an objective fact about it: It holds whatever anybody conceives or thinks. Whatever anybody conceives or thinks, for example, it is possible that the initial constants of the universe may have been different from what they in fact are. Likewise, it is possible (according to the second part of this premise) that someone physically exactly like me might be phenomenally different in some way or the other.

But what justifies the move from conceivability to possibility in this objective sense? Let's first note that we do in fact have a lot of *modal* knowledge, that is, knowledge of what is possible and necessary in this objective sense. For example, right now I know that there is *not* a huge pile of mushy peas on the kitchen floor. But I also know there *could* be such a pile; in other words, it is *possible* that there is. How do I know this is possible? One plausible answer is that I can conceive or imagine a situation that meets the relevant description. I know it is possible that there is a large pile of mushy peas on the kitchen floor because I can conceive that there is. According to the second premise, what is true in this mundane case is true also in the case of physicalism and consciousness.

Premise 3 of CA says that the possibility described in the second premise is ruled out by physicalism: If that situation is possible, physicalism is false. What justifies this premise?

So far, we have interpreted physicalism as a worldview, a systematic account of what the world is like. One thing that means is that it is an exhaustive thesis. It tells us something about every property whatsoever that is instantiated in the world. More specifically, it entails that every instantiated property is either a physical property or else is necessitated by a physical property, where to be necessitated by a physical property means that if something has the physical property, then it *must* also have the property in question. So take the beauty of Paris, which we may understand as a property of Paris, though presumably a very complex property. If physicalism is true, the beauty of Paris either is a physical property itself or else is necessarily connected to a physical property in the sense that if Paris had that physical property, then it must be beautiful in the way that it is. If physicalism is true, what goes for the beauty of Paris goes for every instantiated property.

But the possibility described in the second premise precisely goes against this: It entails that some phenomenal property is neither physical nor necessitated by a physical property. That is why the possibility is inconsistent with physicalism, and that is why the third premise of CA is plausible.

2.2. The Epistemic View

CA is a valid argument for the falsity of physicalism, whose premises are prima facie plausible. How to respond?

There are a number of classical responses to this argument, which we will turn to in a moment. But let's begin by looking at the response of the epistemic view, which I introduced at the beginning of my opening statement.

The epistemic view offers a two-part response. The first part supposes that there is a type of physical fact or property that is relevant to consciousness but of which we are ignorant. As I noted, I call this *the ignorance hypothesis*. This part of the epistemic view is a contingent claim, since it makes a claim about our epistemic capacities and achievements, and the relation between these capacities and achievements and the world. But it is a contingent claim that is extremely plausible, at least prima facie; surely, we can all agree that there are types of facts about consciousness of which we are ignorant!

The second part argues that, if the ignorance hypothesis is true, CA is unpersuasive. To illustrate this second part, let us focus on the phrase "all instantiated physical properties" that occurs explicitly or implicitly throughout the argument; a phrase of this sort is sometimes called a "quantifier phrase" because the word "all" is a quantifier. Here is the first premise again with the phrase italicized:

Premise 1: It is conceivable that there is a situation that is exactly like the actual situation in respect of *all instantiated physical properties* but is different from it in respect of some instantiated phenomenal property, that is, in some respect having to do with phenomenal consciousness.

If the ignorance hypothesis is true, there are two ways to interpret this phrase. It might be interpreted so that the physical properties that are relevant but unknown to us are included in its scope. Or it might be interpreted so that those properties are not included. However, and here is the key point: Either way you interpret this phrase, the argument is unpersuasive.

Why is it the case that however you interpret the underlined quantifier phrase, the argument is unpersuasive?

Well, suppose first that the relevant but unknown physical properties are *not* included in its scope. In that case, the first and second premises of CA will tell us only about *some* of the instantiated physical properties, not about all. So interpreted, these premises entail it is possible that consciousness comes apart from *some* physical facts, not that it comes apart from all.

But the problem is that there is now no reason to accept the third premise. After all, it is not inconsistent with physicalism that consciousness comes apart from *some* physical facts. How could it be? That claim is entirely unsurprising. Certainly premise 3 does not now entail that consciousness is a fundamental element in nature, which, as we will see in a moment, is the conclusion that proponents of CA are usually interpreted as wanting to establish.

So suppose instead that the relevant but unknown physical properties *are* included in the phrase "all instantiated physical properties." Then the problem for the argument is different: It is that its first premise is false, or at any rate could easily be denied by the physicalist. After all, if you don't know what the relevant physical respects are, you can't conceive in the appropriate sense a situation in which all the physical facts are as they are, but some phenomenal fact is different.

What does it mean to say "conceive in the appropriate sense"? Consider again the case in which I know that there could be a huge pile of mushy peas on the kitchen floor, even though there isn't. I know that this is possible because I can conceive or imagine it. But the notion of conceiving here must be quite demanding. You need to know, at least in outline, what it takes for the conceived situation to obtain; otherwise conceiving won't allow me to know this possibility.

The same applies to CA. In order that premise 2 is true, I must know in outline what it takes for the conceived situation to obtain. That means in turn I must know the relevant types of physical properties. But the ignorance hypothesis precisely denies this. Hence, if the quantifier phrase is interpreted in this second way, the first premise of CA should be rejected; you can't and don't conceive in the appropriate sense.

Of course, none of this denies that there might be other notions of conceiving. A good way to bring this out is to contrast conceiving as we have understood it with what philosophers sometimes call "supposing," that is, supposing something to be the case. Supposing something to be the case provides no reason to believe it is possible. You can suppose it is the case that $2 + 2 = 5$, for example, in order to show something about mathematics. But this doesn't justify you in believing it is possible that $2 + 2 = 5$. Likewise, for all the ignorance hypothesis says, it may be that you can suppose the situation described in CA obtains but that would not begin to show it is possible.

2.2.1. The Book of Nature and Ordinary Books

We may bring out the basic idea of the epistemic view by contrasting the book of nature and ordinary books.

Suppose I hold up an ordinary book and say, "It is possible that everything in this book is the case, and yet it is not the case that Charlie Chaplin died in Switzerland." Is what I said true?

The obvious answer is that we don't know, and the reason is we don't know what is in the book. Suppose the book is a biography of Chaplin, focusing on the circumstances of his death. Then what I would have said is false, assuming the book is reliable.

Suppose instead that the book is a cookbook, focusing on Japanese desserts. Then what I would have said is true, assuming it is not an extremely unusual cookbook, which includes sidebars about the lives of 20th-century film personalities.

This example should remind us that we make modal judgments all the time, in this case about what is possible or not as regards some particular book. But it should also remind us that knowledge of such things as books influences what sort of modal judgments we can reasonably make about them.

In fact, you could construct an argument here exactly like the first part of CA. Its first premise is that it is conceivable that everything in this book is the case, and yet Chaplin didn't die in Switzerland; its second premise is that if this is conceivable, it is possible. The conclusion is that it is possible that everything in this book is the case and yet it is not the case that Charlie Chaplin died in Switzerland.

This argument is obviously unpersuasive, and the reason again is we don't know what's in the book. In consequence, we can't conceive of the relevant thing in the appropriate sense. No doubt we can conceive it in some sense or other. For example, we can *suppose* that everything in the book is the case, and yet Chaplin didn't die in Switzerland. But, as we have seen, supposing doesn't justify claims about possibility.

On the epistemic view, what goes for ordinary books goes for the book of nature, the mythical volume that tells us literally everything about the world. We may make modal judgments about it—for example, that every physical thing written down in it could be true without some phenomenal thing being true. And we may construct conceivability reasoning such as CA in support of these judgments. But our ability to make these judgments and sustain this reasoning is sensitive to what we know about the contents of the book. In particular, if we are ignorant of some relevant type of thing written down in the book of nature, CA will be unpersuasive. What the epistemic view is saying is that this is precisely the case.

Zombies and the Inverted Spectrum

The key idea of the conceivability argument is that it is conceivable, and so possible, to have a situation exactly like the one we are in from a physical point of view, but different from it phenomenally. It is common in philosophy to motivate this claim by focusing on two thought-experiments: zombies and the inverted spectrum.

Zombies in the philosophical sense are not the zombies of Hollywood but are rather beings who by definition are physically exactly like us but who lack all phenomenal consciousness entirely. Zombies behave exactly as we do, have exactly the same brains and bodies, and have even the same psychological states, so long as these states are not phenomenal states. The limiting case is a zombie world: a world that is identical to ours, except for the fact that it lacks phenomenal states (see, e.g., Chalmers 1996).

The inverted spectrum hypothesis does not involve beings who lack phenomenal consciousness entirely. It rather focuses on the idea that particular aspects of phenomenal consciousness in one subject may be systematically switched with counterpart aspects in another subject. Max and Moritz, for example, might be identical physically, and yet when Max looks at cherry tomatoes, the associated feeling or phenomenal property he has is precisely the one Moritz has when he looks at cucumbers (see, e.g., Shoemaker 1982).

Both of these examples have proved controversial; a lot of philosophers think there is some hidden contradiction in them. Against the zombie hypothesis for example, some argue that there are necessary connections between being in a phenomenally conscious state and believing that one is, and that, on account of this, very idea of zombies is contradictory. Against the inverted spectrum hypothesis, some argue that there are asymmetries in color perception that rule out any possibility of a straightforward switch.

It is a difficult question whether these apparent inconsistencies are genuine or not; there are many different versions of these thought experiments, and the details of these different versions matter. That is why in the text we focused on a much simpler example, which does not require the absence of phenomenal consciousness entirely or its systematic inversion.

2.3. Alternatives to This View

How does the epistemic view compare with other proposals about how to respond to the conceivability argument?

2.3.1. Dualism and Panpsychism

The dualist accepts CA and concludes that consciousness is a fundamental element of nature.

What is it to say that something is a fundamental element of nature? Think of an ordinary physical object such as the desk in my office. It has various properties, a certain shape, weight, color, and so on. One of its more interesting properties is that, while it is a desk, it is nevertheless made up of things that are not desks. I don't just mean its legs and top, though of course it is made up of them. What I have in mind are stranger things such as atoms, sub-atomic particles, regions of space, and so on. While the desk itself exists, it is not, as we might say, a fundamental object but is rather a derivative one: an object that depends for its existence and nature on the existence and nature of other things.

Extending this from objects to properties, we may also say that the properties of the desk, its color or shape, are not fundamental but are instead derivative: properties that depend for their instantiation on the instantiation of other properties, in this case, the properties had by the fundamental objects, whatever they are, that make the desk up.

When people talk in philosophy of "fundamental elements of nature," they generally mean to apply this way of thinking about the desk to everything whatsoever. The underlying picture is that the world at large is made up of a certain kind of fundamental object or objects, which have a small stock of fundamental properties. Every other existing or instantiated thing, which is most things on the usual development of this approach, is not fundamental but derivative.

From this point of view, what the dualist is saying is that phenomenal properties, such as the property that I had when I had my attack of gout, are fundamental. This view is not logically incoherent, but it is extremely unlikely. After all, it is me who felt the way that I did. And like my desk, I am not a fundamental thing. I too depend for my existence and nature on the existence and nature of other things. So if dualism is true, some non-fundamental objects have fundamental properties too. And that involves a very odd break in the totality of existing things.

To see how odd the break is, consider a diachronic analogy. In a temporal sense, it is plausible that the universe had some initial conditions, which together with the empirical laws, determine or render probable every other event occurring in time. But now imagine someone who looks at an ordinary event in history—for example, Charlie Chaplin's dying in Switzerland—and insists that it too is an initial condition of the universe. A position of this sort is not incoherent. There is no contradiction in claiming that this event has no history. Still, it is extremely improbable, because it involves an odd break. The same is true with the suggestion that consciousness is fundamental.

Dualists respond to arguments like this in several ways. One way that has been influential in recent years is to move to panpsychism: the idea that consciousness is not simply had by non-fundamental objects like humans and animals but also in some form by fundamental objects, whatever they might be. If so, one can obtain the benefits of dualism but without the implausible by-product of an unexpected break in the system of nature.

But panpsychism is implausible too, arguably more so. In its most straightforward version, it entails that a fundamental object—a particular electron, for example—feels pain somewhat in the way that we do. For most of us, this is no more likely than its having a handlebar mustache or being a member of the lumpenproletariat.

Panpsychists will protest this is a caricature. "The phenomenal properties had by fundamental objects," they may say, "are quite different from those had by us."

But while this does indeed remove some of the implausibility of panpsychism, it also raises an awkward dilemma. Suppose the panpsychist says that the phenomenal properties had by fundamental objects are akin to those had by us. Then it is hard to see that the basic implausibility of their position has been avoided. Suppose instead the panpsychist says that the phenomenal properties had by fundamental objects are very different from those had by us; perhaps, for example, we have no idea what these properties are beyond the fact that they combine together with other properties to yield ordinary phenomenal properties. Then panpsychism, despite its name, ceases to have any panpsychist content; it is simply the thesis that the fundamental elements of the world somehow or other have the capability to yield consciousness—and that is not something many people will deny.

2.3.2. Eliminativism and Illusionism

The second response to CA concedes that the argument is sound so long as phenomenal consciousness exists—but then goes on to deny it exists. Clearly it is no objection to physicalism that it is incompatible with the existence of something, if that something does not exist.

This too is not incoherent. It is not logically contradictory to say you have no feelings. Still, this *eliminativist* option (as it is usually called) is also an unbelievable view. I felt a particular way when I had gout; that some philosopher tells me I didn't moves me not at all.

What do eliminativists say to this? Usually, they distinguish two notions of phenomenal consciousness: a *problematic* notion apparently presupposed in CA, and an *unproblematic* notion. What they deny, they say, is only phenomenal consciousness in the problematic sense. This leaves unaffected consciousness in the unproblematic sense, which stops their position from being unbelievable.

But this only disguises the implausibility of eliminativism, perhaps even from eliminativists themselves. One may certainly distinguish different notions of phenomenal consciousness. Consider again the sense-datum theory, on which when I feel a pain in my foot, and so instantiate a phenomenal property, I am acquainted with a mental object. In the light of that theory, one might articulate a particular conception of phenomenal consciousness: phenomenal consciousness as understood by the sense-datum theory. Moreover, one might reasonably go on to say that phenomenal consciousness so understood does not exist, even if consciousness understood in some other way does.

However, while one can distinguish problematic and non-problematic notions of consciousness here, this is no help to the eliminativist. For their view is not merely that there *exists* a problematic conception; it is in addition that this problematic conception is *presupposed* in CA. And that is not so. When we formulated CA, we used the notion of a phenomenal property, but we didn't rely on any particular account of what such properties consist in; we certainly did not rely on the sense-datum theory.

In recent literature, the standard eliminativist position is distinguished from a more elaborate position called *illusionism*. The illusionist is an eliminativist who says not only that there is a problematic conception of consciousness presupposed in CA but in addition we are under a stable introspective illusion that consciousness exists in this problematic sense. One development of this view, for example, is that we are under a stable introspective illusion that the sense-datum theory is true.

This is an interesting position, but it is even more improbable than standard eliminativism. If it is unlikely that consciousness in some problematic sense is presupposed in CA, it is even more unlikely that consciousness in some problematic sense is (a) presupposed in CA *and* (b) is such that we believe we have it in introspection.

2.3.3. Standard Physicalism

A third response to CA is the position I call "standard physicalism." Standard physicalism says that the CA fails, and yet consciousness exists. To that extent it is like the epistemic view. What distinguishes standard physicalism is that on this view CA fails not because of our ignorance but for a quite different reason: either the ignorance hypothesis is false or else it is irrelevant to the assessment of CA.

There are two main ways to develop standard physicalism. The first argues that premise 1 of CA is false because we can give a reductive definition or analysis of phenomenal consciousness in the way I mentioned briefly in the introduction. This sort of view tries to explain phenomenal consciousness in physical terms that we currently understand, such as neural or computational or causal terms.

I won't try to criticize this position here, beyond making two points. First, while this idea is historically important, it is out of favor among contemporary philosophers. Second, people who defend views of this sort often end up in the same position as the eliminativist: They distinguish two conceptions of phenomenal consciousness, the unproblematic one is given a reductive analysis, while the problematic one is eliminated. But this position is no better when given a reductionist twist than an eliminativist one.

A second version of standard physicalism objects to the second premise of CA by appealing to (what is often called) *the phenomenal concept strategy*. This strategy draws a distinction between phenomenal concepts or words, on the one hand, and phenomenal properties, on the other. It then goes on to say that phenomenal concepts have a special feature that renders implausible the inference from conceivability to possibility.

There is an extensive critical literature on the phenomenal concept strategy; I have contributed to it myself (Stoljar 2005). But again, I won't try to review the issues here beyond making two points. First, many philosophers who have held a position like this in the past have now given it up, since the phenomenal concept strategy is subject to a myriad of technical problems. Second, the phenomenal concept strategy is often motivated by appealing to Kripke's (1980) famous book *Naming and Necessity*. But Kripke himself never appealed to a distinction between concepts and properties to undermine arguments like CA, which suggests there is something wrong with the strategy.

2.4. Features of This View*

We've examined the epistemic view and how it contrasts with some alternatives. Let me conclude this statement of it by noting some further attractive features.

2.4.1. Two Parts

I mentioned that the epistemic view has two distinct parts. One is the ignorance hypothesis. The other is the claim that *if* the ignorance hypothesis is true, arguments such as CA are unpersuasive. An attractive feature of the view is that individually each part is very difficult to deny. As I have said, the first part is an empirical thesis, though a very obvious one. And, while the second part is a piece of modal epistemology, which is certainly a controversial area of philosophy, no one can deny that ignorance will have a negative impact on modal reasoning; that is the point of the Charlie Chaplin example.

In my experience, people are often confused by the ignorance hypothesis. In defending it, they want me to give a direct case that takes something like the following form: "Here are the facts of which we are ignorant; if we knew these facts, we could give an account of consciousness." But nobody can rationally give a speech of that sort! The whole point is that we can't say what the facts of which we are ignorant are.

Even if a direct case for the ignorance hypothesis is out of the question, there are several indirect considerations one might advance if for some reason you don't find it as obvious as I do. Here are three:

> *First*, we know from history that we have often mistakenly believed our theories to be complete; it is natural to assume that our current theories are the same.
> *Second*, humans are beings with an evolutionary history and an empirical nature; that makes it very probable that we have a limited understanding of the enormous world around us.
> *Third*, scientific theories involve idealized models or theories that provide only partial information about the bits of the real world they correspond to; that suggests that our current theories provide only a selective account of the physical world.

I've gone into considerations of these sorts in other contexts and won't elaborate here (Stoljar 2010, 2017). The key point for present purposes is that the case for ignorance is multifaceted in this way.

2.4.2. Generalization to Other Arguments

A second attractive feature is that CA is just one of a number of contemporary arguments against the compatibility of consciousness and physicalism, and the epistemic view can be generalized to deal with these other arguments too.

One different sort of argument, for example, is the knowledge argument ("KA" for short), which infers the falsity of physicalism from a premise about knowledge, namely that it is possible to know all the physical facts that obtain in a situation without knowing the phenomenal facts. Nagel offered one sort of knowledge argument in his 1974 paper, but the *locus classicus* of this argument is a number of papers by Frank Jackson (Jackson 1982, 1986).

The epistemic view defeats KA just as much as CA. To see this, notice that we can construct the same argument in the Charlie Chaplin example. Is it possible to know everything in the book I held up and not know that Charlie Chaplin died in Switzerland? We can't assert that, since we don't know what is in the book. Likewise, we can't assert that someone (like Jackson's famous character of Mary) can know everything physical and yet not know some phenomenal fact.

2.4.3. The Meta-problem

A third feature of the epistemic view is that it offers a solution to the meta-problem, the problem of explaining why problems of consciousness, and in particular the compatibility problem we have been focusing on, have such a grip on our imagination (Chalmers 2018).

The epistemic view contains a straightforward prediction about when we are going to find issues about consciousness compelling, namely, when we convince ourselves for whatever reason we know what the physical world consists in either in detail or in outline (Strawson 2019). Actually, the history of philosophy provides several cases of this. Descartes, for example, held a physical theory on which matter is just extension in space; he also thought this theory provided a complete account of the physical world. If you really hold that, it is not surprising that you will be in the grip of the compatibility problem since it is clear that the mind is not extension, as in fact Descartes pointed out.

One might think this provides an account of why the compatibility problem is gripping to philosophers but not to ordinary people. But it is easy to generalize the basic idea. Plausibly, when ordinary people think about the physical, they utilize what Bertrand Russell once called an "imaginative picture of matter," a conception according to which all matter is in principle perceptually available (Russell 1948). If matter is in principle perceptually available, it again will seem obvious that we know what the physical world consists in at least in outline. But then again it is understandable that people find the compatibility problem compelling.

2.4.4. Variations

The final feature of the epistemic view is that it can be held in more and less ambitious forms. This is attractive since, if you disagree with the ambitious forms, you may still accept a modest version.

One ambitious form says not simply that we are ignorant of some relevant fact but that it is impossible for us to come to know these facts given our biological nature, just as it is impossible for other creatures (e.g., foxes) to know complicated philosophical ideas (e.g., the consequentialist view of ethics). We might call this, following (Flanagan 1992), a *mysterian* version of the epistemic view.

You can find an idea like this in many philosophers and thinkers who have defended views akin to the epistemic view in the form that I want to hold it; see, for example, Nagel 1974; Jackson 1982; Chomsky 1986, 2009; McGinn 1989. There is much that is attractive in it, but there is no logical connection between mysterianism and the epistemic view.

For one thing, it's surplus to requirements. To show that CA is unpersuasive, we only need to show that we don't know something relevant; we don't need to go further and show that we could not come to know that something. For another, while it is almost certain that there are limits on human knowledge, it is a matter of speculation exactly what those limits are. Hence it is speculative to say that the facts discussed in the ignorance hypothesis lie outside those limits. To establish that, you would need to know both what the facts in question are and what our limits are. But we know neither of those things, so we shouldn't commit to this ambitious view.

Another ambitious form of the epistemic view is inspired by various remarks of Bertrand Russell and is sometimes called Russellian monism; see, for example, Alter and Nagasawa 2015. The key idea here is that our knowledge of the physical world, at least when we get beyond knowledge based on direct perception or introspection, is limited to properties of a certain metaphysical character. Different theorists will describe these properties in different ways. Some say they are extrinsic, some relational, some dispositional, some structural. These differences won't matter for us. The key idea is that empirical knowledge is limited to knowledge of properties of a certain kind.

Once again there is much that is attractive about this Russellian development of the epistemic view. There is a lively discussion in contemporary philosophy about how to understand it and what its pros and cons might be; I have contributed to it myself and will come back to this topic at a later stage in this discussion.

Nevertheless, there is again no reason why the epistemic view must assume a Russellian form. To show that CA is unpersuasive, we only need to show that we don't know some relevant type of property, we don't need to insist that the type of property is of a particular metaphysical category. Moreover, while again it is almost certain that there are limits on human knowledge, it is unclear that the sort of metaphysical notions that the Russellian monist relies on properly mark those limits.

2.5. Objections to This View

Like any proposal in philosophy, the epistemic view is going to draw several counter-arguments. The remainder of this section is therefore devoted to pushbacks.

2.5.1. The Relevance Objection

This objection says that, while we are of course ignorant in some sense or other, we are not ignorant of any features *relevant* to consciousness. We know those features already, so the ignorance hypothesis is false.

There are various ways to develop this idea. Perhaps the most obvious is to emphasize that consciousness clearly depends on brains in some sense or other, and to say that, thanks to neuroscience, we know here and now what the properties of the brain are (Lewis 1994). We are not ignorant in any required sense, in other words, because neuroscience tells us what the relevant properties of the brain are.

But this objection forgets that neuroscience, like any science, tells a selective story about the parts of nature it is concerned with. From an abstract point of view, neuroscience tells us that the brain is made up of cells (i.e. neurons) and then enumerates various properties of and relations among those cells. But there are two ways in which this only gives us partial information about brains. First, it does not tell us about *every* property of the cells themselves, only those that neuroscience is interested in; in particular, it does not tell us, but rather takes for granted, how the cells themselves are ultimately composed or how this might bear on their behavior. Second, even focusing on the properties that neuroscience does attribute to cells, it does not tell us *every* property of these properties; that is, it tells us that neurons have various properties but not what these properties are capable of. Hence, while we may agree both that consciousness depends on brains and that neuroscience tells us a lot about brains, it is implausible that, at least in its current form, it tells us everything about brains that is relevant to consciousness.

2.5.2. The Persistence Objection

This objection says that, while our ignorance is real enough, we can ignore it when thinking about CA, since that argument can be formulated *whatever we know or learn about the physical world*. The basic idea is that all physical facts, known or not, knowable or not, are of a certain kind, and anything of that kind will be such as to raise the problem.

To sustain this objection, you need to say what kind of fact physical facts are supposed to be. There are various suggestions about this in the literature. Some say that all physical facts are "structural"; some say they are "objective." I've argued elsewhere that these labels do not permit a convincing development of the persistence objection (Stoljar 2006, 2015). I won't repeat those points here. Let me concentrate instead on another idea you find in the literature, namely that physical facts are "third-personal" facts, while phenomenal facts are "first-personal"; see, for example, Frankish 2017. Formulated in terms of this idea, the persistence objection goes like this: while we might be ignorant of many things, any physical fact is a third-personal fact, and as such it will be sufficient to generate a version of CA.

The problem with this version of the persistence objection is that there is no understanding of the first-/third-person distinction that will make it work.

On the face of it, the first-/third-person distinction is a linguistic or syntactic division with no bearing on the issues we are discussing. A sentence like "John is in pain," for example, is third-personal, but it can clearly be used in any formulation of the CA. Likewise, a sentence like "I weigh n kilos" is first-personal, but it expresses a physical fact in any relevant sense.

In ordinary language, when you say you have "first-personal knowledge" of something, you often mean something like "first-hand knowledge," which in turn is close to knowledge based on introspection. Then the contrast between first-personal and third-personal facts amounts to the contrast between facts knowable by introspection (first-personal facts) and facts knowable but *not* by introspection, that is, third-personal facts. But, again, on this interpretation the objection is unpersuasive. For why should it be assumed that there no third-personal facts in this sense that will alter the situation? To say that is simply to deny the epistemic view without offering any reason for doing so.

2.5.3. The Revelation Objection*

This objection says that the epistemic view is inconsistent with a central idea about introspection, sometimes known as "revelation." It is natural to say that when you instantiate some phenomenal property, you can come to know by introspection that you instantiate that property (see the box on pages 109–10). The thesis of revelation goes further: it says that you can come to know, not just that you instantiate the property, but the essence or nature of the property itself.

Why does this put pressure on the epistemic view? On that view, as we have been developing it, phenomenal properties are not fundamental, which means they depend for their instantiation on some other sort of properties. But someone may perfectly well instantiate a phenomenal property and not know this. In turn, that suggests there is some aspect of the essence of phenomenal properties of which we are ignorant. And this is ruled out by revelation.

The first thing to say about this objection is that, while revelation may be inconsistent with the epistemic view, it is also inconsistent with many other views. On a standard physicalist view, or indeed on a panpsychist view, many phenomenal properties depend on some other sorts of properties. Still, it is perfectly possible that someone might instantiate a phenomenal property and not know this. Hence revelation is inconsistent with standard physicalism and panpsychism too.

Of course, that the epistemic view is not alone in lying in the target range of an objection does not show the objection is mistaken—what then is wrong with the revelation objection?

What's wrong is that revelation is false. Consider again the sense-datum theory, which says that to instantiate a phenomenal property is to bear a relation to a sense-datum, a mental particular of a distinctive kind. Let us assume (counterfactually) that the sense-datum theory is true. Then, what revelation entails is that you could know that the sense-datum theory is true, simply by instantiating a phenomenal property. But that is quite implausible. Whether the sense-datum theory is true is something for which you would need considerable argument. It is not something that you could know simply by instantiating the property in question. What you learn by introspection is that you perceive a red thing, but the essence of that perception is something you will only come to know if you have a theory about what it is, a theory which is independent of introspection. If so, we should reject revelation.

What Is Introspection?

The word "introspection" literally means something like "looking within," but its use in philosophy departs from its etymology. Here it is used to mark a distinctive way that you come to know that you are in a conscious state.

Suppose you consciously perceive a cat, and so are in the conscious state of perceiving a cat. How do you know you are in such a state?

Note that to begin with it is a *contingent fact* that you are in that state: You are in it, but you could have failed to be in it—if you shut your eyes for example. And usually, you know contingent facts, when you do, by perception or inference or a mixture of both. If the fact concerns your immediate environment, you will know it by perception. If it concerns something remote from you—the distant past, say—you will know it through inference, in particular, from what others say.

But it is unlikely that you came to learn you are in the conscious state of perceiving a cat in either of these ways. Take something you *did* learn about through perception, for example, that there is a cat in the room. You learned about the cat by perception but you didn't learn that you were perceiving the cat by perception.

What about inference? This can mean different things, but here it means you learned that you are in the conscious state by inference from other things that you know or believe. Again, this is unlikely to have happened in this case. You know that your neighbor is away because you have been told that his lawn needs mowing. In this case you infer that he is away from the belief that his lawn needs mowing. That is not how you came to know you are perceiving a cat.

You know you are in the conscious state of perceiving the cat, but you didn't learn it by perception or inference. Hence there must be some distinctive way that you knew it. If we use the label "introspection" for that way, we may say that you learned you are in this conscious state by introspection.

This way of thinking about introspection leaves open what the nature of this distinctive way is. In philosophy there are several theories about the nature of introspection, some of which reflect more closely the etymology of the label. But we won't go into them here.

2.5.4. The "It's Not Physicalism" Objection*

This objection says that the epistemic view is guilty of false advertising. I have been suggesting it is a type of physicalism, though of a non-standard sort. But isn't it no sort of physicalism at all?

Unlike some of the other objections, I am sympathetic with this one. The reason is that, while we have talked a lot about physicalism so far, providing a precise formulation of the view is a difficult thing to do.

One issue here concerns the relation that must obtain between the physical and everything else if physicalism is true. Physicalism is an exhaustive thesis, but what does this amount to precisely? When looking at premise 3 of the conceivability argument we assumed that the exhaustiveness of physicalism at least means it must entail that every instantiated property either is a physical property or else is necessitated by a physical property. But it has proved controversial whether this necessary condition on physicalism can be understood also as a sufficient condition, and if not, what might be added here to obtain a sufficient condition; for a recent discussion of these matters, see Stoljar (2021).

Perhaps an even more serious issue about the interpretation of physicalism concerns what the physical is in the first place. There are different potential answers to this question, but none is very attractive:

1. "Physical" means ordinary features of matter: position in space, solidity, capacity to move, and so on. *Problem:* Physics itself has shown that not everything is physical in this simple sense, since it tells us about sub-atomic particles, fields, strings in 10-dimensional space, and so on.
2. "Physical" means anything at all discussed in contemporary physics, that is, the physics that we have here and now. *Problem:* This commits a physicalist to an extremely optimistic view of contemporary science, since if physicalism is true, and if it is understood like this, contemporary knowledge is complete, at least of the physical world.
3. "Physical" means that which is discussed in the *true* physics, whatever that turns out to be. *Problem:* This rules out an open possibility, namely, that there are properties that do not appear in the true physics, and yet are physical nonetheless; further, since we have no real idea of what the true physics is, we likewise have no idea about what physicalism does or does not rule out.
4. "Physical" means non-mental. *Problem:* This ignores the possibility that some things may be both physical and mental, while others may be neither; in addition, it offers no positive account of what the world is like if physicalism is true.

In the light of these problems, it certainly looks as if there is something to the "it's not physicalism" objection. How then is it possible that I have talked uncritically about physicalism at several points, not least when I described the epistemic view as a kind of non-standard physicalism? What is going on?

What is going on is that there are different contexts in which people talk about physicalism. In one context, they are engaged in what is sometimes called *speculative metaphysics*. Here the project is to offer a specific, positive, and complete account (and not merely a general, negative, or partial account) of what the world is like. In this context, "physicalism" names one of (or a class of) such accounts. My own view is that the interpretative problems just discussed show that any such account is quite implausible; indeed, I am skeptical of us ever offering a worldview in this sense (see, e.g., Stoljar 2010).

However, a different context in which philosophers talk about physicalism is in philosophy of mind or consciousness. Here, when you say that you are "physicalist," what you typically mean is that you are someone who thinks that consciousness is not a fundamental feature of the world; more generally, in this context, a commitment to physicalism is a commitment to any worldview that entails that consciousness is not fundamental, regardless of whether it is physicalism by stricter or historical standards.

It is this latter usage that I have been employing in this book. Hence there is no harm in saying that the position suggested by the epistemic view is a kind of physicalism in this weak sense, while at the same time denying that it is physicalism by more exacting standards.

2.5.5. The "It's No Explanation" Objection*

The final objection says that any contribution to the problem of consciousness must provide an explanation of consciousness, but the epistemic view provides no such thing: It is just a response to an argument for the incompatibility of physicalism and the existence of consciousness.

This objection is not sufficiently attentive to what is meant by the phrase "explanation of consciousness." One thing you could be asking for when you ask for such an explanation is information about a relevant system of relations that conscious states enter into: what they are caused by, what they depend on or are necessitated by, and what laws if any govern them.

But the epistemic view *does* provide such information, at least in an abstract sense. It tells us, for example, that conscious states are not fundamental and so depend on other things, even if it leaves open what exactly they depend on.

Moreover, while it is natural to want further information here, there is nothing in the epistemic view to stop you from providing it. As we noted at the outset, the epistemic view is designed to solve a particular problem about consciousness, the compatibility problem, but it is not inconsistent with answering other questions. In particular, as we will see in the third section, it is quite compatible with the view that we also pursue the science of consciousness.

Having said this, the phrase "explanation of consciousness" sometimes means something special in philosophy, and it is important to be clear that the epistemic view does not provide an explanation in this sense. We can see this by looking at two of the main meta-philosophical ideas of the 20th century, one often associated with Carnap (Carnap 1937, 1967) and the other often associated with Quine (Quine 1960, 1969).

Carnap's idea is that there is a base language that is sufficient to formulate all the facts of the world, or at least all the knowable facts. From this point of view, an explanation of consciousness would mean either the assimilation of consciousness into the base language or an account of how sentences involving consciousness would follow from sentences in the base language.

Quine's idea is that there is a set of base facts, perhaps provided by contemporary science, in particular contemporary physics. These base facts are sufficient to explain or determine all the other facts of the world. From this point of view an explanation of consciousness would mean either the suggestion that consciousness is a fundamental element, alongside the basic elements described by physics, or else that is something that is explained or determined by those basic elements.

There is much that distinguishes the Carnapian and the Quinean. Carnapians tend to be friendlier than Quineans to the idea that we know or a capable of knowing certain things in philosophy or mathematics a priori, in a way that is in some hard-to-define sense independent of experience. Quineans by contrast tend to emphasize the relations between philosophy and empirical science, since their initial move is to take contemporary empirical science for granted. Nevertheless, both views are similar insofar as they assume something specific about what a philosophical explanation of consciousness should look like: It will involve understanding consciousness in the light of the base language (in Carnap's case) or a base set of facts (in Quine's case).

It is true that the epistemic view departs from these expectations. It does not "explain" consciousness in this sense. But this is more a problem for these expectations than for the epistemic view. Certainly, we would like an explanation of consciousness in the sense mentioned earlier: the provision of relevant information about systems of relations consciousness enters into. But there is no requirement that the information in question be provided in the ways prescribed by Carnap or Quine.

> The main points of this second section are as follows. A central philosophical problem about consciousness concerns whether its existence is compatible with physicalism. The conceivability argument is a valid argument against physicalism. That argument presupposes the existence of consciousness, and so, if sound, it would show that they are incompatible. The epistemic view is a two-part answer to this argument. It says, first, that we are ignorant of a certain type of physical fact relevant to consciousness, and second that if that is so, the conceivability argument is unsound. This view has several good features: It will work against any arguments for incompatibility, it will work no matter what the truth is about modal epistemology, it affords an answer to the meta-problem, and it comes in both modest and ambitious versions. The alternatives to the epistemic view all face well-known problems. The epistemic view faces problems of its own but these can be answered.

3. The Metaphysics of the Science of Consciousness

We've had a good look (in Section 1) at what consciousness is, and suggested it was best to adopt a pluralist approach according to which there are several things it could be. We've also considered (in Section 2) the compatibility problem for phenomenal consciousness, that is, the problem that this notion does not fit with a broadly physicalist worldview, and argued that the epistemic view is the best way to solve this problem.

In this final section, we turn from the philosophy of consciousness to its science. I will be interested in what the science of consciousness looks like in general, and in particular what it looks like after the epistemic view is accepted.

3.1. Case Study: Aaronson Versus Tononi

One of the most revealing episodes in recent science of consciousness occurred a number of years ago, when the computer scientist Scott Aaronson wrote a blog post on why he does not believe what is called the integrated information theory (IIT), developed by the scientist of consciousness Giulio Tononi (see Aaronson 2014; Tononi 2015)

IIT is one of the major contemporary empirical theories of consciousness, championed in different ways not only by Tononi but by Christof Koch, Max Tegmark, and others (Koch 2012; Tegmark 2015). IIT says, roughly, that consciousness is a matter of integrated information, which is information in a system, as Aaronson puts it, that "can't be localized in the system's individual parts." In particular, according to IIT, for any conscious state there is some quantity of integrated information such that, if a physical system instantiates that quantity, it will be conscious, or at least will be associated with a subject that is conscious.

Aaronson proposed a counterexample to this theory. Consider what is called an expander graph, a graph that represents the informational connections between different nodes in a system. (It doesn't matter for present purposes exactly what it is.) Aaronson argued that the expander graph does not have consciousness because it is too simple—yet it also has a high degree of integrated information. Hence the expander graph seems a counterexample to IIT. The reasoning is simple: The theory entails that the expander graph is conscious, but it is not conscious; hence the theory is false.

What happened to this dispute between Aaronson and Tononi? It is fair to say it drifted into a stalemate. Aaronson took it to be obvious that the expander graph was not conscious and so IIT is false. But Tononi took it to be a discovery that the expander graph was conscious, but added that it was conscious only in a very limited way.

In philosophy, a situation like this is described as "one person's modus tollens is another person's modus ponens"—the references are to the Latin names for the various argument forms underlying the dispute. Since we are keeping Latinisms on the index of prohibited words, and more importantly, since the issues here are complex, we won't resolve the dispute here. But what we will do is single out three assumptions that Aaronson and Tononi share, despite their differences.

3.1.1. Three Assumptions

The *first* assumption, which might seem obvious but is worth stressing, is this. Consciousness is a scientific topic: a topic that scientists take an interest in and develop theories of. Indeed, IIT is only one of a number of scientific approaches to consciousness currently on the market. A recent summary distinguishes no less than 13 different theories (Doerig et al. 2020).

To say that consciousness is a scientific topic is not to deny it is a philosophical one. Nor is it to say, as people sometimes do, that philosophers have made no progress on the issue and it is now time for the scientists to take over. Rather it is to say that, like phenomena such as language or democracy, consciousness provokes a multitude of different questions, some philosophical in character, some scientific. The questions we have been considering so far are philosophical, but there are scientific questions too.

The *second* assumption concerns the target of any scientific theory of consciousness; what such theories are theories of. In a sense, the answer is easy: The target is consciousness. But there are many different notions here; which one is at issue for IIT and other theories?

Both Aaronson and Tononi are interested in *phenomenal* consciousness. Indeed, researchers who formulate scientific theories of consciousness routinely say their target is phenomenal consciousness.

This claim is sometimes questioned. In a famous paper, Ned Block argued that, while scientists often *say* they are interested in phenomenal consciousness, in fact they are concerned with access consciousness (Block 1995). Block is right that there is a tendency to conflate different notions. But it doesn't follow that phenomenal consciousness is not the target of scientific research. Another possibility is that scientists are interested in phenomenal consciousness insofar as it is associated with access consciousness. As we saw (see Section 1.5.2), while these notions are distinct, they are also related.

The *third* assumption concerns what questions empirical theories are trying to answer about phenomenal consciousness. Again, the answer seems easy: they are trying to explain consciousness from a scientific point of view.

But that answer while true doesn't go very far. As we noted in Section 2.5.5, phrases like "explanation of consciousness" conceal substantial methodological assumptions. And in fact, both Aaronson and Tononi make a further specific assumption about what explaining consciousness amounts to, which I will call *the laws of consciousness thesis*, or LCT. Roughly, LCT says that the science of consciousness aims to produce systematic knowledge of the empirical laws or principles connecting every state of phenomenal consciousness with a corresponding physical system.

LCT is particularly clear in Aaronson's discussion. He did not simply offer a counterexample to one theory. He argued more generally that IIT and other theories are trying to solve what he called "the pretty hard problem" of consciousness. The pretty hard problem is not the hard problem. Aaronson takes "the hard problem" to be the compatibility problem we talked about in Section 2. The pretty hard problem is rather about what exactly the laws or principles are that connect phenomenal consciousness to the physical. So when he says that the science of consciousness concerns the pretty hard problem, Aaronson commits himself to LCT.

Nor is Aaronson's commitment here an isolated event. Tononi, in his response to Aaronson, disagrees that the expander graph is a counterexample but does not demur from Aaronson's characterization of the underlying issues. And many scientists of consciousness, whether or not they accept IIT, conceive of what they are doing in terms of LCT. David Chalmers' famous book *The Conscious Mind*, for example, has as its subtitle "In search of a fundamental theory" (Chalmers 1996). What does Chalmers mean in this context by a "fundamental theory"? What he means—as he noted in comments on Aaronson's blog post—is a theory of the laws connecting each conscious state with some physical state. He is presupposing that there are such laws and regards the science of consciousness as the attempt to provide information about them—ultimately, the science is nothing less than a specification of each such law.

In thinking about the science of consciousness, my focus will be on the laws of consciousness thesis. The point is not to develop or criticize any scientific theory of consciousness. I'm interested instead in whether LCT properly articulates the basic goals of such a science. This is an issue of concern not only to researchers in consciousness science but also to philosophers reflecting on its nature. What I'm going to suggest is that the LCT can't quite be right and that the science of consciousness should be understood in a more modest and more achievable way.

3.2. The Laws of Consciousness Thesis

According to LCT, the science of consciousness aims to produce systematic knowledge of the empirical laws or principles connecting every state of phenomenal consciousness with a corresponding physical system. Let's first examine this in more detail.

3.2.1. Two Parts

LCT divides into two parts. The first part is the existential or metaphysical thesis that there are laws linking phenomenal consciousness and physical systems. The second part is a recommendation for research, namely, that the science of consciousness should aim to provide systematic information about such laws.

These two parts are distinct, though related. When we talk about laws in this context we mean empirical laws like Newton's laws or the laws of chemistry. The assumption is that laws are high-level features of the world that obtain independently of what anybody says or thinks. Take Newton's first law, that every object will remain at rest or in uniform motion in a straight line unless compelled to change its state by the action of an external force. If Newtonian physics had provided (as we know it does not) a true and complete account of the physical nature of the world, this law would have obtained independently of what anybody (including Newton) thought or said.

The same is true in the case of the laws of consciousness, if they exist. Of course, such laws don't obtain entirely independently of what we think, at any rate what we think consciously. These are laws about consciousness, after all, not the motion of objects. But they do obtain independently of what our *theories* of them are. They would obtain, for example, even if humans never developed scientific thinking at all. And that is enough to sustain the analogy to laws in physics.

In principle, one could agree with the existential thesis, and not accept the recommendation for research. It might be argued that, while there are such laws, it is premature for us to inquire into their nature because, for example, we don't have the methodology to do it (Irvine 2012). That's an interesting issue, but I will leave it aside.

Can one accept the recommendation for research and reject the existential thesis? As we have formulated the issues so far, the answer is no: The recommendation presupposes that there are such laws. Nevertheless, you could accept some modified recommendation without accepting that there are these laws; this is a point we will look at below.

3.2.2. Formulating the Laws

LCT says that there are laws of consciousness; what are these laws exactly?

A good way to think about them is in terms of the notion of a phenomenal property that we introduced in Section 1. As we saw, a phenomenally conscious state is simply a subject's having or instantiating a phenomenal property. From this point of view, the existential claim says this: For every instantiated phenomenal property F, there is a physical property G such that it is a law that if G is instantiated, so too is F. For example, when I had my attack of gout, I instantiated some particular phenomenal property. What the existential thesis says is that there is some physical property that is also instantiated, and this physical property guarantees as a matter of law that I had this phenomenal property.

So understood, the existential thesis can be developed in several different ways. For example, some researchers in the science of consciousness offer computational theories, some biological theories, and some informational theories; some even offer theories that look very much like the higher-order and access approaches we considered in Section 1 but interpret them as empirical proposals about phenomenal consciousness rather than alternative definitions of what consciousness is.

Such approaches are not inconsistent with LCT. They simply understand the physical properties that appear in the relevant laws in different ways. We won't need to go into these or other variations here.

3.2.3. LCT and Physicalism*

We noted earlier that physicalism is an exhaustive thesis. It applies not just to consciousness and related phenomena but to everything else too: Tuesdays, steamships, pumpkins, pumpkins on Tuesdays, pumpkins inside steamships on Tuesdays, and so on. Likewise, it applies not just to these particulars but to their distinctive properties: the property of being a Tuesday, being a steamship, being a pumpkin, being a pumpkin inside a steamship on a Tuesday, and so on. But it is not plausible that everything for which physicalism is true participates in laws. There are no laws about the behavior of pumpkins inside steamships, for example.

One might think that, if physicalism is true, there *must* be laws connecting conscious states and physical states. Doesn't physicalism entail, as we saw earlier, that every property is either a physical property or is necessitated by a physical property?

Yes, but it doesn't follow that there is a law here. After all, the same thing is true in the case of pumpkins in steamships, but there are no laws about such things. More generally, the world contains a potential infinity of particulars each of which instantiates a potential infinity of properties. Only a subset of these enters into laws.

These observations show that LCT is a distinct commitment from physicalism. LCT says that phenomenal properties enter into laws. But physicalism by itself makes no such commitment. As far as it is concerned, the property of perceiving a red thing, for example, might be like the property of being a pumpkin inside a steamship on a Tuesday. It may be instantiated, and physicalism may be true of it, but it does not participate in any laws. Physicalism, in short, leaves the question of laws open.

3.2.4. Motivations*

Why do so many people accept LCT? One plausible answer is that it has been mistakenly conflated with physicalism. Another is that it dovetails with dualism. Dualists take phenomenal properties to be fundamental, but they usually go on to say that there are empirical laws connecting the instantiation of such properties with physical systems, a position which itself is close to LCT.

But there is plausibly a more basic element at work here: the assumption that the ignorance hypothesis we have been discussing throughout is false. For what could be the aim of the science of consciousness be in a context in which we already know what the relevant facts or properties are? Answer: to provide systematic information about the relations that hold among items whose nature is assumed to be clear. Dualists will typically say that the relations at issue here are ones of contingent law. Standard physicalists will typically say the relations are ones of identity or necessitation or something similar.

If this is right, we arrive at another illustration of the point I made at the outset: that while the epistemic view doesn't solve questions about consciousness apart from the compatibility problem, it nevertheless helps to clarify them. In this particular case, it helps to make it clear that there is nothing inevitable about LCT, which means that this thesis will need to be defended or criticized on its own terms.

> ### Consciousness of What Is Not There
>
> One of the most famous lines of reasoning in philosophy of consciousness, particularly as regards perception, is the so-called "argument from hallucination." This argument begins from a consideration of a pair of possible situations like this.
>
> *Situation 1:* There is a yellow banana on the desk in front of me. I am in good light. My cognitive and perceptual faculties are functioning as well as can be expected. I perceive the banana and therefore come to know it is on the desk.
>
> *Situation 2:* I have been kidnapped by the goons from the Timothy Leary Society. They have me strapped to a gurney and have injected me with a hallucinogen that characteristically produces rich and realistic hallucinations, but of a mundane and boring sort. As a result, I hallucinate that there is a banana on the desk in front of me.
>
> There is a sense in which these situations are different and a sense in which they are the same. They are different because in situation 2 there is no banana, and I don't know there is a banana—if there isn't one, you can't know that there is. They are the same because they are indistinguishable from my point of view. How it feels for me in situation 1 is exactly how it feels in situation 2.
>
> While S2 is certainly outlandish, both situations are possible logically speaking. But the argument from hallucination suggests that the mere possibility of these situations leads to the highly controversial conclusion that the sense-datum theory is true. On that theory, in both situations 1 and 2 what I perceive in the first instance is something quite unexpected: it is a banana that is a mental thing, rather than a physical thing.
>
> Here's one way to formulate the reasoning. Premise 1: In both situations, I am in the same conscious state, namely, the conscious state of perceiving a banana. Premise 2: If I perceive a banana, there is a banana that I perceive. Interim conclusion:

in both situations, there is a banana that I perceive. Premise 3: In situation 2, the banana that I perceive is mental (because there is no physical banana that I perceive). Premise 4: If I perceive a mental banana in situation 2, I likewise do so in situation 1 (because I am in the very same conscious state in both cases). Final conclusion: in both situations, I perceive a mental banana; that is, the sense-datum theory is true.

There is no question of accepting this reasoning. The sense-datum theory, while it is historically important, is surely mistaken. What on earth is a banana that is mental rather than physical?

What then has gone wrong? What is often called relationalism denies Premise 1. On that view, when I perceive a banana, I stand in some relation to a physical object, such as a banana. Since I don't stand in that sort of relation in S2, I don't perceive a banana in that case. What do I do? Answer: I hallucinate a banana, which, according to the relational theory, is a psychological state disjoint from perceiving. Perceiving and hallucinating are, on this view, as different from one another as knowing and imagining.

What is often called representationalism, by contrast, denies premise 2. On that view, perceiving a banana is a way of representing a banana, something I do in both situations. However, since I can represent a banana without there being a banana I represent, premise 2 is false. What is it to represent a banana? Representationlists traditionally understand this on the model of belief. Just as in both situations I may believe that there is a banana, in both situations I may represent (perhaps in a perceptual way) that there is a banana.

Both these views face problems. The problem with relationalism's denial of premise 1 is that it is plausible that I am in the same conscious state in both situations. The problem for representationalism's denial of premise 2 is that perception seems to involve a relation to an object in a way that belief does not. What I believe is a proposition, but what I perceive is a thing, namely a banana, and there is no such thing in situation 2.

How to move forward? The best option is to draw a distinction in how representation is understood, which allows a synthesis of the relational and representational accounts. In general, expressions such as "I represent a banana" have two readings, sometimes called a relational and a notional reading (see, e.g., D'Ambrosio 2019; D'Ambrosio and Stoljar 2021). On its relational reading, to represent a banana is to stand in some relation to a banana. On its notional reading, to represent a banana is, roughly, to be in a state that is correct if and only if you stand in that relation to a banana; from this point of view, you can represent a banana without there being one, so long as the state you are in is incorrect.

Applying this to the argument from hallucination, we may agree with representationalism that, in both situations, I perceive and so represent a banana. The difference is that representation here is not understood on the model of belief. I don't simply represent *that* there is a banana—I represent *a banana*. Likewise, we may agree with relationalism that there is a distinction between situation 1 and situation 2: in the first but not the second, I represent the banana in a relational sense. The difference is the states I am in in these situations are not disjoint: both are states of representing a banana, one correct, the other not.

3.3. Are There Laws of Consciousness?

We've examined what LCT is and why it's attractive; let's turn to why it can't be right.

3.3.1. Degrees of Consciousness*

One argument against LCT concerns the possibility that consciousness comes in degrees. Suppose you are presented with a huge series of creatures ranging from paramecia to human beings and asked to draw a line between those that are conscious and those that are not. On the face of it, drawing any line is arbitrary, even though it is clear (or so we may suppose) that humans are conscious and paramecia are not. For many people, this suggests that consciousness comes in degrees, somewhat in the way that height or tallness comes in degrees. In other words, there is such a thing as someone's having some amount of consciousness, just as there is such a thing as a person's having an amount of tallness.

That consciousness comes in degrees is central to IIT. That theory entails not simply that a system is conscious if it has such and such a degree of integrated information; it entails also that a system has a higher degree of consciousness if it has a higher degree of integrated information. Indeed, Tononi exploits this point in his reply to Aaronson; the expander graph is conscious, he says, but only to a limited degree.

But there is nothing special about IIT here. In the light of LCT, any scientific approach to consciousness at all will associate phenomenal properties with physical properties. Since these physical properties are themselves likely to come in degrees, phenomenal properties are likely to as well. Hence LCT seems to entail that it is at least possible that consciousness comes in degrees.

But many writers question the very coherence of the idea that consciousness comes in degrees. Bayne, Hohwy, and Owen, for example, argue that "the notion of degrees of consciousness is of dubious coherence. . . . consciousness resembles being a member of the United Nations rather than being healthy, which clearly can come in degrees" (Bayne et al. 2016, 405; see also Pautz 2019).

This suggests a very straightforward argument against LCT, which we can call *the degrees of consciousness argument*:

> *Premise 1:* If LCT is true, it is possible that consciousness comes in degrees.
> *Premise 2:* It is not possible that consciousness comes in degrees.
> *Conclusion:* LCT is false.

This argument is valid, and premise 1 is hard to disagree with. But one might question premise 2.

One objection to premise 2 points out that, expressions like "conscious of" bear some of the hallmarks of what linguists call *gradable* adjectives, which suggests that the states they report come in degrees (Brogaard 2010). We can talk of someone being tall*er* than someone else, for example, or of being very tall. Likewise, we can speak of someone being more conscious of something than another or of being very conscious of something.

This objection is suggestive, but to deal with it properly involves tricky issues we won't pursue here. As we noted at the outset, phenomenal consciousness is not reflected well in the word "conscious" in any case. Moreover, some expressions have the hallmarks of gradable adjectives even though the things they pick out do not come in degree. A potential example is "knowledge"; we can say that someone knows very well that such and such, or knows better than someone else that such and such, without assuming that knowledge comes in degrees (Pavese 2017).

For present purposes, a better objection to premise 2 points out that, quite apart from how we talk, phenomenal consciousness is strongly associated with things that do come in degrees. Feelings can be more or less intense. They can be in systems more or less complex. They can be more or less accessible to introspection. Given that phenomenal consciousness is associated with these obviously gradable things, it is likely that it too comes in degrees.

Skeptics about degrees of consciousness will reply, I think, that, while correct, this doesn't alter the underlying point. On the phenomenal account, a subject is conscious if and only if the subject feels some way or other. But either you feel some way or you don't. This is an on-off affair. If so, phenomenal consciousness doesn't come in degrees.

But there is an error in this line of thought. Let's look again at height, taken as a property of people. This paradigmatically comes in degrees. One person can be greater in height than (i.e., be taller than) another. Nevertheless, there are complex properties defined in terms of height that do not come in degrees. Take the property of *being the same height as Napoleon*. You can't have that property to a greater or lesser degree; either you are the same height as Napoleon or you aren't.

The same applies to phenomenal consciousness. When you feel pain, you feel it to some degree of intensity. If so, phenomenal properties come in degrees. Nevertheless, there are complex phenomenal properties that do not come in degrees. Take the property of *having some phenomenal property or other*, or the property of *feeling pain to some degree of intensity or other*. These properties do not come in degrees even though other phenomenal properties do.

This suggests that the situation as regards phenomenal consciousness is analogous to the situation as regards height. Some properties associated with height (e.g., being tall) admit of degree, while others don't (e.g., being the same height as Napoleon). Likewise, some properties associated with phenomenal consciousness (e.g., feeling pain) admit of degree, while others don't (e.g., having some phenomenal property or other). It is true the phenomenal account defines a subject's being conscious in terms of a property that does not admit of degree. It says that you are conscious if and only if there is some phenomenal property that you have. This property, being such that you have some property or other, does not come in degrees. But it remains the case that other phenomenal properties do come in degrees, and so may figure in laws that entail that they come in degrees. And that is all that is required for LCT.

3.3.2. Nomological Properties

Even if the argument about degrees of consciousness is no threat to LCT, there is a second argument that is. The germ of this argument is a point mentioned earlier, namely, that only a subset of all the properties that are instantiated are of the sort that enter into laws. Suppose we call properties in this restricted class, *nomological properties*— "nomos" means having to do with laws. Then we may say that only a subset of all the properties that are instantiated is nomological.

If that is so, we may go on to ask whether all phenomenal properties are nomological. Of course, LCT entails they are. It says that there are laws connecting every conscious state to a physical system. What this means is that for every phenomenal property F, there is a physical property G such that it is law that if a system has F, it has G. That can't be true unless all phenomenal properties are nomological.

This suggests a second argument against LCT, which we can call *the nomological properties argument*:

> *Premise 1:* If LCT is true, every instantiated phenomenal property is a nomological property.
> *Premise 2:* Not every instantiated phenomenal property is a nomological property.
> *Conclusion:* LCT is false.

This argument too is a valid argument against LCT, and its first premise is hard to deny. What of the second premise?

Unlike the previous argument, here the second premise is plausible. When we first introduced phenomenal properties, we noted that there are several ways to think about their metaphysical structure; this issue comes up again in the context of the argument from hallucination and the issue of what to make of consciousness of something that isn't there (see the box on pages 121–3). No matter what the precise theory of these matters is, however, it is plausible to think at least this: phenomenal properties are relational properties.

In general, a property is a relational property if and only if when you have it you bear a relation to something else. Consider the property of *being 3950 kilometres from Darwin*. That is a relational property because when you have it, you stand in a relation to a certain thing, namely Darwin, that is, you are a certain distance from Darwin. (I have in mind the city not the scientist, though you could also be that distance from the scientist; if you did, you would have a different relational property.)

When I say that phenomenal properties are relational, I don't mean that when you have one you must bear a relation to a *physical object* like Darwin. That is true on *some* theories of the metaphysical structure of phenomenal properties, but not on all. What I mean instead is that when you have a phenomenal property you bear a relation not to a physical object but to a *property*, and, moreover, a property that is not itself a phenomenal property.

This is a somewhat confusing idea, so let me illustrate it with an example. Suppose again you perceive a red thing, and so instantiate a phenomenal property, the property of perceiving a red thing. On a plausible view of the metaphysical structure of that property, when you have it you bear a certain relation to the property of being red. (Different theories will have different views about what the relation is, but set this aside.) But the property of being red is *not* a phenomenal property in our sense. It is property had by physical objects, like handkerchiefs and traffic lights, not a property had by subjects like me or Alice B. Toklas. In sum, when you perceive a red thing, and more generally when you have a phenomenal property, you bear a relation to a property that is not itself phenomenal.

Once we realize that phenomenal properties are relational properties of this sort, however, it is a short step to thinking that they are not nomological. For suppose we apply what we just learned about perceiving a red thing to a different example: perceiving a pumpkin inside a steamship on a Tuesday. If perceiving a red thing involves bearing a relation to the property of being red, then, likewise, perceiving a pumpkin inside a steamship on a Tuesday involves bearing a relation to the property of being a pumpkin inside a steamship on a Tuesday. But this latter property is not a nomological property; indeed, we used this example before to illustrate how some properties are not nomological. Not only are phenomenal properties relations to properties that are non-phenomenal but are relations to properties that not nomological.

Suppose, then, that when you instantiate a phenomenal property, you bear a relation to a property that is not nomological; that makes it very natural to think that phenomenal properties are not nomological either. If there isn't a law about the property of being a pumpkin inside a steamship on a Tuesday, then there isn't a law about the complex property of being in some relation to property of being a pumpkin inside a steamship on a Tuesday. If so, phenomenal properties are not nomological, and LCT is false, just as the nomological properties argument says.

3.4. Consciousness Science Without the Laws?

The nomological properties argument is a valid argument against LCT, whose premises are prima facie plausible. How to respond?

Some people might resist the idea that phenomenal properties are relational properties. However, while this is certainly suggested in the literature (Papineau 2021), it is difficult to sustain given the facts about hallucination (see the box on pages 121–3). Others might object to the underlying metaphysical assumptions of the argument; maybe it's a mistake in the first place to assume a distinction between nomological properties and all the rest? But at least if one accepts that there are properties of the sort that we have been discussing—for example, being a pumpkin and so on—it is hard to see that they are nomological.

There is, however, a better way to respond. When you think about it, LCT presents an extremely ambitious goal for the science of consciousness. It makes a claim not about *most* or *some* phenomenal properties but about *all*. It says that for *every* instantiated phenomenal property, there is a law connecting that property and a physical system, and that the science of consciousness is the project of coming to understand those laws. It is this claim that comes under attack by the argument from nomological properties.

However, once we appreciate how ambitious LCT is, it should be clear how to react to the nomological properties argument: to sketch ways in which the science of consciousness might proceed without making a strong presupposition of this kind. There are two different possibilities here.

The first is that, while there aren't laws that apply to every phenomenal property, there may nevertheless be laws that apply to some. In particular, it may be that phenomenal properties of general or abstract kind participate in laws, even if highly specific phenomenal properties do not. For example, it is sometimes said that there are global states of consciousness (see, e.g., Bayne 2016; Doerig et al. 2020); perhaps these global states enter into laws, even if specific states do not. To take a different example, consider the properties of perceiving a red thing and perceiving a yellow thing. These are distinct phenomenal properties, but they nevertheless have something abstract in common; both are cases perceiving a thing. Perhaps there are laws that apply to this more general kind of phenomenal property, even if there is none that apply to more specific kinds.

Of course, it is an open question whether there are laws of this general kind and what these more abstract phenomenal properties might be; that is something that may become clear as empirical inquiry proceeds. The key point is that there is no threat to the existence of the laws of this more abstract kind from the nomological property argument. That argument tells us that not all phenomenal properties are nomological, but leaves open that some are. If so, it becomes possible to understand the science of consciousness in a slightly different way from that suggested by LCT, namely, as aiming to understand laws of this general sort.

The second way we might react to the nomological properties argument is by saying that you don't need laws to do the science of consciousness. Admittedly, the word "science" is often used in English in such a way that it picks out rational inquiry into laws or nomological properties. But there are many forms of rational inquiry that are not scientific in this narrow sense. Historians, for example, are interested in getting to the truth about Watergate, but Watergate is not something that constitutively involves the instantiation of nomological properties.

For all the nomological properties argument says, consciousness may be like Watergate: It admits of detailed investigation and description even if it is not governed by laws. What would the outcomes of such an inquiry be like? One example might be the inquiry that we have been undertaking. The philosophy of consciousness is a systematic inquiry into the nature of conscious states, but it does not presuppose that every phenomenal property is nomological. For another example, consider this passage from George Orwell (Orwell 1962):

> Suddenly, in the very middle of saying something, I felt—it is very hard to describe what I felt, though I remember it with the utmost vividness. . . . Roughly speaking it was the sensation of

being at the centre of an explosion. There seemed to be a loud bang and a blinding flash of light all round me, and I felt a tremendous shock—no pain, only a violent shock, such as you get from an electric terminal; with it a sense of utter weakness, a feeling of being stricken and shrivelled up to nothing. The sandbags in front of me receded into immense distance. I fancy you would feel much the same if you were struck by lightning. I knew immediately that I was hit, but because of the seeming bang and flash I thought it was a rifle nearby that had gone off accidentally and shot me. All this happened in a space of time much less than a second. The next moment my knees crumpled up and I was falling, my head hitting the ground with a violent bang which, to my relief, did not hurt. I had a numb, dazed feeling, a consciousness of being very badly hurt, but no pain in the ordinary sense.

(Orwell 1962, 137–138)

Here Orwell is describing the feeling he had when (TFW) he was shot through the throat, something that happened to him while he was fighting in the Spanish Civil War. In our terminology, Orwell in this case had some phenomenal property, and what he is doing is carefully describing that property. There is nothing in the nomological properties argument to prevent Orwell from doing this. Nor indeed is there anything to prevent any of us from doing something similar (though perhaps not as well, and perhaps with respect to less dramatic conscious states).

3.5. Consciousness Science After Ignorance

There is much more to say about what the proper goals of a science of consciousness are. I think the truth will combine both forms of inquiry we have distinguished. If one is interested in a science of consciousness in the sense of a mathematized investigation of empirical laws, abstract laws (i.e., laws that involve abstract phenomenal properties) will be of interest. If one is interested in a science of consciousness in the sense of a complete description of conscious states, close analysis, and description, that will be more important.

I won't pursue those issues further here. Let me instead end the overall discussion by returning to the theme we started with: that while people often accept that we are ignorant in the ways that the epistemic view says, they routinely fail to see the relevance of this to philosophical and scientific questions about consciousness.

I hope it is clear by now how mistaken this attitude is. In the case of the compatibility problem, as we saw in Section 2, the ignorance hypothesis is what allows us to solve the problem. And in the case of the science of consciousness, while the hypothesis of course doesn't achieve the goals of that science, it nevertheless brings those goals into sharper focus. Moreover, the hypothesis itself is perfectly compatible with achieving those goals. We can accept the hypothesis and still aim at systematic knowledge of the lawful relations that obtain between abstract states of consciousness and their abstract physical counterparts. Likewise, we may accept this hypothesis and still provide a careful description and analysis of individual conscious states. In short, the epistemic view I have been recommending not only solves the compatibility problem, the problem most people think of as "the" problem of consciousness in philosophy, it also allows a clearer view of the scientific study of consciousness.

> The main points of this third section are as follows. The dispute between Aaronson and Tononi is revealing of a number of key assumptions in contemporary science of consciousness. The most important of these is the laws of consciousness thesis, according to which (a) there are laws connecting every conscious state to some physical state, and (b) the goal of the science of consciousness is to produce systematic knowledge of these laws. The thesis is distinct from a commitment to either physicalism, though it is strongly suggested by dualism and standard physicalism. There are a number of arguments against (b). One, which is based on skepticism about degrees of consciousness, is implausible. Another, based on the idea of nomological properties, is plausible. Hence the laws of consciousness thesis should be rejected in favor of a more modest thesis which either restricts laws of consciousness to conscious states of an abstract kind or else relaxes the commitment that the science concerns laws, or (more plausibly) some combination of both.

First Round of Replies

Chapter 3

Ignorance Is No Defense
Reply to Daniel Stoljar

Amy Kind

Contents

Introduction	135		4.2. Great Past Success Does Not Necessarily Mean Great Future Success	150
1. An Analogy	136			
2. Why Should We Believe the Epistemic View?	138			
3. What Does the Epistemic View Tell Us About the Metaphysics of Consciousness?	144		4.3. Considerations of Simplicity Do Not Settle the Matter	151
			4.4. Should the Epistemic View Benefit From the Presumption in Favor of Physicalism?	152
4. Where Does the Burden of Proof Lie?	148			
4.1. Denying Physicalism Does Not Commit One to Something Spooky or Supernatural	150		5. Where Does That Leave Us?	153

Introduction

According to a famous proverb, what you don't know can't hurt you. But according to Daniel Stoljar's analysis of the problem of consciousness, the proverb gets things decidedly wrong. What we don't know can hurt us. In fact, it can cause us to go seriously astray in our assessment of the viability of physicalism.

Stoljar's opening statement covers a lot of ground, but in this response, I want to focus on his discussion and defense of *the epistemic view*. The epistemic view is put forward to solve what Stoljar calls *the compatibility problem*, that is., the problem of how physicalism can be compatible with the existence of consciousness. This terminology for referring to the problem is unique to Stoljar.

DOI: 10.4324/9780429324017-5

In my own opening statement, I talked about *the problem of phenomenal consciousness* or *the hard problem of consciousness*, both phrasings that are in widespread use. As I'll discuss later, I have some reservations about Stoljar's way of framing the problem. But I think we're both focused on roughly the same general issues, so to make things simpler for readers of this debate, I'll try to adopt his terminology as much as possible for the purposes of this response.

The epistemic view can be understood as the conjunction of two claims. The first claim is what Stoljar calls *the ignorance hypothesis*. According to this hypothesis, we are ignorant of a physical fact or property that is relevant to consciousness. The second claim is that this ignorance is what accounts for the apparent incompatibility underlying the compatibility problem. As Stoljar helpfully summarizes things: "We are profoundly ignorant of the nature of the physical world, and ignoring this ignorance is what generates the problem" (this volume, 64).

How successful is the epistemic view in solving the compatibility problem of consciousness? It's no doubt unsurprising that I am considerably more pessimistic on this score than Stoljar is. Before I get into a closer and more direct look at the epistemic view, I'll give a rough sense of my overall reaction to it by way of an analogy. This will then lead to my case against Stoljar, which will proceed in three parts. First, I'll look more closely at his defense of the epistemic view and show why I think it falls short. Second, I'll raise some related considerations about the relationship between epistemic claims and metaphysical claims in discussions of consciousness. And third, I'll turn to questions about where the burden of proof lies in this debate.

1. An Analogy

In line with the Scandinavian crime series motif running through the introduction to Stoljar's opening statement, the analogy I'll use will revolve around a detective who is trying to solve a homicide.

So let's consider this detective, Detective Stoelgaard. From very early on in the investigation, it becomes clear that signs point strongly to a suspect we'll call Fyssikberg. There's lots of evidence at the crime scene that shows that Fyssikberg had been there. Fyssikberg has a strong motive. They were seen threatening the victim. The murder weapon is found hidden away in their residence. It short, it seems that any sort of rational approach to the investigation demands charging Fyssikberg with the crime. Unfortunately, however, Detective Stoelgaard eventually discovers that Fyssikberg has what appears to be an ironclad alibi for the time of the crime. Fyssikberg's alibi is incompatible with their having committed the crime.

When the alibi is first brought to the detective's attention, it seems eminently reasonable that there would be some pushback. Surely we don't yet know the exact window of time in which the crime had to have been committed . . . couldn't that window have started a bit earlier, or closed a bit later? Couldn't something have been done to the body to make the time of death appear vastly different from what it in fact was? And surely even alibis that initially appear ironclad are often undercut by later discoveries. Couldn't the receipts proving Fyssikberg was in a different city have been tampered with somehow? Couldn't the security camera footage have been digitally manipulated? Couldn't the witnesses who claim to have seen Fyssikberg elsewhere have been mistaken?

So when the detective initially claims that we're mistaken to think there's really an incompatibility here, that there's too much we don't know, the claim seems pretty plausible. But then suppose the time of death window is confirmed by the autopsy, the authenticity of the receipts is verified, the metadata of the security camera footage shows no evidence of manipulation, and the witnesses' testimony continues to hold up after repeated questioning and attempts to undermine it. At this point, the detective's position starts to seem less reasonable. Why the single-minded focus on Fyssikberg? Why is that the only explanation for the crime?

"But there's still so much we don't know!" says Detective Stoelgaard. And, in a sense, this is undoubtedly correct. Yet when we push on this and ask the detective to articulate what kind of facts we're missing, what we should be exploring, and what information is needed, we don't really get much of a response. All Detective Stoelgaard can tell us is that we're ignorant of some fact that's relevant to dissolving the incompatibility. It's some new fact that's different from all the facts we've already uncovered. And that's all that can be said about it. Once we uncover this fact, insists the detective, we'll see how it's true both that Fyssikberg committed the murder and that Fyssikberg was in an entirely different location (verified by video footage, receipts, and witnesses) at the time of the crime, even though the compatibility of those two things seems entirely unfathomable given the present state of the homicide investigation.

How satisfying is Detective Stoelgaard's insistence here? How successful is it at showing us that the apparent incompatibility between our conclusion that Fyssikberg committed the murder and Fyssikberg's alibi is not really an incompatibility after all? To my mind, the answer to both questions is: not very. As the analogy here is very thinly veiled, it should be easy to see the moral for Stoljar's epistemic view. Though I grant that there's still plenty we don't know, I don't see how this dissolves the apparent incompatibility between consciousness and physicalism, and I don't see how it sheds any real light on the nature of consciousness.

Having given this rough sense of the kind of line I want to offer in reply to Stoljar's opening statement, I'll spend the rest of this response fleshing it out in more detail.

> In part 1 of my first response to Stoljar, I begin my criticism of his epistemic view by way of an extended analogy to a Scandinavian crime drama. When confronted with a problematic incompatibility that one wants to dismiss, it may well be reasonable to note that the apparent incompatibility will be dissolved once we learn more, as might happen when a key suspect's alibi is incompatible with their having committed the crime under investigation. Ultimately, however, once a lot more investigative work has been done and the alibi still seems ironclad, it becomes considerably less plausible for the detective to insist that the problem is simply our ignorance of some relevant facts. Likewise, I find it implausible to think that the compatibility problem about consciousness arises wholly due to ignorance.

2. Why Should We Believe the Epistemic View?

Stoljar offers very little direct support in making the case for the version of physicalism that he favors. Instead, his strategy is largely based on an attempt to undermine a key set of considerations in favor of dualism, a set of considerations he groups together under the heading of the Conceivability Argument (CA). As stated, his version of the CA most closely parallels the structure of the zombie case that I considered in my opening statement. According to Stoljar, though we may think that the zombie case is conceivable—that a being can be exactly like a given human in all physical respects yet different from that human phenomenally—the only reason this seems conceivable to us is that we're ignorant about a certain kind of physical fact relevant to consciousness. Once we recognize this ignorance, he says, we see that the CA is unpersuasive. Though the CA as stated does not map directly onto the structure of the other cases that I considered in my opening statement (i.e., Nagel's bat case and Jackson's color scientist case), because those cases also rely on facts about conceivability they could plausibly be treated in a similar way. So, for example, Stoljar might say that although we think it's conceivable that Mary could know all the physical facts in the black-and-white room and yet still come to learn a new fact when she exits the room, the only reason this seems conceivable is that we're ignorant about a certain kind of physical fact relevant to consciousness.

Upon hearing this diagnosis, it's natural to want to know more about what fact or kind of fact is the subject of our ignorance. But of course, Stoljar can't tell us anything further on this score. That's his whole point. We're ignorant about it! All he can say is that it's a physical fact and that it's relevant to consciousness.

One might wonder why we should believe him. Why should we believe that his ignorance hypothesis is true? Stoljar seems to take this claim to be an obvious one, one not in need of defense. Describing this claim as rather plausible, he notes that there are surely facts about consciousness of which we are ignorant.

By setting things up this way, Stoljar makes it appear that it would be irrational to proceed as I'm proceeding here. It's bad enough even to ask for a defense of the ignorance hypothesis, let alone to deny it. This is one place where appearances are deceiving. There's been some sleight of hand. Look closely at the claim that is described as the "rather plausible" one, the one that we can "surely" assume. It's the claim that there are facts about consciousness of which we are ignorant. Importantly, however, this is different from saying that there are *physical* facts about consciousness of which we are ignorant. And, more to the point, it's different from saying that there are physical facts about consciousness of which we are ignorant *that are relevant to the compatibility problem.*

Do we know absolutely everything there is to know about consciousness? Surely not. Stoljar is undeniably right on this score. Do we know absolutely everything physical there is to know about consciousness? Again, surely not, and we can probably answer this second question with just about the same level of confidence that we had when answering the first question. Stoljar is right on this score as well. But now consider a third question: Are the facts of which we're ignorant relevant to the compatibility problem? Or, more to the point, are the *physical* facts of which we're ignorant relevant to the compatibility problem? Here I don't see how we can have anywhere near the same level of confidence that we had with respect to the first two questions. Though it seems immensely plausible that we're ignorant in various ways, it's less plausible that our ignorance is what makes physicalism seem incompatible with consciousness.

Think again about our Scandinavian detective and the analogy I gave in the previous section. There are all kinds of facts still unknown about Fyssikberg's actions and whereabouts on the night of the crime. We could make a very long list of unanswered questions. To mention just a few:

- How many times did Fyssikberg sneeze on the night of the homicide?
- What herbs were in the pickled herring that Fyssikberg had for dinner that evening?
- Exactly how many kroner were in Fyssikberg's wallet?
- How tightly were Fyssikberg's shoelaces tied?

It's hard to see how answering these questions and thus coming to know all these additional facts will be relevant to the incompatibility between Fyssikberg's alibi and Fyssikberg's having committed the crime. For us to have good reason to question this incompatibility, the detective has to give us some sense of why the facts we don't know would dissolve the incompatibility, what the facts might look like, or what kinds of facts we're missing. Short of that, what the detective does seems like mere fist pounding or stubbornness.

Here it would obviously be question-begging for the detective to tell us: *Well, the facts we don't know must be relevant. After all, that's the only way to dissolve the incompatibility, and we know that this kind of incompatibility must be dissolvable.* The parallel moves by Stoljar would be just as problematic. Yes, there's lot we don't know about consciousness, but we can't rely on our sense that the incompatibility must be dissolvable to defend the claim that what we don't know is relevant to that dissolution—or at least, we can't do that if we also want to defend our sense that the incompatibility is dissolvable by pointing to that set of relevant facts.

Let's consider one specific example just to make things more concrete. Scientists know a lot about the brain processes involved in dreams, and they know a lot about various roles that dreams play in the life of the organism, from boosting brain function to regulating the immune system. But there's also a lot they don't know. One of the biggest unsolved mysteries in dream research concerns the function of dreaming; that is, why did humans (and other mammals) evolve so as to dream? When it comes to the science of dreaming, there are facts that we don't know, and moreover, at least some of the facts are undoubtedly physical facts. We can say this with a high degree of confidence. But can we also say with a high degree of confidence, even a moderately high degree of confidence, that these unknown physical facts are relevant to the explication of the phenomenology of dreaming, that is, to the explication of its conscious nature? Without knowing what the facts are, and without any explanation as to why filling in those details will make a difference to our understanding of the phenomenology of dreaming, to have a high level of confidence that the unknown facts are relevant to this understanding seems epistemically questionable.

The kinds of considerations that I've been raising in this section can be applied directly to Stoljar's invocation of the ignorance hypothesis in an attempt to diagnose the problem with the Conceivability Argument (CA). As Stoljar states the first premise of the argument:

> It is conceivable that there is a situation that is exactly like the actual situation in respect of all instantiated physical properties but is different from it in respect of some instantiated phenomenal property, that is, some respect having to do with phenomenal consciousness.

He then homes in on the phrase "all instantiated physical properties." Are the hypothesized relevant-but-unknown physical properties included in this set? There are two options. Suppose first that they're not included. In that case, the premise might well be true but the argument isn't going to be successful. The CA would then show only that consciousness comes apart from a subset of the physical facts (the known ones), and that is not enough to show that physicalism is false. So that means we must take the second option. The relevant-but-unknown physical properties must be included in this set of all instantiated physical properties. But, when we take this option, Stoljar denies that the first premise of the CA is true: "if you don't know what the relevant physical respects are, you can't conceive in the appropriate sense a situation in which all the physical facts are as they are, but some phenomenal fact is different" (this volume, 96).

    Let's grant Stoljar that the relevant sense of conceiving must be a demanding one. Indeed, this was something I explicitly acknowledged in discussing conceivability arguments in my opening statement. As I indicated, not every stray thought that pops into someone's head counts as their having adequately conceived of a scenario. And with respect to zombies in particular, I considered the worry that someone who takes themselves to have conceived of a zombie might be mistaken: Though they have aimed to conceive of a being who is microphysically identical to them, what they have really conceived of is a creature who is extremely physically similar to them. The ignorance hypothesis now enters to give this worry particular force. It's not just that we've inadvertently fallen a bit short of the appropriately demanding standard in our conceiving, perhaps because we haven't fleshed things out in enough detail. Rather, it's that this standard can't be met given our state of ignorance. Our ignorance makes it impossible for us to flesh things out in enough detail.

    I agree that there's cause for concern here. But it's not clear to me that the concern is nearly as significant as Stoljar makes out. To see this, we first have to think more carefully about what's involved in meeting the demanding standard for conceiving. Let's think about a case in which an act of conceiving plausibly meets the standard, that is, a case in which an act of conceiving a given scenario justifies us in concluding that the scenario is possible. Suppose you are contemplating buying a large desk and trying to decide whether it can be adequately rotated to fit through the doorway of your home office. There may be lots of things you don't know about the desk. You might not know its exact weight. You might not know how well-made it is, or what kind of wear and tear it will withstand, or whether its drawers glide easily. So, none of these factors can be perfectly represented in your conceiving. But as none of these factors matters for the question under consideration—the question of whether it can be rotated so as to fit through the doorway—this won't affect your ability to meet the demanding standard. You can probably see where this is going. Our ignorance of various facts is not in and of itself a bar to our meeting the demanding standard for conceiving. This will only be a problem if the facts are relevant ones. It's only if we have reason to believe that we're missing relevant facts that we should believe that we can't meet the demanding standard of conceiving. Stoljar has not provided us with any such reason. To my mind, this point alone is enough to undermine Stoljar's rejection of the CA.

But there's a further point that's also important. As a general matter, meeting the demanding standard for conceiving a scenario does not require that every detail of the scenario be embedded and fully worked out in the conception itself. Consider a high school student who is studying for a standardized college admission test. In the United States, this is the SAT. They are trying to conceive of themselves getting a particular score that they're aiming for, a 1400 (out of 1600) say. As they conceive of the scenario, they build in information about the format of the test and the number of total questions being asked. They also build in information about the pace at which they work and the number of questions they'd have to get right. But to conceive of this scenario adequately, and to meet the demanding standard, they don't have to build in the details of each and every question, let alone the answers to those questions. It's not that this information is irrelevant. It's just that it doesn't need to be represented in detail in the conception being undertaken. That's not the kind of detail that even the demanding standard of conceiving requires. It's a mistake, yes, to take just any old conceiving as adequate for use in conceivability arguments. We shouldn't overly deflate our standard. But to avoid this mistake, we need to be careful not to push too far in the opposite direction. We also shouldn't overly inflate our standard. It's just as much a mistake to require that a conceiving represent every single aspect (even every relevant detail) of a scenario in complete and exhaustive detail. If we did that, then conceivings could never be useful to us for drawing conclusions about possibility. That's simply not a standard that could ever be met.

Note here that Stoljar himself accepts that there are indeed plenty of scenarios in which I can make a judgment of possibility on the basis of something that we've conceived. (Recall his mushy peas example: I can conclude that it's possible that there be a huge pile of mushy peas on the kitchen floor because I can conceive it.) Thus, as Stoljar should agree, we need to make sure that our demanding standard of conceiving strikes the right balance between deflation and inflation. Having recognized this point, however, we further undermine Stoljar's rejection of the CA.

> In this section I offer several reasons to worry about Stoljar's epistemic view. I begin by exploring whether we really have reason to believe that the facts of which we're ignorant and that are relevant to the problem of consciousness are physical facts. I then turn to Stoljar's attempted rejection of the Conceivability Argument. As I suggest, Stoljar's discussion relies on an overly inflated standard of what counts as conceiving of a scenario. A proper interpretation of the notion of conceiving must strike a balance between being overly inflated and being overly deflated, but on any such balanced interpretation, we have no reason to think that the Conceivability Argument fails.

3. What Does the Epistemic View Tell Us About the Metaphysics of Consciousness?

In the previous section, I presented reasons to worry that the case for the epistemic view is not as strong as Stoljar thinks. In this section and the next, I want to raise a different kind of worry. For even if you're not fully convinced by what I've already argued, and you think there's more reason to believe that the epistemic view is correct than I think there is, it's still not clear that the view is successful in solving the compatibility problem or establishing the truth of physicalism. In his opening statement, Stoljar anticipates this kind of response:

> "Ah," people sometimes say, "but even if what you say is right, that would at most show that various arguments for incompatibility [CA] fail. It doesn't show positively that physicalism is true."
> (this volume, 65)

Call this the you're-not-done response, or YND for short. Interestingly, Stoljar grants that the response is correct. What he denies, however, is that it's as important as it sounds. Why not?

To answer this, we need first to note that Stoljar takes physicalism to be an empirical thesis. Its truth cannot be established a priori. Though not all physicalists agree with this claim, many of them do. So, for example, the identity theorists of the 1950s, in pointing to mind-brain identity claims such as "pain is identical to C fiber firing," thought that such claims should be understood to be analogous to scientific discoveries along the lines of "lightning is electrical discharge" or "temperature is mean kinetic molecular energy." These claims are not true by definition, and we cannot determine their truth without empirical investigation.

> ### A Priori Versus A Posteriori Claims
>
> Take the claim "squares have four sides." This claim is knowable independent of any particular experiences with squares. The claim is true definitionally, and so if you know the definition, you know that the claim is true. When a claim can be known independently of any particular experience, it can be said to be knowable *a priori*. Now compare the claim "The square logo used by American Express has a blue background." This claim is not true by definition. In order to know that it's true, you have to have seen the logo (or had someone reliable tell you about the logo). You've had to have some particular experiences. Thus, this claim is not knowable a priori, but rather is known *a posteriori*.

If physicalism is not an a priori claim, and if it cannot be shown to be true by definition, then a complete defense of the view has to wait until a full scientific story can be told, that is, until science progresses to the point at which it explains consciousness. Physicalists are thus in a kind of "wait and see" holding pattern. Note, however, that even if physicalism cannot be shown to be true in advance of that scientific work, it could be shown to be false in advance of that scientific work. That's what the arguments put forth in my opening statement aim to do. If we can show that consciousness does not supervene on the physical, then we've shown that physicalism cannot adequately explain consciousness—or, to put it in Stoljar's terms, that physicalism and consciousness are incompatible with one another. Demonstrating that these arguments fail is thus a matter of some urgency for the physicalist. That is what is truly of importance for the physicalist, says Stoljar, and that is what he takes himself to have done.

Certainly Stoljar is right that it's extremely important for the physicalist to undercut the CA. But here's where YND comes in. Is he also right that it's not important for a physicalist like him to do more? Having undercut the CA, is his case for physicalism complete? Is it really not important that Stoljar has no positive case to offer on behalf of his theory? Unsurprisingly, this is a matter on which we disagree.

To some extent, this disagreement may turn on considerations about who has the burden of proof. I'll address those considerations in the next section. First, I want to raise a different kind of worry about the adequacy of Stoljar's case. Let's return to a point that I foreshadowed at the start and consider his framing of the problem of consciousness. (There are many problems of consciousness, but both he and I have focused on a single one of them for the purposes of this debate, and so when I refer to *the* problem of consciousness, I mean to be pointing to that one.)

As we've seen, Stoljar thinks that we can best capture the problem of consciousness by thinking of it in terms of the compatibility problem. The problem of consciousness, in his view, is the seeming incompatibility between consciousness and physicalism. Note something interesting about this way of framing the problem. When the problem is thought of this way, it seems to presume that physicalism must be correct. The problem is not one of developing an adequate account of consciousness. Rather, the problem is one of developing an adequate account of physicalism, that is, of showing how physicalism can be seen to be an adequate account for consciousness.

Perhaps there's a sense in which it might seem that his framing allows for other options. Couldn't we deny physicalism? Couldn't we deny the existence of consciousness? To some extent, I'll concede that his framing does not preclude these possibilities. But note that these don't really count as *solutions* to the problem. When a problem is put in terms of apparent incompatibility between A and B, there's really only one way to solve it, namely, to find some way of understanding both A and B so that they are not incompatible after all. To deny the existence of either A or B is, in essence, to give in to the incompatibility, not to solve it. Framing the problem in terms of A and B's apparent incompatibility, and then looking for an adequate solution to that problem, creates a strong presumption that we want to hold on to both A and B.

The more standard ways of framing the problem of consciousness— ones that are put in terms of an explanatory gap or in terms of the hard problem—do not do this. Perhaps Stoljar thinks they go too far in the opposite direction, that is, that they presume that we must reject physicalism. On that I'd disagree. Regardless, it's easy enough to come up with a more neutral framing of the problem. In fact, the framing that I use in my own Opening Statement is neutral on just this point. It presumes neither the truth nor the falsity of physicalism. On the very first page of this statement, I cast the consciousness problem as "a question about the nature of consciousness: What is consciousness, and what is its relationship to the brain and body (and, more generally, to the physical world)?" (this volume, 3).

When we put the problem this way, Stoljar's claim that we shouldn't be bothered by the fact that the epistemic view does not establish the truth of physicalism seems much less plausible. Suppose that all the epistemic view can do is show us that the CA fails. This makes some headway on the compatibility problem. It doesn't show us definitively that consciousness and physicalism are compatible, but it deprives us of a major obstacle to thinking that they are. In doing that, however, it doesn't answer the consciousness problem. It doesn't tell us what consciousness is, and it doesn't tell is what its relationship is to the physical world. When we move away from framing the problem of consciousness as the compatibility problem, YND has much more bite.

To some extent this shouldn't be surprising. The problem of consciousness is a metaphysical problem, a problem about the metaphysics of consciousness. In general, we should be worried about attempts to solve metaphysical problems in terms of epistemological facts. What we know or don't know does not by itself tell us anything about the nature of a thing. It's thus not surprising that a view called *the epistemic view* would be unable to solve the problem we're trying to solve. We may be ignorant of certain metaphysical facts, but that ignorance does not settle anything about what those metaphysical facts are.

One way to see this is to consider the relationship between the epistemic view and other versions of physicalism, for example, the identity theory or eliminative materialism. In fact, the epistemic view is largely compatible with both of these metaphysical views. Granted, the strategies that these other versions of physicalism utilize in response to the compatibility problem are different from the strategy used by the epistemic view (this volume, 101–3). They might not accept the claim that the ignorance hypothesis solves the compatibility problem.[1] But if we think about what they say about the metaphysics of consciousness, there is no conflict between them and the epistemic view. The lack of metaphysical conflict between the epistemic view and these standard versions of physicalism is harder to see when we focus on the compatibility problem—a fact that gives

---

1. Actually, I think there's a sense in which eliminativists *do* accept the ignorance hypothesis or at least something very much like it, and they also think that our ignorance is an important factor in solving the compatibility problem. But in addition to accepting the ignorance hypothesis, they also seem to deny or nearly deny the existence of phenomenal consciousness. In virtue of this denial, the eliminativists' strategy for addressing the compatibility argument departs from the one employed by the epistemic view.

us more reason to worry about framing the debate in those terms. When we instead focus on what I've called the problem of phenomenal consciousness, when we focus on the metaphysics of phenomenal consciousness, we can see that the epistemic view makes no metaphysical commitments that keep it from collapsing into a standard version of physicalism.

> In this short section, I argue that the epistemic view doesn't really tell us anything about metaphysics of consciousness. It offers no positive account of how consciousness can be understood in physical terms. Moreover, because it is compatible with standard versions of physicalism such as the identity theory, it's not clear that it is as non-standard a response as Stoljar would have us believe.

4. Where Does the Burden of Proof Lie?

As we saw in the previous section, Stoljar accepts that the epistemic view does not actually show us that physicalism is true. But if he has successfully undercut the CA, as he takes himself to have done, then he has removed the main impediment to accepting physicalism. Though the scientific work that is needed to remove our ignorance still awaits completion, we no longer have any reason to think that physicalism must be false. Given this, one might think that physicalism wins by default. In the *Oxford Dictionary of Philosophy*, Simon Blackburn (2016) notes that "if in some situation there is a proper presumption that something is true, anyone seeking to prove its opposite is said to bear the burden of proof." If the CA fails, then then one might think that there is a "proper presumption" that physicalism is true and thus that the burden is on the dualist to make the case otherwise.

Though Stoljar does not explicitly make this move, I think it is implicit in his overall case. He does briefly mention some indirect reasons to think that the ignorance hypothesis (and hence physicalism) is correct, but he does not develop them in any detail. And, in explicating the two "big ideas" that underlie the compatibility problem, Stoljar notes that physicalism is a world-view "that many people think you must believe if you hold a vaguely scientific or rational approach to the world" (this volume, 64). That sounds a lot like the kind of proper presumption just mentioned. With this presumption in place, it seems that the burden of proof would have to lie with physicalism's opponents.

I confess, however, that I simply don't see why this presumption should be in place. In the final section of this response, I'll offer four sets of considerations that call into question this assessment of where the burden of proof lies. Though I don't take these considerations to shift the burden of proof to the physicalist, I do take them to show that we can't simply assume that the burden must be solely and wholly borne by the dualist. With the playing field leveled, we can see that it's not enough for Stoljar to pose objections to the dualist's arguments and then rest on their laurels without presenting any arguments of their own. Rather, to defend physicalism, Stoljar needs to show us what can actually be said on behalf of the view.

Burden of Proof

The notion of burden of proof is a familiar one in legal contexts. According to Article 11 of the Universal Declaration of Human Rights, everyone charged with a criminal defense has the presumption of innocence until proved guilty in a court of law. Thus, in criminal matters, the burden of proof lies with the prosecution. If the prosecution does not meet this burden, then the defendant is found not guilty—even if the defendant has not mounted any case of their own.

How does the notion of burden of proof work in philosophical contexts? Suppose we think of the two competing positions in a philosophical debate as being on opposite sides of an evenly balanced scale. The arguments in support of each side can be seen as weights. As one side accumulates more argumentative weight, the scale tips in its favor, and that side can be seen to have won the debate. But when one side has the burden of proof, the balance does not start out even. Suppose Side A has the burden of proof. In that case, the scale starts off tipped toward Side B, and so Side A needs to provide argumentative weight just to level the scale.

4.1. Denying Physicalism Does Not Commit One to Something Spooky or Supernatural

The thought that physicalism is the only rational approach presumably arises in large part from the sense that a rejection of physicalism commits one to something spooky or supernatural. But as I discussed in some detail in my opening statement, this is a mistake. Perhaps it would be true if we were still holding on to the kind of dualism that was endorsed by philosophers like Descartes in the 17th century. But the view has moved well beyond that. Tarring contemporary dualists with the mistakes of their predecessors would be like tarring contemporary astronomers with the mistakes of their predecessors. We don't indict contemporary astronomy on the ground that Copernicus thought the sun revolved around the earth. Likewise, we shouldn't indict contemporary dualism on the grounds that Descartes thought that the truth of dualism depended on the existence of God or that the pineal gland was the locus of interaction between the mind and the body.

From the perspective of the 21st century, these Cartesian claims may strike us as howlers. But we can find similar howlers in the history of physicalism as well. Democritus tried to explain the mind in terms of smooth, round atoms. Aristotle believed that the heart was the seat of intelligence and sensation while the brain simply functioned as a radiator that kept the heart from overheating. In the 19th century, Karl Vogt famously compared the brain to the liver or the kidneys; on his view, thought should be understood as the secretion of the brain, just as bile should be understood as the secretion of the liver. Just as we detach contemporary physicalism from the mistakes of its past, appropriately recognizing that the view has moved on, we should detach contemporary dualism from the mistakes of its past and recognize that the view has moved on. Once we've done so, it's no longer clear why physicalism counts as the only rational approach, and if it's not, then we would need a good reason to think that its opponents must bear the burden of proof.

4.2. Great Past Success Does Not Necessarily Mean Great Future Success

Perhaps one thinks that the burden of proof lies with the dualist because of the record of past success surrounding physicalist theories in science. Interestingly, however, this past success cuts both ways for someone who holds the epistemic view. On the one hand, yes, physicalist science has been successful. But, on the other hand, we are crucially ignorant about some of the physical facts relevant to consciousness. The ignorance suggests that these facts are importantly different in some way from the facts we already know—they are a different *type* of fact. But depending on how fundamental this difference is, it might be that the theory in which these facts are embedded is significantly different from our past theories. With such a significant difference between this future theory and other theories that have been successful in the past, however, why should we judge the likelihood of the future theory's success on the basis of this record of past success? It's not clear why one should be connected with the other, and certainly not clear enough to shift the burden of proof to the non-physicalist.

4.3. Considerations of Simplicity Do Not Settle the Matter

In my opening statement, I noted that physicalism is often thought to gain support from considerations of simplicity. However, as I also noted, in order for considerations of simplicity to even come into play, we must be adjudicating between two theories that have equal explanatory power. Here's one way to see this point. Idealism, the view that everything that exists is mental, is just as simple a theory as physicalism. Likewise for panpsychism. So physicalism can't be taken as the default view about consciousness just on grounds of simplicity.

The fact that considerations of simplicity come in only when we have two theories of equal explanatory power makes things tricky for a proponent of the epistemic view. Given the ignorance hypothesis, we don't know what the physical properties are that account for consciousness. We don't really have much of a sense of exactly what the theory will look like once we do finally gain this knowledge. So it is hard to adjudicate whether the physicalist theory (in particular, the epistemic view) and the dualist theory have equal explanatory power. Thus, it's hard to see how considerations of simplicity could work to shift the burden of proof to the dualist. Even worse, if the unknown physical properties are really so different from the known physical properties, then one might reasonably wonder whether the view we end up with is really simpler than the dualist view. Though the unknown properties might well count as physical (in some sense of physical), they might be as different from the known physical properties as the dualist's nonphysical properties are. In that case, the view that we end up with—though physicalist—would not really have the advantage of simplicity over dualism.

4.4. Should the Epistemic View Benefit From the Presumption in Favor of Physicalism?

The final consideration I'll raise concerns the status of the epistemic view. Suppose one is not convinced by the previous three considerations. Suppose one still maintained that, in general, the presumption is in favor of the physicalist. The physicalist and the dualist do not compete on a level playing field; rather, the physicalist is exempt from making a positive case, while the dualist must carry the burden of proof. Even if one were inclined to make this presumption, a question arises: Does this presumption also apply to the *epistemic view*? According to the proponent of the ignorance hypothesis, we're ignorant of some physical properties that are relevant to consciousness. But, as we've seen, these physical properties are very different from your run-of-the-mill physical properties. Physicalism might have to expand dramatically to accommodate them, so dramatically that it would be hard even to recognize them given our current understanding of the notion of physical. In fact, if we really are ignorant about some physical properties relevant to consciousness, it's possible (even likely) that our ignorance arises at least in part from a misconception about what counts as physical. In light of all this, it's not clear whether (and if so, how) the theory we will end up with resembles our past and current physicalist theories. So why should it benefit from a presumption in their favor?

One might pursue this point by questioning whether the theory that we end up with should even count as a physicalist theory. Stoljar tries to address this issue in his opening statement. I'm going to sidestep this issue. Suppose it makes sense to count the theory that we end up with as a physicalist theory in the weak sense of "physicalist" that Stoljar wants to adopt. We can then put the point as follows: When we talk of there being a presumption in favor of physicalism, that presumption applies only to physicalist theories in a more exacting sense.

This fourth point that I'm making is in many ways a generalization of the previous two points. One reason we might think that there's a presumption in favor of physicalism is its past record of success. Another reason we might think there's a presumption in favor of physicalism has to do with considerations of simplicity. As I have suggested, however, the non-standard nature of the epistemic view means that these presumptions do not straightforwardly apply to it. My point now is that this same kind of worry can likely be raised no matter how we attempt to flesh out the claim that there is a presumption in favor of physicalism. In short, though the epistemic view may gain some plausibility by departing from the standard versions of physicalism on offer, this departure means that it cannot shift the burden of proof to its non-physicalist opponent. We're owed a substantive explanation for why we should believe it.

> In this section I take up the question of where the burden of proof lies in the debate about consciousness. Though the physicalist often seems to presume that the burden lies with the dualist, I offer three reasons to show why this is mistaken. First, denying physicalism does not commit one to something spooky or supernatural. Second, the great past success that has been enjoyed by a given theory does not necessarily mean that the theory will enjoy great future success. And third, despite what the physicalist often suggests, considerations of simplicity do not settle the matter. Finally, I take up a fourth consideration. As I argue, even if there is some general presumption in favor of physicalism, it is not clear that the epistemic view in particular should benefit from this presumption.

5. Where Does That Leave Us?

Let me once more return to the analogy with which I started this response. When we're watching a Scandinavian crime show on Netflix, we ultimately want some kind of resolution. Perhaps it's fine if the detective does not tie up every loose end. Perhaps we like our Scandinavian crime shows to leave some questions unanswered. But we're looking for the detective to solve the crime. If at the series' end, all the detective can do is insist that some unknown facts will undercut the lead suspect's alibi, then it's not going to be a very satisfying experience for the viewers. The show's score on Rotten

Tomatoes is not going to be very high, and the show is unlikely to be renewed. There's no comparable website to Rotten Tomatoes for philosophical views, and to be honest, I'm glad of that. But when I think about the epistemic view, I'm left with the same kind of dissatisfaction that would be felt by viewers of this crime show. Just like them, I'd rather explore my other options.

Chapter 4

Taking Non-Standard Options Seriously
Reply to Amy Kind

Daniel Stoljar

Contents

Introduction	155	7. Kind and the Structure and Dynamics Argument	167
1. Russellian Monism	157	8. Dualism 2.0 and the Conceivability Argument	169
2. Kind's Critique	158		
3. Must We Say What the Properties Are?	160	9. The Mathematics Analogy	170
4. The Combination Problem	162		
5. False Advertising	164	10. Reconsidering the Space of Options	171
6. Non-standard and non-Russellian?	166		

Introduction

Amy Kind defends what she calls *dualism 2.0*. This is intended to be a thoroughly modern dualism, a dualism shorn of the various things that are sometimes associated with it. There is no religious element in Kind's dualism. There is no after-life. Hers, she says, is a naturalistic dualism, the sort of position any scientist or anyone sympathetic with science might accept.

I agree with Kind that dualism can be detached from these associations and be defended in the context of a certain sort of naturalism. But I don't think it's true. So that is one thing that distinguishes us. She thinks dualism is true, I don't.

Associated with this disagreement are several others; indeed, this is a typical situation in philosophy in which disagreements come in clumps rather than on their own. One is over the definition of the physical. Another is over how to react to the conceivability argument. Another is over the reasons for thinking that dualism is implausible.

DOI: 10.4324/9780429324017-6

If I am not mistaken, however, there is a more basic disagreement between us, which influences and shapes these others. In my opening statement I spoke of *standard* physicalism. Standard physicalism is the sort of physicalism for which the ignorance hypothesis—the hypothesis that we are ignorant of a type of physical fact relevant to consciousness—plays no role: Either that hypothesis is false or it makes no difference to the dialectical situation. It is standard physicalism that Kind takes as her opponent. She argues that standard physicalism has no response to arguments like the conceivability argument, except perhaps to adopt a kind of eliminativism. So for her the basic options are standard physicalism, dualism, and eliminativism.

As between these options, I can sympathize with someone who views dualism as the best bet, though I think it is more correct to say it is no worse than any of the others.

But I disagree these are the options! I think there is a fourth option here, namely, the epistemic view, or equivalently, non-standard physicalism. Once that option is factored in the entire issue assumes a very different shape. In particular, this position is clearly preferable to any of the standard options, including Kind's dualism. Hence the more basic disagreement between us is not so much whether dualism is true but what the theoretical options are in thinking about whether it is true.

When I say that the sort of position I have in mind is not regarded by Kind as an option, I don't mean she doesn't mention it. She does mention it, or at least one version of it, the one that is usually called "Russellian monism." What I mean is that, while she mentions this option, it plays no significant role. In fact, Kind argues it plays no significant role, an argument she has also made in other work (Kind 2015). She thinks that factoring Russellian monism into the discussion makes no difference. I think that is wrong and that positions like this have a transformative effect on how we understand the issues. So once again, the issue boils down to what the options are.

In this response to Kind, I am going to focus on why we should take non-standard options seriously. I will concentrate initially on the case of Russellian monism, since that is the version Kind discusses. But the basic message is more general: it is that non-standard positions, whether of a Russellian or non-Russellian kind, open up an entirely different way to approach the dialectic around the conceivability argument, and more generally, the place of consciousness in the physical world.

1. Russellian Monism

Russellian monism consists of three main theses. The first thesis is that physical theories, and empirical theories in general, tell only a limited story about nature; namely, they tell us only about the instantiation of properties of a certain kind.

There is a dispute in the literature on these matters about what kind of properties these are: dispositional properties, relational properties, or structural properties. I will mainly refer to "dispositional" properties, but this is simply for ease of presentation; anything I say can be formulated if we wish in terms of the other notions.

What reason is there to believe this first thesis? As I understand it, the Russellian monist thinks we know this thesis a priori. We know a priori, that is, that physical theory has a certain important limit; namely, it tells us only about dispositional (or whatever) properties. Of course, this is a major assumption. Not everyone will agree that we can make substantive a priori claims about the nature of empirical inquiry, and not everyone will agree that, even if we can, this is the right one. But I won't try to assess the reasons for the first thesis further here.

The second thesis is that, while (in accordance with the first thesis) physical theories tell us only about the instantiation of properties of a certain kind, it is also the case that properties of a complement kind are instantiated. So, in particular, if some dispositional property is instantiated, some non-dispositional property is also instantiated.

What reason is there to believe this second thesis? The answer is again a priori, at least on most developments of this view. We know a priori, according to the Russellian monist, that if dispositional properties are instantiated, then non-dispositional properties are also instantiated. Suppose we come to know that some dispositional properties are instantiated, for example, by an application of physical theory; we may then infer that some non-dispositional properties are instantiated too. Once again, this is a major assumption; can we really be so sure of this conditional claim, that if dispositional properties are instantiated, non-dispositional properties are also instantiated? But again, I am going to let this assumption stand for the purposes of this discussion.

The third thesis is that these non-dispositional properties are relevant to the nature of consciousness. Here the idea is that, while dispositional properties alone do not ground or necessitate phenomenal properties, non-dispositional properties, perhaps together with further dispositional properties, might do so.

What reason is there to believe this third thesis? The answer this time is that, when combined with the other two theses, this thesis makes available the response to the conceivability argument offered by the epistemic view.

As I said in my opening statement, the epistemic view says, first, that we are ignorant of a certain type of physical property that is relevant to consciousness, and, second, that if this is so, the conceivability argument fails, and indeed fails for quite understandable reasons: From the epistemic point of view, when we think about consciousness and its relation to the world, we are in the position of somebody considering the book of nature we looked at in the Charlie Chaplin example.

Russellian monism offers a distinctive version of this epistemic response. The three theses we just reviewed together entail that there is a class of instantiated non-dispositional properties, of which we are ignorant and which are relevant to consciousness. If we accept that there is a sense in which these properties are physical, which on at least some ways of thinking about the physical we may do so, we have arrived at the ignorance hypothesis.

2. Kind's Critique

Now that we know what Russellian monism is, let's look at Kind's criticisms of it. As I understand it, her critique falls into two parts.

In the first part, Kind divides Russellian monism (RM) into four different versions, each of which takes different stances on the nature of the non-dispositional properties the view is committed to. The four versions are as follows:

(A) *Panpsychist Russellian Monism*: On this view, the non-dispositional properties are phenomenal properties, though of an extraordinary sort. *Ordinary* phenomenal properties attach to human beings such as Alice B. Toklas or me, and to animals such as my cat Django. *Extraordinary* phenomenal properties attach, not to objects like Alice or Django but rather to the fundamental objects of the world, whatever they happen to be. These extraordinary phenomenal properties, according to panpsychist RM, are the non-dispositional properties identified in the second and third theses that make up the doctrine.

(B) *Panprotopsychist Russellian Monism*: On this view, the non-dispositional properties are properties that have the following feature: They are such as to necessitate ordinary phenomenal properties, at least when combined with other dispositional properties. It is in this sense that they are "panprotopsychist" properties; the expression is due to David Chalmers (see Chalmers 2015).

(C) *Physicalist Russellian Monism*: On this view, the non-dispositional properties are physical properties on at least one legitimate conception of the physical. This view need not deny that they fail to be physical properties on some other legitimate conception; indeed, it is usual for a proponent of this view to operate with more than one such conception. This is a point I have been interested in in the past; as Kind mentions, I have distinguished various different versions of what a physical property might be, and at least on some of them, these non-dispositional properties may count as physical (see, e.g., Stoljar 2001).

(D) *Neutral monist Russellian Monism*: On this view non-dispositional properties mentioned in the second thesis are identical to properties that are neither mental nor physical. This sort of position is sometimes thought of as the most "Russellian" of the various versions Russellian monism, that is, the version that is closest to Russell's actual views. But in fact the interpretation of Russell's views is difficult, not least because he changed his mind on these issues at different points in his career (see, e.g., Wishon 2015). We won't try to pin anything on Russell here.

In the second part of her critique, Kind levels various objections against these theses so understood. There are three main objections.

Kind's first objection is that panprotopsychist and neutral monist RM (i.e., positions B and D) fail a condition of adequacy. Any version of RM, she says, must provide an account of what these non-dispositional properties are; yet properly understood these versions of the view do not do so; hence, they are inadequate.

While Kind does not say this explicitly, I think this objection, if it is any good, should also be directed at physicalist Russellian monism: position C. It is true that a proponent of this sort of account may say, "Of course, I can tell you the nature of these non-dispositional properties: they are physical." Still, saying that a property is physical without going on to say more is to under-describe it, especially in a context in which there is more than one conception of the physical in play. So, position C is in the same boat as position D and B.

What about panpsychist RM, position A? As I noted briefly when discussing panpsychism in my opening statement, it is not always clear what panpsychists have in mind when they attribute consciousness to the fundamental elements of nature. However, so long as we take them at their word and assume that the relevant non-dispositional properties are genuine phenomenal properties, though of an extraordinary sort, we might regard position C as avoiding this particular objection (whatever other problems it faces).

Kind's second objection to Russellian monism is that both panpsychist RM (position A) and panprotopsychist RM (position B) face a well-known problem called "the combination problem." This problem is traditionally a problem for panpsychism, but Kind says it is a problem for panprotopsychism too. Once again, while she doesn't say this explicitly, it is hard to see why it is not also a problem for neutral monist and physicalist Russellian monism (C and D), at any rate if it is a problem for panprotopsychism.

Kind's final objection—in her view this is the most serious of the three—is that all four positions are guilty of false advertising. The Russellian monist is presented by its proponents as a non-standard view, a view that moves us beyond the ordinary options; indeed, this is exactly how I presented it. But Kind argues that this is the wrong way to see the situation. When all is said and done, she says, position A is a version of dualism, and positions B-D are versions of physicalism. Hence, if we adopt RM, we are in the same philosophical predicament we always were: we still need to decide between physicalism and dualism. In sum, adopting RM provides only the illusion of progress.

What can we say about this critique of RM? In what follows I will respond to each of these three objections before turning to other points of disagreement with Kind.

3. Must We Say What the Properties Are?

Kind's first objection is that the positions B and D fail a condition of adequacy in that they "owe us an account" of what the non-dispositional properties are. My reply is that this is not a condition of adequacy. These positions don't owe anyone an account of what these properties are; in fact, they don't owe nobody nothin'.

To explain why this is so, let me back up a little. According to positions B and D, we don't know the nature of the relevant non-dispositional properties. The point is not that we know nothing *at all* about these properties. They could hardly figure in Russellian monism in the first place if that were true. You have to know at least a little about a property in order to talk at any length about it. It is rather that, if RM is true, what we know about these properties is abstract and negative. We know that they are not dispositional, that they are instantiated, that they are instantiated if dispositional properties are, and that they are relevant to consciousness. Beyond that, we don't know what they are.

But this claim is in effect the whole point of RM, or at any rate of versions B and D. This is why saying that these positions "owe us an account" misses the point. It is a bit like saying that Immanuel Kant, the 18th-century German philosopher, "owes us an account" of noumena, that is, the "things in themselves" that according to him exist but of which we have no knowledge. It may be that Kant needs to provide an argument for why we should believe that there are noumena, but the whole point of his position is that there is no account of the nature of noumena. You can disagree with Kant all you like, but you can't say he "owes us an account' of noumena.

There is also a different way to bring out that positions B and D do not owe us any account of the nature of non-dispositional properties. The idea that we don't know the nature of these properties is not something that merely happens to be true on these proposals. On the contrary, this is the feature that allows them to respond to the conceivability argument. As we have seen, the conceivability argument is an argument, or is often taken to be an argument, that phenomenal properties are fundamental. The Russellian monist who holds any position like B, C, or D (let's set aside A for the moment) is committed to the view that the argument is a failure. Why does it fail according to them? Answer: our ignorance of non-dispositional properties. In other words, each of B-D appeals to the ignorance hypothesis to answer the conceivability argument. Of course, on this style of view, we don't know the nature of these properties; that is the central idea.

So the objection that positions like B and D owe us an account misses the point. Why has Kind missed it? One reason, I think, is that nowhere in her critique of Russellian monism does she explicate how the positions like B, C, and D respond to the conceivability argument. These theories entail that consciousness is not fundamental; hence they must answer the conceivability argument somehow. The key element of the response is the assertion that there is something relevant about the world we don't know. To say "but you must tell us what the nature of the world is!" entirely misjudges these sorts of position.

4. The Combination Problem

Kind's second objection is that positions A and B face the combination problem. My reply is that, while position A faces the combination problem, position B does not. The combination problem is a problem for panpsychism. Since A is a version of panpsychism, it faces the problem. But, since B is not a version of panpsychism, it does not.

What is the combination problem? That is a big issue, but for our purposes we may think of it in the way that Kind suggests. Its first premise is that it is *not* possible for a collection of feelings to constitute one overall feeling; as Kind (p. 43) puts it, "Suppose we have 100 different feelings and we now bundle them together. No matter how tight the bundle is, there is no way for the feelings to intermix with one another." Its second premise is that, if panpsychism is true, this *is* possible. The conclusion is the panpsychism is false.

Contemporary philosophers have discussed this problem at some length, distinguishing various versions of it, and various replies (see, e.g., Goff 2017, and for criticism see Stoljar 2020b). Since I have no brief for panpsychism I will set this aside. Let me note only what is clearly true: that panpsychism faces the combination problem.

But panprotopsychism does not face the combination problem! All panprotopsychism says is this: The non-dispositional properties that necessitate the dispositional properties physical theory describes have a certain abstract feature, namely, the capacity to necessitate or partially necessitate phenomenal properties. That is quite consistent with them being entirely non-phenomenal; indeed, it is consistent with them being entirely non-psychological. But if this position does not entail that such properties are phenomenal, it does not face the combination problem.

How has Kind missed this? I think the answer this time is that she has been misled by the label "panprotopsychism." To describe a position as "panprotopsychism" conveys very strongly that it is a sort of panpsychism or at least that it would be a form of panpsychism if only it had the courage of its convictions—a kind of "spirit" panpsychism rather than "letter" panpsychism.

But to convey that about position B is quite mistaken. Take the most straightforward kind of materialism, say the sort defended by

Hobbes, on which the only fundamental objects are atoms and the void. That view will of course permit (since it is not eliminativist) that there are non-fundamental objects, such as human beings, who are conscious. But then Hobbes' position too may be described as a kind of panprotopsychism, since it too entails that fundamental objects such as atoms have the capacity within them to come together to form complex objects that have phenomenal states. But nobody thinks that this classical version of materialism faces the combination problem, whatever other problems it faces. The same applies to B.

One might reply that, while position B does not face the combination problem in the sense that panpsychism does, it nevertheless faces a related problem that is almost as bad. For surely position B must agree that there is some account of how non-dispositional properties combine together, perhaps with dispositional physical properties, to generate consciousness. There is some story to be told, in other words, about how the fundamental elements of nature, with their suite of dispositional and non-dispositional properties, come together to produce consciousness.

However, while this is true, there are two reasons why it is no objection to position B. The first is that, while B is committed to the existential claim that *there is* such an account, it is not committed to the much stronger claim that *we can provide* that account. On the contrary, it says directly that we cannot do so, at any rate in present epistemic circumstances.

The second is that, while position B is committed to there being such an account, it avoids the usual reasons for thinking that such an account is impossible. In the case of panpsychism, position A, there is a positive reason for thinking that such an account (or a parallel account) is impossible; the combination problem is precisely such a reason. Likewise, in the case of standard physicalism, such as that defended by Hobbes, there is a positive reason for thinking that such an account is impossible; the conceivability argument is precisely such a reason. But position B faces neither of these arguments; indeed, it is designed to avoid them.

There is a further point to be made here about Kind's classification of panpsychism as a version of Russellian monism. This is certainly standard in the literature. In David Chalmers' influential (2015) discussion of these matters, Russellian monism is understood as coming in two forms: panpsychist and panprotopsychist. But there is good reason to resist this way to look at things. It is true that both positions A and B are Russellian in character, which means in this context that they appeal to a distinction between dispositional and non-dispositional properties. Still, panpsychism is a very different doctrine from panprotopsychism, as in effect Kind points out in her critique of RM. In particular, panpsychism accepts that consciousness in a distinctive form is fundamental; panprotopsychism does not. Since that the fundamentality of consciousness is in effect the central issue, any taxonomy that regards them as the same sort of view is extremely strange.

5. False Advertising

Kind's third objection is that Russellian monism is guilty of false advertising. Russellian monism is advertised as getting us beyond the physicalist-dualist divide. But Kind argues on the contrary that the divide is preserved. Position A is just a souped-up version of dualism; at any rate it has the key consequence that consciousness in some form is a fundamental element of nature. Positions B-D, by contrast, are just souped-up versions of physicalism, for the parallel reason that for them consciousness is not a fundamental element. Hence, she argues, if you decide to become a Russellian monist, and so decide that one or other of A-D is true, you will still face the choice between the dualist view that consciousness is fundamental and the physicalist view that it is not. But that is exactly the choice you faced before becoming a Russellian monist; in fact, it is just the choice you faced all along.

My reply is that this is not the choice you faced all along. One way to see this is to forget about the label "Russellian monism" for a moment and just focus on the choice between A, on the one hand, and B-D, on the other. This is a choice between panpsychism, on the one hand, and a certain category of non-panpsychist position, on the other. All the members of this latter category have a very distinctive feature: They make available a version of epistemic response to the conceivability argument and related arguments for the conclusion that consciousness is fundamental. All of them, in other words, are committed to the ignorance hypothesis. Hence, while these positions can be understood as versions of physicalism, they are also versions of non-standard physicalism. Putting this together, the choice between A, on the one hand, and B-D, on the other, is a choice between panpsychism and non-standard physicalism.

But this is not at all the choice we faced all along; at any rate, it is not the usual choice between dualism and physicalism. There are several points of difference.

First, the usual choice between dualism and physicalism assumes that the ignorance hypothesis is either false or irrelevant to the conceivability argument. The usual choice, in other words, is between dualism and standard physicalism: It presupposes that we have complete information about what type of facts or properties are physical; the only issue is what relation holds between phenomenal properties and physical properties so understood.

Second, the usual choice between dualism and physicalism is a choice between a view that entails that ordinary phenomenal properties of the sort had by humans and other sentient creatures are fundamental and a view that entails they are not. Dualism entails the first, while physicalism entails the second. But the choice between A and B-D is not that. In fact, none of these options entail that ordinary phenomenal properties are fundamental—not even panpsychism.

The third reason why the choice between A and B-D is not the choice we faced before is perhaps the most serious one. The choice between dualism and standard physicalism is a very difficult one in the following sense: Whichever way you go, you have a position that is almost impossible to believe. The dualist holds that ordinary phenomenal properties are fundamental elements of nature, properties that logically speaking are on a par with the charge of the electron. That is not incoherent from a logical point of view, but it is impossible to believe—at least for most of us. The standard physicalist, by contrast, focuses instead on properties that we know we have and which we already know the ins and outs of—properties like having a particular cell assembly or being disposed to call your mother. The position of the standard physicalist is that ordinary phenomenal properties are identical to or necessitated by these well-known physical properties. That too is almost impossible to believe. It is true that these properties are instantiated, but the suggestion that feeling a pain in your foot is really one of them seems as outlandish as the idea, to use an example Frege used in a different context, that Julius Caesar might be a number.

The choice between A and B-D, however, is not at all a difficult one. Option A is panpsychism, which is perhaps best understood as a sort of generalization of standard dualism from subjects like me and Alice B Toklas to every fundamental object. That too is almost impossible to believe, quite apart from technical problems such as the combination problem. But options B-D, by contrast, are completely different. What they say is there is a type of physical property that is unknown to us but which is relevant to consciousness. That is of course a substantive assumption; it may or may not be true. But it is not impossible to believe.

6. Non-standard and Non-Russellian?

I have been suggesting that Kind's critique of Russellian monism is mistaken. But at this stage I should emphasize a point made in my opening statement, namely, that Russellian monism is not the only form of non-standard physicalism, or, to put the point in the terms of Kind's critique, that positions B-D are not the only forms of non-standard physicalism.

In general, non-standard physicalism is any position that says that consciousness is not fundamental and appeals to our ignorance of the physical world in the defense of that claim. Positions B-D express this underlying idea within a Russellian framework in which empirical inquiry is assumed to be limited in important ways to dispositional (or structural or relational) properties.

But there is a parallel position that expresses that idea in a framework that makes no commitment about the a priori limits of empirical inquiry. David Chalmers (Chalmers 2010) calls this view "Type-C materialism," but it would be confusing to use that label in the context of Kind's discussion, since for her "C" already denotes something else. We might perhaps call it "non-Russellian non-standard physicalism," but now the number of negations is becoming oppressive. Here I will simply refer to it as the "non-Russellian epistemic view" in contrast with the Russellian epistemic view we have been discussing so far. In other words, we have what Kind calls positions B-D, which are versions of the Russellian epistemic view, and then in addition we have a non-Russellian version of the same view.

It should not be surprising that there is a non-Russellian version of the same view. After all, the parallel point applies in the case of panpsychism. Position A is a distinctively Russellian form of panpsychism, and there may be good reasons for focusing on that version of the view. Still, there are many versions of panpsychism that are not Russellian in this sense. It would be wrong to insist that Russellian panpsychism and non-Russellian panpsychism are entirely different views.

What then happened to this non-Russellian form of the epistemic view? While it dominated my own opening statement, it makes no appearance at all in Kind's discussion! In the case of Russellian monism, she at least considers it and argues that it plays no role. But non-Russellian epistemic view has gone entirely missing. It is present only as a Gramscian subaltern; it has been entirely othered.

7. Kind and the Structure and Dynamics Argument

What explains the absence of non-Russellian forms of the epistemic view in Kind's discussion?

I suspect that Kind is here influenced by an argument suggested by David Chalmers and developed and defended by Torin Alter, namely, *the structure and dynamics argument* (Alter 2016; Chalmers 2015). The point of this argument is that the non-Russellian epistemic view of the sort I have been recommending is not a genuine option: pushed one way, it becomes Russellian monism, but pushed another way, it becomes standard physicalism.

Here is how the structure and dynamics argument goes, at least in a simplified form that connects with the issues we have been discussing. Let us suppose first that there are physical properties of which we are ignorant but which are relevant to consciousness; this is a presupposition of both the Russellian and the non-Russellian epistemic view. Presumably, these properties are either dispositional or non-dispositional. If they are non-dispositional, however, then the allegedly "non-Russellian" view stands exposed as a kind of Russellian monism. After all, it is now committed to the view there are non-dispositional properties of which we are ignorant but which are relevant to consciousness, and that is precisely what the Russellian monist says.

What then of the alternative possibility: that the properties of which we are ignorant are dispositional? In that case, insists the proponent of the structure and dynamics argument, the conceivability argument will re-emerge. Moreover, in attempting to answer that argument, the non-Russellian will be forced to make the same moves as the standard physicalist. But if you make the same moves as the standard physicalist in response to the conceivability argument, you are a standard physicalist! Conclusion: The non-Russellian epistemic view is either a kind of Russellian monism or a kind of standard physicalism.

This is certainly a challenging objection to the position I have been recommending. In my opening statement I didn't discuss precisely this problem, but I did discuss a more general problem of which this is an instance, namely what I called there "the persistence objection." Elsewhere, however, I have argued against the structure and dynamics argument at length (Stoljar 2015, 2020a). In my view, the argument greatly overemphasizes the difference between Russellian and non-Russellian forms of the epistemic view. Moreover, it faces a lot of technical problems over how to interpret its key distinction between dispositional properties and non-dispositional properties (or, to put it more accurately, between structural properties and non-structural properties; as its name suggests the argument focuses on structural properties rather than properties of other sorts).

I won't repeat or elaborate on these criticisms of the structure and dynamics argument here. For present purposes, it is more important to make two points. First, the attitude of proponents of the structure and dynamics argument is rather like Kind's attitude to Russellian monism in general. The point of the structure and dynamics argument is to limit the set of options we have available to us. Kind's argument about Russellian monism is similar. In fact, if we combine Kind's argument with the structure and dynamics argument, we are back with the standard options for thinking about the place of consciousness in the physical world.

Second, while there is this similarity between Kind's positions and the friend of the structure and dynamics argument, in fact, the latter argument is not available to her. For that argument rests on a particular conception of a physical property, a conception implicit in the first thesis of the three that constitute Russellian monism. A key move of the argument is that we know a priori that physical properties are of a certain logical or metaphysical type—for example, they are dispositional or extrinsic or structural—and that no property of that type will alter the dialectical situation with respect consciousness. Hence the only way in which that situation can be altered is if one adopts Russellian monism.

The reason that Kind cannot endorse this argument is that she rejects any conception of a physical property that limits it to a type of that sort. Instead she adopts a view defended by Jessica Wilson, Barbara Montero, and others, which is sometimes called the *via negativa* (Wilson 2006; Montero 1999). On this view, at least as Wilson develops it, a physical property is a property expressed by any physical theory at all, so long as it is not both a fundamental property and a mental property. As Kinds puts this position (p. 58), "However physicalism is to be defined—whether it's in terms of current physics or future physics, or some other way entirely—we should see the theory as committed to an important constraint: physicalism can be true only if phenomenality is not a primitive aspect of the world."

There are several issues that arise with the via negativa. In other work, I have argued that while it is a plausible account of what philosophers often have in mind when they speak about the physical, it is not a good account of what a physical property actually is (Stoljar 2010). The key point for present purposes, however, is that the via negativa does not serve the purposes of the structure and dynamics argument. The reason is that a view of this sort is quite compatible with the key element of the ignorance hypothesis; the via negativa permits that there is a type of physical property that is relevant to the consciousness but of which we are ignorant, and it makes no demands on the metaphysical or logical character of that type of property. So you can't defend the structure and dynamics argument if you hold the via negativa.

8. Dualism 2.0 and the Conceivability Argument

I will come back explicitly to the issue about options in the concluding section of this reply, but before doing so, let me make two remarks about the option that Kind herself thinks is the best one, namely, dualism 2.0.

The first concerns the motivation for this kind of dualism, and indeed dualism of a more traditional sort as well. Obviously, the motivation is the conceivability argument and similar arguments. If the conceivability argument is sound, and if consciousness exists, then presumably it is fundamental. That is the key commitment of dualism 2.0.

But of course, if the options I have been talking about are on the table, things look completely different. If options B-D are available, for example, the conceivability argument is unsound. And the same is true for the non-Russellian shadow of options B-D, namely the non-Russellian epistemic view.

This puts Kind's attempt to narrow the options in a different light. For her the point is not simply academic, as we might say; it does not simply concern the abstract possibility of these options.

Rather, to properly motivate dualism 2.0, Kind will need to show that none of these options are available, for, if those options are available, the key argument for dualism 2.0 goes away. As I have been suggesting, however, her arguments to rule out B-D are unpersuasive, and her arguments to rule out the non-Russellian epistemic view are non-existent.

9. The Mathematics Analogy

The second remark concerns what is perhaps the main objection to dualism rather than the motivation for it. On any version of dualism, including Kind's, ordinary phenomenal properties turn out to be metaphysically fundamental. As I have mentioned a number of times, my own view is that, while this is not a priori impossible, it is extremely unlikely.

Kind does not confront the issue in quite this form but she is certainly sensitive to objections along these lines. Her main suggestion is that dualism may be defended against this objection using a mathematics analogy. "The fact that something cannot be reduced to the physical," she says, "does not mean that it is magical or mystical." She continues:

> Take mathematics, for example. Mathematicians are committed to the existences of numbers, like the number 2 or 17 or 24 . . . so too are the rest of us. But while numbers can be represented physically with a numerical inscription, numbers themselves don't seem to be physical things. I can have 17 peas on my plate, for example, but I can't have the number 17 on my plate. And mathematics commits us not only to rational numbers like 2 or 17, but also mathematical constants like π and e (known as Euler's number), irrational numbers, and even imaginary numbers. Some of these mathematical entities may be strange, but their strangeness doesn't get characterized as spooky—as in some way magical or mystical. (this volume, 54)

I am sympathetic with Kind's attitude to mathematics as expressed in this passage. I think there are mathematical entities and I don't think we should view them as spooky or magical or mystical—at least I don't have a clear sense (and I don't think anybody else has a clear sense) of the standards of spookiness (etc.) that would make them spooky.

Still, I don't think it helps the defense of dualism. Kind's idea is that while, according to dualism 2.0, consciousness is fundamental and is not physical, you can't object to it on that count, since mathematical objects and properties are also fundamental and not physical. One problem with this is whether it's true that mathematics isn't physical. That depends, of course, on what notion of the physical one has in mind. Certainly on some views, including Kind's own version of the via negativa, there is no problem with classifying the mathematical as physical.

But a different problem is whether mathematics is fundamental in the relevant sense. As several recent philosophers have argued, a property is fundamental just in case (a) it is the sort of property apt to be grounded, or hold in virtue of, some other property; and (b) it is not grounded in any other property (Rabin 2020; Dasgupta 2015). Dualism 2.0 entails that phenomenal properties are fundamental in this sense: They are both apt for being grounded, and yet are not grounded. But mathematical properties, one might argue, are not even apt for being grounded; indeed, perhaps this is true of topic-neutral properties in general. If so, they are not fundamental in the first place, and the mathematical analogy is misplaced.

10. Reconsidering the Space of Options

Turning finally to an explicit statement of the set of options before us, as I said at the outset, the key disagreement between Kind and me is what exactly is included in this set. We may bring that out by articulating various sets of options and asking about the relative plausibility of their members.

The first set of options is the basic one:

[dualism, eliminativism, standard physicalism]

Kind thinks that, out of these options, dualism is best and appeals to a mathematical analogy to make that plausible. I think myself that, as between these three, each is equally bad. In fact, that is what makes the compatibility problem as standardly presented so difficult, since it is standardly presented as a forced choice among these options.

The second set expands on the basic one, including not just these options but in addition the four versions of RM Kind considers. So this set is:

[dualism, eliminativism, standard physicalism, position A (panpsychism), position B (panprotopsychism), position C (physicalist monism), position D (neutral monism)]

Kind thinks again that, out of these options, dualism is best. That is because, as we have seen, she thinks that, out of the basic set of options, dualism is the best bet, and in addition, as we have also seen, that A-D don't alter the option space. As I have said, I disagree with this. I don't think position A is plausible, but the disjunction of B-D seems to me easily preferable to any of the other positions in this second set. On the issue of which of B-D to opt for, I tend to agree with Kind that these are all basically physicalist options, at least in the sense that they all entail that consciousness is not fundamental. Beyond that I see no reason at this stage to fight over which is preferable.

The third set expands on the second set, including not just all the options on the second list (the basic set, plus A-D) but also a non-Russellian form of the epistemic view. So the third set is:

[dualism, eliminativism, standard physicalism, position A (panpsychism), position B (panprotopsychism), position C (physicalist monism), position D (neutral monism), non-Russellian epistemic view]

Kind does not even consider this expanded set of options, and she provides no argument against doing so, though as I have noted, there is an argument, namely the structure and dynamics argument, which entails that the third set of options reduces to the second. My view, as I have said, is that options B-D are attractive, but I think the non-Russellian epistemic view is even more so. This is because it puts no weight at all on the idea that physical theory, and empirical theory in general, is limited a priori to dispositional properties (or some similar sort of property); nor more generally does it place any weight on the distinction between dispositional and non-dispositional properties or any similar distinction. Maybe there is such a distinction, and maybe there are a priori limits on empirical inquiry, but I don't think it is necessary or desirable to rely on that in order to solve the issue of whether physicalism is compatible with the existence of consciousness.

The key points of my reply to Kind's opening statements are these. The most obvious difference between Kind and me is that, while she as a dualist thinks that consciousness is a fundamental element of nature, I don't. Lying behind this difference is a less obvious but more important one, namely, what the space of options is. I think there are several non-standard options available, whereas Kind does not. Some of these non-standard options go under the label "Russellian monism." As regards these, Kind argues in her statement that they do not change anything as far as the philosophical issues surrounding consciousness go. I reject this argument on several grounds, the most important being that Russellian monism, unlike any standard option, makes available an epistemic response to the conceivability argument. In addition to the various versions of Russellian monism, there is also the option of holding a view that is both non-standard and non-Russellian—that is in fact the position I defend in my own opening statement. Kind neglects this entirely; it does not even appear in her discussion as an object of criticism. Nevertheless, a position of this sort is more attractive than any other position, standard or not. Finally, the mathematics analogy that Kind uses to defend her version of dualism is misplaced.

Second Round of Replies

Chapter 5

The Consciousness Slugathon
Reply to Daniel Stoljar's Reply

Amy Kind

Contents

Introduction	177	2. Is Dualism Impossible to Believe?	186
1. The Non-Russellian Epistemic View	179		

Introduction

To start, it will be useful to review the overall dialectic of our discussion. Roughly speaking, there are two main options for solving the problem of consciousness: dualism and physicalism. While I am defending dualism, Stoljar is defending physicalism. But the kind of physicalism that he is defending is a non-standard version of the view.

So whereas the debate as traditionally construed looks like this:

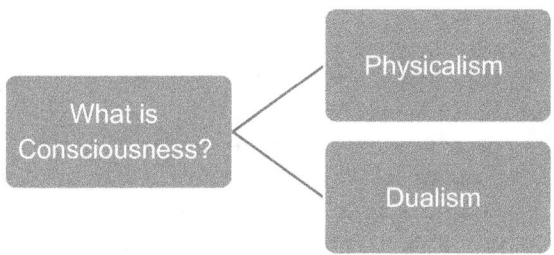

DOI: 10.4324/9780429324017-8

Stoljar has broadened the debate so that it looks like this:

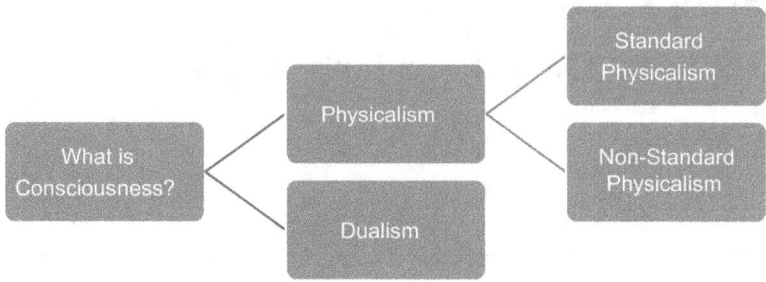

If that's the way the debate looks, then showing that standard physicalism fails is not enough to establish dualism. I would also have to show that non-standard physicalism fails. And that's what Stoljar charges that I haven't done. This is the primary thrust of his response to my opening statement.

Here I'm reminded of one of my family's favorite board games: Titan. As described on the box, the game is a Monster Slugathon Fantasy Wargame. Each player builds an army of mythological monsters (such as gargoyles, trolls, cyclops, and behemoths) that are divided into various legions. At various points in the game, one of a given player's legions will engage the legion of an opposing player in battle. Battles take place over seven rounds, with the outcomes in each round determined by various series of dice rolls. Without getting caught up in the details, which are pretty complicated, what matters for us here is that the players take their turns in the battle rounds sequentially, but we're meant to imagine them as happening simultaneously. So if I go first, and one of my unicorns kills one of my opponent's ogres, then when it's my opponent's turn, we treat the ogre as if it's still alive. Its attack is understood as happening at the same time as my unicorn's attack.

This debate is a little bit like Titan—not in the sense that I take myself and my opponent to be mythological monsters, but in the sense that our salvos should be imagined as occurring simultaneously. In Round 1, we each wrote our opening statements without seeing the other's opening statement, in Round 2, we each wrote our first responses without seeing the other's first response, and now in Round 3, we each are writing our second responses without seeing the other's second response. Why is this important? When

Stoljar makes the accusation in Round 2 that I have failed to take non-standard views like his epistemic view seriously, this was written as a reaction to what had happened in Round 1. Indeed, in the very same round where Stoljar was making that accusation, I was ("simultaneously") making a serious attempt to grapple with the epistemic view. One of my main goals in that response was to show why and how his defense of the epistemic view falls short.

In short, Stoljar is right that in my opening statement, I was concerned to defend dualism against (primarily) the standard physicalist options. I was treating the debate as it is depicted in the first diagram above. But in Round 2, I tried to meet him on his terms, and I shifted to treating the debate as it is depicted in the second diagram. I tried to show why dualism comes out as the winner even in a battle against non-standard versions of physicalism like the epistemic view.

But of course, there's more that could be said. So now in Round 3, as we ("simultaneously") offer our second and final responses to one another, I'll stay focused on his epistemic view and attempt to address some of the new points that arose in Round 2. In particular, given that Stoljar's Round 2 responses help to flesh out the contours of his own preferred version of the epistemic view, I will try to focus more closely on that view and show why, even given this fuller picture of it, it should not be seen as preferable to dualism. These matters are complicated, and so I should warn you in advance that parts of my response will tread into some difficult territory. But I will make every effort throughout to keep things as simple as possible.

1. The Non-Russellian Epistemic View

As Stoljar notes, my opening statement did contain a discussion of Russellian monism (see Section 4.3, Chapter 1), though I did not characterize the view as a version of non-standard physicalism. But in my opening statement I didn't discuss Stoljar's preferred version of non-standard physicalism, what he characterizes as the Non-Russellian Epistemic View (what I'll call *NRE*, for short). Though he does not think that NRE is the only version of non-standard physicalism that beats out dualism, it is the version of non-standard physicalism that he finds most attractive.

Stoljar notes that there are some arguments—in particular, an argument often referred to as the *structure and dynamics argument*—that aim to take NRE off the table, that is, that push us back to the standard views available. Put very roughly, if all physical properties are structural and dynamic properties, then even if there are physical properties of which we're now ignorant, they too will be structural and dynamic properties. This means the consequences of our ignorance are much less dramatic than it may have seemed. Most significantly, our ignorance doesn't allow us to escape the traditional dialectic surrounding the conceivability argument. As we've discussed, the conceivability argument is very powerful support for dualism. Between the bat case, the knowledge argument, and the zombies, there is good reason to think that consciousness escapes the physicalist net. When the physicalist is pushed back to the standard options I discussed in my opening statement—options like the identity theory and functionalism—they don't have a good response to the conceivability argument, and dualism might plausibly be taken to emerge victorious. Think of things in terms of the following equation:

STRUCTURE AND DYNAMICS ARGUMENT + CONCEIVABILITY ARGUMENT → NRE FAILS

That sounds like a pretty good result for the dualist, you might think. And indeed, it is! But Stoljar thinks that I am not the kind of dualist who can make use of this result. Given the kind of dualism that I have espoused, he thinks that the structure and dynamics argument is unavailable to me, and so he does not think I have both of the pieces that I need to use the above equation and thereby push the physicalist back to the standard options. I disagree. (Shocking, I know.) Be warned that the issues here are complicated. Moreover, engaging in a full discussion of them would take considerably more space than I have here. Nonetheless, I'm optimistic that I can help to show why Stoljar is mistaken without having to get down too much into the weeds.

I'd suggest we can see Stoljar as arguing something like the following:

Stoljar's Argument Against Kind

1. To claim that all physical properties are structural and dynamic requires one to make a substantive commitment about what it is to be a physical property.
2. Kind disavows any substantive commitment about what it is to be a physical property (i.e., on Kind's view, the notion of the physical can be defined only negatively).

3. Therefore, Kind cannot claim that all physical properties are structural and dynamic. [From 1,2]

On Stoljar's view, if I can't make the claim all physical properties are structural and dynamic, then I haven't adequately made my case for why our ignorance doesn't matter, and I'm wrong to dismiss NRE, his epistemic view. Again, as the above equation suggests, to conclude that NRE fails, I need the structure and dynamics argument to add to the conceivability argument. If I don't have the structure and dynamics argument, I don't reach my conclusion.

But why don't I have the structure and dynamics argument? The key claim is the second premise in Stoljar's Argument Against Kind. To support this premise, he quotes the following passage from my Opening Statement: "However physicalism is to be defined—whether it's in terms of current physics or future physics, or some other way entirely—we should see the theory as committed to an important constraint: physicalism can be true only if the phenomenality is not a primitive aspect of the world." Relatedly, I also say: "What counts as physical may adapt as physical theory evolves, but the notion cannot adapt so far as to include primitive phenomenality within it." This is what I call the No Fundamental Mentality constraint (NFM). To my mind, however, these passages do not imply—and I did not mean to imply—that I disavow the possibility of making a substantive commitment about what it is to be a physical property. Rather, I was simply trying to sidestep the issue for the purpose of the debate. In this regard, there are two key things to note.

First, one might reasonably think that it's the physicalist, not the dualist, who owes us a characterization of the notion of the physical. But the dualist cannot remain entirely silent on what the physical is, since the claim that consciousness is something over and above the physical can only be understood if we have at least some sense of what the physical is. To make some effort in this regard, my intention in the quoted passage was not to provide a definition of the notion of the physical but rather to lay down a necessary condition for the physical. Specifying that condition puts a constraint on being president of the United States, but it does not give us a definition of that notion. Sometimes when one gives a set of necessary conditions for a given phenomenon, they amount to a definition of that phenomenon, but we can give necessary conditions without aiming to give a definition. For example, here are some necessary conditions for being president of the United States that don't define the notion for us: To be president of the United States, you must be at least 35 years old, you must be a US citizen, and you must have been born in the United States. When it comes to the notion of the physical, I want to leave open what the definition is, but I do think there are some constraints on the physicalist for what such a definition must allow, and the NFM was meant in that spirit.

Necessary Versus Sufficient Conditions

Suppose that you go to the county fair and you want to go on the Tilt-a-Whirl. When you get to the front of the queue, you see a sign with a line across it saying, "You must be this tall to go on this ride," where the line indicates a height of 46 inches. One way we might put this is to say that being at least 46 inches tall is a *necessary condition* for going on the Tilt-a-Whirl. If you're not at least 46 inches tall, you will not be let on the ride. But is that a *sufficient condition*? No. You also need to have a valid ticket. Together, however, these two factors are jointly sufficient for your being let on the ride. If you're at least 46 inches tall, and you have a valid ticket, then you will be let on the ride.

Second, the passage does not deny that a substantive definition of physicalism can be given. It's true that I don't offer a substantive definition of physicalism, either in the quoted passage or elsewhere. (Remember: sidestepping.) And it's also true that I leave open whether the definition should be in terms of current or future physics. (Remember, again: sidestepping.) But this is compatible with the claim that even a future physics must be limited to structural and dynamic properties. It might be different from current physics in all sorts of ways, but given that it is a *physical* theory, its properties must be of that sort.

With the rejection of premise 2, Stoljar's argument fails. So there's no reason that I can't help myself to the kinds of insights underlying the structure and dynamics argument. I have both pieces I need for the equation to go through. Stoljar himself noted a suspicion that I had something like this argument in mind while making the case for dualism in my opening statement, and that suspicion was indeed correct. It also was undoubtedly in the background of the arguments I made in my first response. Let me thus stop sidestepping and simply take that commitment on board, and let me also endorse the equation we've been working with. Doing so helps to go a long way toward showing why I'm underwhelmed by NRE and, correspondingly, why I haven't taken it as seriously as Stoljar thinks I ought. In short, I think there is considerably less room in which to maneuver than there would need to be in order for NRE (or indeed, for any version of the epistemic view) to be at all plausible. Let me explain why.

Stoljar needs three things to be true:

(i) We are ignorant about some properties relevant to consciousness
(ii) The properties of which we are ignorant are physical properties.
(iii) The properties of which we are ignorant are importantly different from all the physical properties of which we're not ignorant.

As I said in my previous response to Stoljar, I'm happy to grant (i). This claim is an extremely plausible one. My worry comes from the conjunction of (ii) and (iii). In order for our ignorance to have the power that Stoljar needs it to—in order for it to provide us with "an entirely different way to approach the dialectic around the conceivability argument" (this volume, 156)—the physical properties of which we're ignorant have to be very different from your run-of-the-mill physical properties. After all, given that we don't yet have a completed neuroscience, nearly everyone—including the dualist—likely accepts that there are physical properties of which we're ignorant that are relevant to consciousness. But this just takes us back to a form of the standard debate between dualism and physicalism: The dualist thinks that completing neuroscience isn't going to help to solve the hard problem of consciousness, while the (standard) physicalist thinks that it will.

As David Chalmers notes, a physicalist might think that we can close the epistemic gap once all the information is in and neuroscience is completed, that is, that this gap is closable "in the limit," because at that point

> we will see that explaining the functions explains everything, and that there is no further explanandum. It is at least coherent

to hold that we currently suffer from some sort of conceptual confusion or unclarity that leads us to believe that there is a further explanandum, and that this situation could be cleared up by better reasoning.

(Chalmers 2002)

But as Chalmers also notes, this ends up being just a version of a standard physicalism, and Stoljar does not take himself to be defending a physicalism of the standard sort. What matters for defending a non-standard physicalist view like NRE is that the unknown physical properties are not just more of the same. They have to be different enough so that we make an important mistake when we take ourselves to be able to imagine, say, that zombies are physically identical to us or that Mary the color scientist has all the physical facts in the black-and-white room. They have to be different enough so that it's plausible that, at present, given our meager conceptual resources, we are not appropriately situated to engage in the imaginings.

But—and this is the crux of the matter—how different could those properties be and still be *physical* properties? Even if we don't know exactly how to define the notion of physical—as I had suggested in the passages that Stoljar had quoted from my opening statement—we know enough to know that there must be some constraints on that notion in order for it to be a substantive one. I explicitly committed myself to one such constraint, namely, the no-fundamental-mentality (NFM) constraint. But there can be other constraints as well. Though we know that a future physics will likely look very different from current physics in all sorts of ways, ways that are not predictable from our current vantage point, in order for it to be a future *physics*, as opposed to a theory of another sort, it has to be recognizable as a physical theory.

The dilemma faced by a non-standard physicalist like Stoljar is thus easy to see. He has two options: He can argue that is open to future physical theories to accept physical properties that go beyond structure and dynamics, or he can argue that this is not open to them. Suppose he takes option one. To my mind, the futility of this option can be easily demonstrated, and once again I'll rely on some remarks from Chalmers to help do so:

[G]iven the character of physical explanation, it is unclear what sort of theory this could be. Novel physical properties are postulated for their potential in explaining existing physical phenomena, themselves characterized in terms of structure and dynamics, and it seems that structure and dynamics always suffices here.

(Chalmers 2002)

Presumably here Stoljar will again invoke ignorance: We don't know what the relevant novel physical properties would be, and we don't know (and indeed, can't know—for this isn't something that can be known *a priori*) that they wouldn't be able to be explanatory, not structural or dynamic in nature, and yet still physical. Moreover, if we try to push Stoljar to give some characterization of how this could be, if we try to tell him that he owes us more, he'll tell us that we've missed the point. He doesn't owe us anything, much the way that Immanuel Kant, the 18th-century German philosophy doesn't owe his readers an account of noumena. According to Kant, all objects can be understood either as phenomena or as noumena. Though we can think about phenomena, in his view the noumena are by their very definition outside the realm of human knowability. This means that to ask him to tell us what they are is to fail to take what he's saying seriously. As Stoljar says,

> It may be that Kant needs to provide an argument for why we should believe there are noumena, but the whole point of his position is that there is no account of the nature of noumena. You can disagree with Kant all you like, but you can't say he "owes us an account" of noumena.
>
> (this volume, 161)

The Kantian analogy is a clever one, but I don't think it's successful. First, the properties Stoljar is positing are not meant to be *unknowable in principle*. He is not saying that there is no way to explicate their nature. Rather, he says that we're precluded from doing so given our current state of knowledge. More importantly, however, note that even if we take the analogy seriously, it allows us to demand that Stoljar provide us an argument for why we should believe there are such properties. What I've tried to suggest in my previous response—see especially my discussion of the burden of proof in Section 4 of Chapter 3—is that he simply hasn't done what he needs to do in this regard.

So, if the first option of the dilemma doesn't work, suppose that Stoljar takes option two. On this route, it looks like he would have to argue that it is open to future physical theories to include consciousness itself among its basic properties. As should be clear, however, it's precisely this kind of move that's ruled out by the NFM constraint that I've committed myself to. Might he then try to deny this constraint? In my view, doing so would be tantamount to throwing in the towel on defending physicalism, even a non-standard form of physicalism, and crossing over the divide into the dualist camp—or, perhaps better, it is tantamount to collapsing the two views into one another. If what it takes to be a physicalist is to accept phenomenality as a fundamental part of reality, then there really isn't any principled way to draw a line between physicalism and dualism. But I take it that one of the few points of agreement between Stoljar and me is that there is such a line; that is, physicalism and dualism are distinct positions.

> This section responded directly to an important argument that Stoljar made in his Reply to my Opening Statement. Though Stoljar claims that I cannot make use of an important argument against non-standard versions of physicalism—the structure and dynamics argument—I think this claim is mistaken. I first show why this argument is available to me. I then show why this argument presents a deep problem for Stoljar's Non-Russellian Epistemic View. In brief, it's not clear that there's room for the unknown physical properties posited by this view to be sufficiently different from ordinary physical properties to do the kind of work they need to do in solving the Compatibility Problem.

2. Is Dualism Impossible to Believe?

I didn't say much about my dualist view in my first response to Stoljar's Opening Statement, and I haven't said much about it in this second response thus far, but before I close out my contribution to this consciousness slugathon, I want to return my attention to the view for which I have been arguing. Let me first note some good news: In his reply to my Opening Statement, Stoljar acknowledges that dualism may be the best bet when considered against the range of standard options—or at least, he explicitly expresses sympathy for this claim. Of course, he doesn't like the standard range of options very much, but still, I'll take whatever good news I can get.

One of the reasons that Stoljar doesn't like the standard range of options is that he thinks they are almost impossible to believe. When it comes to standard physicalism, we're in agreement. Like Stoljar, I too find it very hard to believe that a pain or an itch in your foot or your sensation of blueness or your experience of despair is simply identical to, or even grounded in, an ordinary physical property. Stoljar notes that this suggestion "seems as outlandish as the idea . . . that Julius Caesar might be a number" (this volume, 165), and I wholeheartedly agree. Alas, he also thinks that the dualist view is outlandish, and so this is where our agreement comes to an abrupt end. On his view, the dualist's claim that phenomenal properties, while non-physical, are nonetheless as fundamental as properties like an electron's charge, while not logically incoherent, "is impossible to believe—at least for most of us" (this volume, 165).

But, of course, many philosophers do believe the dualist view—or at least, they claim to believe it, and I see no reason to question their own belief reports on this score. In my opening statement, I reported results from the 2009 PhilPapers survey that showed that approximately 29% of the surveyed philosophers report that they accept of lean toward non-physicalism. In the time since I wrote that statement, the eagerly anticipated results of the 2020 PhilPapers survey have been released, and support for dualism has held steady and indeed even slightly increased with almost 32% of participants reporting that they accept or lean toward non-physicalism. While this is considerably less than the percentage who accept or lean toward physicalism (approximately 52%), it is still a sizable number.[1]

For Stoljar, one of the things that his epistemic view has going for it, in contrast to dualism, is that it's not impossible to believe. In fact, he thinks it's rather plausible. But as I discussed in reply to his opening statement (and to some extent in the previous section), while it's rather plausible that we don't know absolutely everything physical there is to know about consciousness, it's much less plausible that the physical facts of which we're ignorant are relevant to the compatibility problem. And, given the standards that Stoljar seems to be employing in judgments about what's impossible to believe, I think I might go so far as to count this claim as something that's almost impossible to believe.

---

1. Note that the survey does not distinguish between standard and non-standard forms of physicalism, so I presume that some of the philosophers who indicated that they accept or lean toward physicalism embrace non-standard versions like Russellian or non-Russellian versions of the epistemic view.

In this section, I won't retread that ground. Here I want to focus on dualism, and so I'll make one last attempt to show why it's not as hard to believe as Stoljar suggests. I'll start first with an ad hominem point. Though the notion of "ad hominem" is often associated with a certain type of fallacious reasoning, not all ad hominem arguments are fallacies; see the following box.

> ### AD Hominem Arguments
>
> The Latin phrase "ad hominem" means "to the man" or "to the person." Sometimes, an arguer responds to an opponent's reasoning not by attacking the reasoning but by attacking the opponent themselves. So, for example, suppose that two politicians, Senator Simon and Senator Murray, are debating how best to respond to school shootings. After Simon makes an argument, Murray responds by saying: "How could we ever trust someone who's wearing such an ugly outfit?" Even if Simon's outfit is indeed ugly, that fact seems entirely irrelevant to the strength of the reasoning they had offered for their claim. By attacking Simon, and not Simon's reasoning, Murray commits the ad hominem fallacy.
>
> But now suppose that Murray makes a different claim: "You argued last week that we should privatize all schooling. But if you think schools should be privatized, then you can't argue now for increased police presence in schools, since schools would not be part of the public sector." This response isn't irrelevant. It aims to show that a certain line of argument is unavailable to Simon given other beliefs that they have. This kind of response is personal, in that it depends on other beliefs that the arguer themselves has. But the fact that it's personal in this way does not make it problematic.
>
> We can see the first example, the fallacious ad hominem attack, as being against the person. We can see the second example, an ad hominem argument, as being to the person.

Someone like Stoljar, who holds the epistemic view, has to believe in the existence of physical properties that are quite unlike the physical properties that we already know about. For the Russellian versions of the view, these properties have to be non-dispositional in nature. Non-Russellian versions of the view don't make this commitment, but they nonetheless have to be committed to the claim that the properties in question are of a significantly different type than known properties (as we discussed in the previous section). Whatever the properties are, they are non-standard. But why is it any easier to believe in the existence of such non-standard properties than it is to believe in the existence of fundamental phenomenal properties? The only thing that could possibly make a difference is that the former properties are considered to be physical. But if we take seriously the non-standard nature of these properties, that doesn't help very much. After all, such properties lie entirely outside the scope of present physical theory; that is, we'd have to adopt a different physical theory to accommodate their existence—and we have no way of knowing what that physical theory would have to look like. The claim that these properties are physical thus can't do much work in helping them to gain traction with respect to believability. And now consider a slight extension of the point: Once we accept the claim that our ignorance plays a starring role in the Compatibility Problem, why must that ignorance be of something physical? Why couldn't the ignorance that's causing all the trouble instead be an ignorance of how phenomenal properties are fully integrated into a naturalistic worldview?

All that said, I don't want to rest my case solely on this ad hominem line of argument. Let's focus on the believability of dualism on its own merits. To motivate my own version of dualism, dualism 2.0, in my opening statement I offered an analogy to mathematics. Just as we don't find it at all difficult to believe in the existence of numbers, even though numbers are non-physical, we shouldn't find it difficult to believe in the existence of non-physical phenomenality. Stoljar doesn't like this analogy, as he thinks it breaks down in various ways. In particular, he raises two problems. First, given my own understanding of the notion of physical, numbers may in fact turn out to be physical. Second, numbers are unlikely to be fundamental in the way that phenomenality would be on my version of dualism.

Our earlier discussion of the notion of the physical helps to defuse the first point. If the notion of physical was *defined* in terms of the non-mental, if the NFM constraint was meant to be giving us a definition of the notion of the physical, then insofar as numbers are non-mental then, contrary to our natural inclinations, numbers might have to be treated as physical. But if the NFM constraint is seen not as providing a definition of the physical but rather as laying down a necessary condition of the physical, then this would not follow.

What about the second point? One way to respond would be to explore the notion of fundamentality in more detail and show that there's a relevant understanding of it that can be employed in the context of mathematics. Perhaps numbers might not turn out to be fundamental on this understanding, but there might be other more primitive mathematical entities that would be. For example, if arithmetic could be reduced to set theory, along the lines of famous work by Peano and Frege, then we might plausibly see sets as fundamental in the relevant sense. But exploring this response would get us into technical matters about mathematics that don't seem worth considering here. Instead, I'm inclined to make a different kind of response. In short, I think Stoljar is trying to place more weight on the analogy than it was meant to bear.

As I noted in my opening statement, what's central to dualism is the treatment of phenomenality as irreducibly real. It's that point that the analogy to mathematics is meant to support. Just as we view numbers as irreducibly real without worries about spookiness, so too can we treat phenomenality as irreducibly real without worries about spookiness. But something being irreducibly real is different from something's being a property like mass and charge, that is, a property that exists at the fundamental level of reality. Dualism 2.0 need not take mass and charge to be the appropriate model for phenomenality. Thus, the fact that numbers are not like mass and charge is irrelevant, since phenomenality need not be understood to be like mass and charge either.

So is dualism impossible to believe—or even just very, very hard to believe? To my mind, the most troubling concerns for dualism's believability arise from considerations of causation, that is, from considerations about how irreducible phenomenality can play a role in the causation of bodily actions (and vice versa), or more generally, how they can fit into a causal network at all.[2] Epiphenomenalism—the view that phenomenality plays no causal

---

2. Note that these are not concerns that Stoljar himself is pushing. Perhaps that's because we also don't have a good sense of how the non-standard physical properties that NRE posits would fit into a causal network. It might be that issues relating to causation are just about as troubling for his view as they are for mine.

role—is highly counterintuitive, and so if that's the only option available to the dualist, then the worry about unbelievability becomes more pressing. But, importantly, there's more that can be said. First, as I suggested in my opening statement, any solution to the problem of consciousness is likely to require us to bite some bullet at some point. It's hard to see how we can hold on to all of our intuitive beliefs. (This point, in fact, constitutes the essence of the Compatibility Problem as Stoljar has framed it.) Second, as I also suggested in my opening statement, once we start to take seriously the existence of phenomenality as irreducibly real, and we work to develop laws that integrate the phenomenal and the physical, then we might be able to make better progress on the causal relations between these two domains.

As a parting shot, however, I'd like to leave you with what may seem like a radical suggestion. Far from being impossible to believe, or even almost impossible to believe, dualism is actually quite easy to believe. Though you might not realize it, I bet many of you do believe it, or at least, that you believe various things that more or less imply it—and I say this without making any presumptions about your religious beliefs (recall that my defense of dualism 2.0 is entirely independent of religious-based considerations). Do you sometimes find yourself inclined to view yourself as at odds with your bodily urges, seeing them as not really yours? Do you talk of your brain and body using possessives—"my brain," "my body,"—analogous to the way you would talk about your clothes or car? Are you inclined to think that your thoughts and emotions are *caused by* various brain processes, thereby suggesting that they're something different from the brain processes themselves? Do you find promising the idea that you could upload your mind to a computer or to a robot body? When you watch *Avatar*, do you take the character Jake Sully to have successfully transferred his consciousness from his human body to his avatar body, becoming a member of the Na'vi? When you watch *Freaky Friday*, do you take the daughter and the mother to have swapped places, with the daughter's consciousness now in the mother's body and the mother's consciousness now in the daughter's body? When you watch *Star Wars*, do you find the notion of the Jedi mind trick coherent?

In fact, a number of researchers have suggested that dualism is in many ways the default view, the view that we believe as children. As I noted in my opening statement, psychologist Paul Bloom thinks that we are all "natural born dualists."³ The dualist view is not something that we have to talk ourselves into believing but rather something that we would have to talk ourselves into giving up. Whether this is something we should do has been the very point at issue in this debate. To my mind, there is a strong case to be made for dualism, and I think it is a stronger case than can be made for physicalism—be that physicalism standard or non-standard. Insofar as we talk ourselves into giving dualism up because we think that it's not scientifically respectable, or that it's spooky, I think we'd be making a mistake. Once we recognize that a commitment to dualism is by no means tantamount to a rejection of science but rather entirely consistent with a naturalistic worldview, we can see not only that the view is believable but also that it's by far our best bet for solving the problem of consciousness.

> In this final section, I attempt to provide some further support for dualism 2.0. More specifically, I take up Stoljar's worry that dualism is impossible to believe. As I argue, not only is it possible to believe in dualism, but it's actually the common-sense view. Many of us have strong dualist inclinations. One can't dismiss it on the grounds that the view is counter-intuitive. In fact, there seems good reason to think that Stoljar's Non-Russellian Epistemic View is the more counter-intuitive of the views presented in this debate.

---

3. Bloom is not himself a dualist, but he thinks of dualism as the common-sense view.

Chapter 6

Even More Seriously
Reply to Amy Kind's Reply

Daniel Stoljar

Contents

Introduction	193	3. Burden of Proof	197
1. Details Don't Matter	194	4. Is Ignorance a Defense?	198
2. You're Not Done	196		

Introduction

In her response to my opening statement, Kind offers three objections to the view I defend concerning the main metaphysical problem about consciousness, the epistemic view.

The first objection is that, while we are indeed ignorant in some sense or other, just as the view says, this would not have the advertised effect on such key arguments as the conceivability argument and the knowledge argument; these arguments, she stresses, don't require that we know every single detail of the situation imagined in order that they are successful.

The second objection is what Kind calls the "you're not done" objection. This objection concedes for the sake of argument that the epistemic view undermines arguments like the conceivability argument, but points out that there are further issues about consciousness that the view does not address. In that sense, the view is incomplete.

The final objection is a burden of proof objection. This objection says that the epistemic view assumes that physicalism is a default hypothesis, and defends it at all costs. Kind says it should not be thought of as a default hypothesis.

In these remarks I will first explain why these objections put no pressure on the epistemic view; I will end by taking up the theme in the title Kind gives to her remarks, namely "ignorance is no defense."

DOI: 10.4324/9780429324017-9

1. Details Don't Matter

In developing her first objection, Kind begins by summarizing the epistemic view as the conjunction of two claims:

> The first claim is what Stoljar calls *the ignorance hypothesis*. According to this hypothesis, we are ignorant of a physical fact or property that is relevant to consciousness. The second claim is that this ignorance is what accounts for the apparent incompatibility [of physicalism and the existence of consciousness].

With the view stated in this way, Kind's objection is that the second claim is false: The ignorance hypothesis does not in fact account for the apparent incompatibility of physicalism and the existence of consciousness, because it does not show what is wrong with the conceivability argument and related lines of reasoning. The key point is that, in a particular episode of imagining or conceiving, you don't need to imagine or be aware of every detail of the scenario in order to be convinced that it is possible. You might be convinced that it is possible for your sofa to go through the doorway, for example, on the basis of imagining it doing so, but you don't need to imagine every aspect of the situation. Inferences from imagination to possibility are epistemically demanding, Kind says, but not that epistemically demanding.

Kind is right to emphasize that, in many such arguments, details don't matter, or, to put it more positively, in many cases of modal reasoning, we abstract away from specific features of the imagined scenarios. But this has no bearing on plausibility of the epistemic view. For the epistemic view does not say that ignorance *of any sort at all* undermines the conceivability and similar arguments. It says instead that ignorance *of a relevant type of fact or property* undermines them (Stoljar 2006, 70–72).

Here, the reference to a *type* of fact or property is crucial. It is quite consistent with the epistemic view that ignorance of a particular fact which is of a type already in our possession—in other words, a detail—does not undermine the conceivability argument. What it requires instead is that there is a type of fact quite distinct from what we know. Indeed, if you look again at the passage above, you will see that Kind has not stated the view correctly. Her formulation leaves out this crucial element. The ignorance hypothesis in the form I defend it does not say merely that we are ignorant of a fact or property that is relevant to consciousness. It says we are ignorant of a *type* of fact or property that is relevant to consciousness.

Kind might perhaps respond with skepticism about the notion of a type of fact or a type of property. But this is a notion we use all the time in philosophy and in modal reasoning in particular. To adopt an example I have used elsewhere, take the well-known perfect actor argument against behaviorism (Stoljar 2007). In at least one version, this argument says that it is conceivable and so possible that I have a behavioral duplicate who is psychologically different and concludes from this that behaviorism is false. Most people who have thought seriously about this argument regard it as convincing. But consider the behaviorist who resists it by pointing out, plausibly enough, that we may well be ignorant of details of any particular behavioral situation. Is that a good response? Of course not. What is at issue in the perfect actor argument is the thought that no fact of a particular kind, namely a behavioral fact, is sufficient by itself for consciousness; hence it presupposes the coherence of the notion of a type of fact.

Or again consider the standard physicalist who accepts the perfect actor argument but who also does not think dualism about consciousness is true; for them there is a type of fact, namely a physical fact that is not also a behavioral fact, which is relevant to consciousness. That response to the perfect actor argument likewise presupposes the coherence of the notion of a type of fact. Moreover, what is true for the perfect actor argument is true for modal reasoning generally: If you are going to address reasoning like this any serious way, you must accept the notion of a type of fact.

Kind might alternatively respond that we have been given no reason to accept the ignorance hypothesis in the form I have been describing—that is, in the form that concerns a type of fact rather than a particular fact. I accept of course that we are not in a position to say what the type of facts is of which we are ignorant. That, as both Kind and I agree, is the whole point. But, as I noted in my opening statement, while we can't say directly what this type of fact is, there are several indirect reasons to suppose that we are ignorant in this way. For one thing, there are historical precedents to our current problems with consciousness. For another, from a biological and psychological point of view, humans like every other creature are highly cognitively limited, and subject to all manner of biases and blind spots. Finally, scientific theorizing itself is highly selective about the systems it aims to explain. I have gone into these considerations elsewhere and how they support the ignorance hypothesis, I and won't try to repeat any of that here (e.g., Stoljar 2006). The key point is that if anything along these lines is right, the ignorance hypothesis has a considerable degree of plausibility, even if we cannot provide anything like a proof that it is true.

Might Kind insist finally that, even if we are ignorant of a type of fact (or a type of property), this will not alter the philosophical situation, either because as a matter of fact we know all the relevant types or because the issues would persist were we to know them? This is to advance either the relevance objection or the persistence objection, as I called them in my opening statement, or perhaps a combination of both. But since I have already criticized these forms of objections, I again won't try to add anything here.

2. You're Not Done

Turning to Kind's second objection, what she has in mind here is that, even if we concede that the ignorance hypothesis is true, this can scarcely be the end of the matter. For the truth of that hypothesis would tell us at most that the existence of consciousness is compatible with physicalism. But even if we accept that, there is surely much more to say, for example, about what the nature of consciousness is, or how one might go about explaining it.

I am befuddled by this objection. Of course there is much more to say. As I emphasized right at the outset of my opening statement, there are many questions about consciousness that are not solved by saying that we are ignorant of something, and hence by solving the compatibility problem. And in both Part 1 and Part 3 of that statement, I set out several ideas about what consciousness is and what it means to do the science of consciousness. From this point of view, Kind and I are in furious agreement.

I suspect that in the back of Kind's mind here is the idea not simply that there are further questions to be answered but in addition that answers to these questions must take a particular form. In particular, I think Kind is assuming that nothing counts as an answer to these questions unless it is expressed ultimately in terms of one or other of the options that dominate her presentation, namely, standard dualism or standard physicalism.

So, for example, if you are interested in the question of what makes a psychological state a conscious state, the answer will on this view have to be something like "to be conscious a state has to instantiate (or involve the instantiation of) a fundamental property" (standard dualism) or "to be conscious a state has to have a property identical to or grounded in a property of a type familiar from contemporary cognitive or neural science" (standard physicalism).

If that is what is lying behind Kind's second objection, however, then my agreement with her ends. Yes, there are plenty of further questions to ask, but no, answers to them need not be restricted to these standard views. You can provide lots of illuminating information about what it is for a psychological state to be conscious without presupposing what the ultimate nature of the world is one way or the other; indeed, you can even do the science of consciousness without presupposing what the ultimate nature of the world is. As I said in my statement, we do that all the time when explaining other things; why should consciousness be any different?

3. Burden of Proof

Turning to Kind's third objection, this has to do with the burden of proof. There is a way of thinking about the problems of consciousness in which you assume that physicalism is true and then ask what this tells us about consciousness; you try to "fit" consciousness into a world in which physicalism is assumed to be true. Kind is hostile to this way of thinking. She thinks it betrays a set of false and selective assumptions. She thinks it stacks the decks against her dualism 2.0.

I am sympathetic with Kind's opposition to those who assume uncritically that physicalism is true and dualism false. But I don't make any such assumption. If we look past the labels and ask what Kind's dualism 2.0 amounts to, the answer is this. When you have the property of feeling a certain way in your foot, you instantiate a fundamental property of the world, one of the very sparse building blocks of reality. As I mentioned a number of times, that is a quite remarkable thing to say. When I had my attack of gout, did I instantiate a fundamental property? Surely not. At any rate, you would need a very, very big argument to make that plausible. Does Kind have such an argument? No; for the arguments she offers for such an amazing conclusion, the conceivability argument and similar arguments, all presuppose that we currently know exactly what the physical or non-experiential world is like. It is true I have no proof that this presupposition is false, but assumptions like this have been false many times in the past, and we have very good indirect reasons to think the same is true now.

Of course, it remains the case that a word like "physicalism" as I have emphasized in my opening statement (see Section 2.5.4, Chapter 2), is highly difficult to keep track of. Sometimes when people use that word, they mean only to register that a dualist position like Kind's is mistaken. In that very weak sense, there is no harm in my saying I am a physicalist; as I explained, that is the sense in which I usually use the word "physicalist" in this discussion.

But in a different sense a physicalist is someone who advances an overall worldview: a positive and detailed account of what the world is like in general. As I have noted, I doubt there is anything meeting that description that is both true and deserves the name (see Stoljar 2010). So in fact I am a vastly bigger critic of physicalism than Kind is. She thinks it's false and shouldn't be assumed uncritically. I think there is nothing here even to be false or assumed in the first place, at least no single thing. Hence there is no sense in which I uncritically rely on it.

4. Is Ignorance a Defense?

What, finally, of Kind's title: "ignorance is no defense"? It won't surprise you to learn that I have had similar remarks directed at me many times before. The implication is that proponents of the epistemic view appeal to ignorance in a self-serving or technical way, in order to avoid some sort of responsibility that they should properly be held to. The further implication is that talking about ignorance is simply sophistry that does not get to the heart of the matter.

But this is all misleading. When people repeat this legal principle, what they generally mean is something like this: The mere fact that a person is ignorant of a law they have broken does not entail that they are not legally responsible for breaking it. This has very little to do with epistemic view and the topic of consciousness more generally. Here what is at issue is not legal responsibility but the goodness of various arguments. In general, if an argument presupposes a certain epistemic claim, and that claim is false, then the argument is no good; issues of legal responsibility are irrelevant.

Moreover, even if we look past the obvious difference between assessing people for legal responsibility and assessing arguments for goodness, there is a separate reason for denying that the principle that ignorance is no defense constitutes any sort of criticism of the epistemic view.

For while it is easy to understand the principle in an impressionistic way, it is in fact unclear from a legal and philosophical point of view exactly what it amounts to and how it should be applied in particular cases; an illuminating discussion is Husak (2016). One potential justification for the principle, for example, derives from the fact that, in a properly organized legal system, laws should be publicly and widely available. If you get caught going the wrong way down Marcus Clarke St, you can't plead ignorance of the law to avoid legal responsibility, even if you are in fact ignorant, since the laws about the direction of traffic on Marcus Clarke St are open to all responsible citizens; in that sense, ignorance is no defense.

But suppose counterfactually that the laws were somehow not available, that they had been passed by the legislature in secret, and had for some reason not been communicated to the public. In that case, it might well be reasonable to plead ignorance, either to remove legal responsibility entirely or else to minimize any ensuing punishment.

Once we see things that way, however, it emerges again that the legal principle that ignorance is no defense has little negative bearing on the epistemic view. For the whole point of that view is to emphasize, as against the established traditions of thought in philosophy of mind, represented very ably in this discussion by Kind, that the relevant facts about consciousness and the rest of the world are in fact not available. If so, ignorance would indeed be a defense in at least this sense: If we are ignorant, as from an historical and empirical point of view it is extremely reasonable to assume, the key arguments for the fundamentality of consciousness, and so for Kind's dualism 2.0, are entirely unpersuasive.

> The key points of my response to Kind's reply to my opening statement are these. Kind offers three main objections to the epistemic view. The first is that details don't matter in modal reasoning: we can remain ignorant of them, and yet arguments like the conceivability argument will still go through. I agree that ignorance of particular details don't matter, but a crucial feature of the epistemic view I defend is that, if it is true, we are ignorant of a type of fact relevant to consciousness, and that certainly does matter in modal reasoning. The second is that, even if the epistemic view is correct, there are still lots of questions to

answer. I agree, so long as these questions are not stipulated to require answers inconsistent with the epistemic view itself; in fact, a major theme of my opening statement was what answers to these further questions would be like. The third is that it is a mistake to approach the philosophy of consciousness assuming that physicalism is true and dualism is false. Once again, I agree, but the epistemic view makes no such assumption. Finally, the common charge against the epistemic view that "ignorance is no defense" is misguided on two counts: It is goodness of arguments that is at issue here, not legal responsibility, and in any case what is behind that legal principle is plausibly a publicity requirement on a proper legal system, but there is no parallel publicity requirement on the nature of the world.

Suggested Further Readings

Amy Kind and Daniel Stoljar

Further Reading (Amy Kind)

For a comprehensive and accessible introduction to the mind-body problem, see my *Philosophy of Mind: The Basics* (Kind 2020). For an accessible introduction to the problem of consciousness, see *A Dialogue on Consciousness* (Alter and Howell 2009). For accessible treatments of a variety of issues relating to the problem of consciousness (including overviews of many of the key theories), see *The Routledge Handbook of Consciousness* (Gennaro 2016). Many seminal readings about consciousness are collected in *The Nature of Consciousness* (Block et al. 1997).

A classical statement of dualism can be found in *Meditations on First Philosophy* (Descartes 1641/1986). For an influential contemporary treatment of dualism, see *The Conscious Mind* (Chalmers 1996). A short and accessible treatment of many of the key issues of the book can be found in "The Puzzle of Conscious Experience" (Chalmers 1995a).

For two of the thought experiments that play a key role in motivating dualism, see "What Is It Like to Be a Bat?" (Nagel 1974) and "Epiphenomenal Qualia" (Jackson 1982).

One very accessible contemporary defense of dualism comes in "In Defense of Mind-Body Dualism" (Gertler 2007).

For a more advanced treatment of some of my objections to physicalist theories of consciousness, see my "What's So Transparent About Transparency" (Kind 2003), "The Case Against Representationalism About Moods" (Kind 2013), and "Pessimism about Russellian Monism."

Further Reading (Daniel Stoljar)

On phenomenal consciousness, see Nagel 1974; Jackson 1982, 1986; Churchland 1983; Dennett 1990, 1991, 2005; Akins 1993; Nida-Rümelin 1995; Kind 2008; Siegel 2011; Drayson 2015. On higher-order consciousness, see Armstrong 1968, 1981; Byrne 1997; Gennaro 2004, 2012; Rosenthal 2005, 2011; Block 2011; Brown et al. 2019. On access consciousness and attention, see Baars 1988, 2002; Block 1995, 2008; Schlicht 2012; Watzl 2017; Graziano 2019; Stoljar 2019b; Jennings 2020. On relations between them, see Block 1980; Shoemaker 1980, 1996; Williamson 2000; Kriegel 2007; Cohen and Dennett 2011.

On the conceivability argument in general, see Cleve 1983; Yablo 1993; Chalmers 1996, 2010; Balog 1999. On the epistemic view, see Montero 2001, 2010; Stoljar 2001, 2006, 2007; Strawson 2019. On dualism and panpsychism, see Nida-Rümelin 1995; Strawson 2006; Mørch 2014; Goff 2017. On eliminativism and illusionism, see Dennett 1990; Lewis 1995; Frankish 2017. On standard physicalism, see Lewis 1994; Braddon-Mitchell and Jackson 2007. On the formulation of physicalism more generally, see Montero 1999, 2001; Papineau 2001; Wilson 2006; Stoljar 2010.

On the science of consciousness in general, see Chalmers 2010; Irvine 2012; Koch 2012; Barron and Klein 2016; Godfrey-Smith 2016; Brown et al. 2019; Graziano 2019; LeDoux 2019; Doerig et al. 2020. On IIT in particular, see Tononi 2008, 2015, 2018; Aaronson 2014; Tegmark 2015; Mindt 2017; Bayne 2018; Mørch 2018, 2019; Pautz 2019. On laws in the science of consciousness, see Chalmers 1996; Koch 2012; Lee 2021. On the idea that consciousness comes in degree, see Bayne 2016; Simon 2017; Lee 2020, 2022.

Glossary

Access consciousness: A state is conscious in the sense of access consciousness when it is poised for use in reasoning and in guiding action. In Stoljar's opening statement, the notion is generalized to other related phenomena.

Argument: A piece of logical reasoning containing a claim or set of claims offered to support some further claim. The claim being supported is called the **conclusion**, while the reasons offered in support of it are called **premises**.

Cognitive phenomenology: A distinctive kind of phenomenal feel that some philosophers claim is had by cognitive states such as thoughts and beliefs.

Conclusion: The final claim of an **argument** and the one that the argument is put forth to support. The other claims in the argument are called **premises**.

Combination Problem: The problem of explaining how individual conscious experiences combine to create larger conscious experiences. This problem is often raised against **panpsychism** and more generally against **Russellian monism**.

Compatibility Problem: The problem of whether physicalism is compatible with the existence of consciousness.

Deductive Argument: An **argument** in which the **premises** are put forth in an effort to guarantee the truth of the **conclusion**.

Dualism: The theory of mind that claims that there are two fundamentally different kinds of things in the world: those that are physical and those that are mental. Dualism is usually contrasted with **monism**, and more specifically, with **physicalism**. It comes in two main versions: **substance dualism** and **property dualism**.

Epiphenomenalism: A view about mental causation that claims that, although non-physical mentality exists, it has no causal efficacy.

Eliminativism: The view that consciousness does not exist. Eliminativists often say that consciousness in one sense does not exist, even if, in the other sense, it does.

Epistemic View: The view that **the ignorance hypothesis**, that is, we are ignorant of relevant aspects of the physical world, explains our sense that physicalism is incompatible with the existence of consciousness.

Functionalism: A theory of mind that claims that mental states should be understood in functional terms. For the functionalist, a mental state is the state that it is because of its function not because of its constitution.

Hard Problem of Consciousness: The problem of explaining why and how phenomenal experience arises from the physical processing of the brain. The hard problem contrasts with other easier (though by no means easy) problems about consciousness that explore about psychological processing and functional mechanisms.

Hempel's Dilemma: A dilemma that faces physicalists about how to specify the nature of the physical—should it be in terms of the currently accepted theory of physics or in terms of some ideal, future theory of physics. This dilemma was articulated especially clearly by philosopher Carl Hempel.

Higher-Order Theory: A theory of consciousness that suggests that what distinguishes conscious states from non-conscious states is the presence of an appropriate higher-order representation, that is, a representation that is about the relevant state. Higher-order theory comes in various forms, such as higher-order thought theory (**HOT theory**) and higher-order perception theory (**HOP theory**).

HOT Theory: A version of higher-order theory that claims that what distinguished conscious states from non-conscious states is the presence of an appropriate higher-order thought, that is, a thought about the relevant state.

HOP Theory: A version of higher-order theory that claims that what distinguished conscious states from non-conscious states is the presence of an appropriate higher-order perception, that is, a perception of the relevant state.

Idealism: A version of **monism** that claims that everything that exists is immaterial/nonphysical. Idealism is usually contrasted with **materialism/physicalism**.

Identity Theory: A version of physicalism that claims that mental states are identical to brain states.

Illusionism: A version of **eliminativism**, according to which we are under a stable introspective illusion that consciousness exists, even though it does not in fact exist.

Ignorance Hypothesis: The hypothesis that human beings are currently and perhaps always will be ignorant of a type of physical property or fact that is relevant to consciousness.

Inductive Argument: An argument in which the **premises** are put forth in an effort to make the truth of the **conclusion** more probable.

Inscrutables: The fundamental intrinsic properties that underlie and ground all of the structural and relational properties of things. If physics deals only with structural and relational properties, inscrutables cannot come under the scrutiny of physics. **Russellian monism** claims that the **inscrutables** are responsible for consciousness.

Intentionality: The aspect of our mental states in virtue of which they are about events or things or states of affairs, that is, in virtue of which they are representational. In this sense, intentionality has nothing to do with our intentions; it is completely independent of whether a state is deliberately or voluntarily formed.

Intentionalism: A theory of consciousness often referred to as **representationalism** (see entry below).

Introspection: The way that we come to know that we are in conscious states, when we are; introspection is usually thought to be distinctive in that it is different from ordinary perception and inference.

Logical possibility: When something is possible in this sense, it follows the laws of logic; that is, it does not involve any logical contradiction or incoherency.

Materialism: A theory of mind that claims that everything that exists is made of matter, or at least bears the right sort of relation to matter. Contemporary versions of materialism are generally referred to as **physicalist** views.

Monism: The view that there is one fundamental kind of thing in the world. Monists divide primarily into two categories: **idealists**, who believe that everything that exists is immaterial/nonphysical, and **materialists** (also called **physicalists**) who believe that everything that exists is material/physical. A third kind of monism, Russellian monism, claims that one fundamental kind of thing cannot be described in terms of either traditional idealism or traditional materialism.

Neural correlates of consciousness: The neural mechanisms that are sufficient to bring about consciousness.

Neutral monism: A version of **Russellian monism** that claims that the **inscrutables** are neither phenomenal nor physical properties but rather should be classified as something neutral between the two.

O-physical properties: One of two different ways (along with the **t-physical**) of classifying what counts as a physical property. O-physical properties are those required by a complete account of the intrinsic nature of paradigmatic physical objects and their constituents plus those that supervene on the sort of property required by such an account.

Panpsychism: A theory of mind that claims that mentality is fundamental to the universe and omnipresent; that is, everything that exists has mental properties. Panpsychism is typically considered to be a phenomenal version of **Russellian monism.**

Phenomenal consciousness: A state is conscious in the sense of phenomenal consciousness when there is something that it is like to experience that state.

Phenomenal monism: A version of **Russellian monism** that claims that the **inscrutables** are phenomenal properties.

Phenomenal Property: In Stoljar's opening statement, someone has a phenomenal property when there is some way that they feel.

Physical monism: A version of **Russellian monism** that claims that the **inscrutables** are physical.

Physical possibility: When something is possible in this sense, it is permitted by the laws of physics.

Physicalism: A theory of mind that claims that everything that exists is physical and thus that the mind is nothing over and above the physical. Physicalism is often characterized in terms of **supervenience**, that is, the claim that the mental supervenes on the physical. Physicalism, which used to be referred to as **materialism**, comes in several varieties, including the **identity theory.**

Pluralism about consciousness: The view that there are several different but equally legitimate concepts of consciousness, for example, higher-order consciousness, access consciousness, and phenomenal consciousness.

Premise: One of a set of claims put forth in support of a further claim, called the **conclusion**. The premises and conclusion together make up an **argument**.

Property dualism: A version of **dualism** that claims that there are fundamentally two different kinds of properties in the world: mental properties and physical properties. Property dualism is compatible with the claim that there is only one kind of substance in existence, that is, physical substances. It thus contrasts with **substance dualism**.

Protophenomenal monism: A version of **Russellian monism** that claims that the **inscrutables** are protophenomenal. While these properties are not themselves phenomenal, they give rise to phenomenal character when a sufficient level of complexity has been reached.

Qualia: The qualitative properties of experiences. What it feels like, experientially, to taste a cherry lollipop is different from what it feels like to taste a lemon lollipop. The qualia of these experiences are what give each of them its characteristic "feel" and what distinguish them from one another. "Qualia" is a plural term; the singular is "quale."

Reductio: A kind of argumentative strategy that aims to show that a claim is false by showing that it leads to an absurd consequence. The full name of the strategy is *reductio ad absurdum*—Latin for reduction to the absurd.

Relationism about Perception: A theory of perception on which whenever it is true that you perceive something, for example, a tomato, you stand in a relation to a physical object, for example, a tomato.

Representationalism: A theory of consciousness that attempts to explain phenomenal consciousness in terms of **intentionality** by reducing the phenomenal character of our conscious states to the intentional content of such states. This theory is also often called **intentionalism**.

Revelation: The idea that when you are in a phenomenally conscious state, you can tell by introspection what the essence of that state is.

Russellian Monism: A monist view that attempts to strike a balance between traditional dualist views and traditional physicalist views. On this view, there exist fundamental properties that ground all structural and relational things. These fundamental properties, called **inscrutables**, give rise to consciousness. Russellian monism comes in several versions that differ from one another on the basis of their view about the nature of the inscrutable properties.

Sense-datum theory: A traditional view of perception on which, when you perceive something, for example, a tomato, you stand in a relation to something mental.

Standard Physicalism: In Stoljar's opening statement, standard physicalism is the version of physicalism that makes no theoretical use of the ignorance hypothesis; non-standard physicalism is the version of physicalism that is not standard.

Structure and dynamics argument: An argument targeting non-standard physicalism that claims that all physical properties are structural and dynamic in nature.

Substance dualism: A version of **dualism** that claims that there are fundamentally two different kinds of substances in the world: minds and bodies. This view is associated with Descartes and contrasts with **property dualism**.

Supervenience: When some fact A supervenes on some fact or set of facts B, there cannot be a difference with respect to A unless there is a difference with respect to B. **Physicalists** typically claim that the mental supervenes on the physical, that is, that there can be no difference with respect to the mental facts of two beings unless there is a difference with respect to the physical facts of those beings.

Thought experiment: A method used in philosophy to explore hypothetical scenarios. Typically, the imagined scenario sheds light on the coherence of a theory or its implications.

T-physical properties: One of two different ways (along with the **o-physical**) of classifying what counts as a physical property. T-physical properties are those that physical theory tells us about plus those that **supervene** on the sort of properties that physical theory tells us about.

Transparency of experience: The claim that we cannot directly attend to the intrinsic properties of experience; rather, we "see" right through our experience to the objects represented. This claim, which is not universally accepted, is often invoked in defenses of representationalism.

Zombie: A creature who is physically and behaviorally indistinguishable from a human being but who is completely devoid of phenomenal consciousness.

References

Aaronson, S. (2014). "Why I Am Not an Integrated Information Theorist, or the Unconscious Expander." *Shtetl-Optimized: The Blog of Scott Aaronson*. Available at https://scottaaronson.blog/?p=1799

Akins, K. (1993). "A Bat Without Qualities." In G. W. Humphreys and M. Davies (eds.), *Consciousness: Psychological and Philosophical Essays*. Oxford, Blackwell: 345–358.

Alter, T. (2016). "The Structure and Dynamics Argument Against Materialism." *Nous* 50(4): 794–815.

Alter, T., and Howell, R. (2009). *A Dialogue on Consciousness*. Oxford, Oxford University Press.

Alter, T., and Nagasawa, Y., eds. (2015). *Consciousness in the Physical World: Perspectives on Russellian Monism*. New York, Oxford University Press.

Armstrong, D. M. (1968). *A Materialist Theory of the Mind*. London, Routledge.

Armstrong, D. M. (1981). *The Nature of Mind and Other Essays*. Ithaca, NY, Cornell University Press.

Armstrong, D. M., and Malcolm, N. (1984). *Consciousness and Causality: A Debate on the Nature of Mind*. Oxford, Blackwell.

Baars, B. J. (1988). *A Cognitive Theory of Consciousness*. Cambridge, Cambridge University Press.

Baars, B. J. (2002). "The Conscious Access Hypothesis: Origins and Recent Evidence." *Trends in Cognitive Sciences* 6: 47–52.

Babbie, E. (1975/2020). *The Practice of Social Research*. Boston, MA, Cengage Learning.

Balog, K. (1999). "Conceivability, Possibility, and the Mind-Body Problem." *The Philosophical Review* 108(4): 497–528.

Barron, A. B., and Klein, C. (2016). "What Insects Can Tell Us About the Origins of Consciousness." *Proceedings of the National Academy of Sciences* 113: 4090–4098.

Bayne, T. (2018). "On the Axiomatic Foundations of Integrated Information Theory." *Neuroscience of Consciousness* 1: 1–8.

Bayne, T., Hohwy, J., and Owen, A. M. (2016). "Are There Levels of Consciousness." *Trends in Cognitive Sciences* **20**(6): 405–413.

Blackburn, S. (2016). *The Oxford Dictionary of Philosophy*, 3rd ed. Oxford, Oxford University Press.

Block, N. (1978). "Troubles with Functionalism." *Minnesota Studies in the Philosophy of Science* **9**: 261–325.

Block, N. (1980). "Are Absent Qualia Impossible?" *Philosophical Review* **89**(2): 257–274.

Block, N. (1995). "On a Confusion about a Function of Consciousness." *Behavioral and Brain Sciences* **18**(2): 227–247.

Block, N. (2008). "Consciousness and Cognitive Access." *Proceedings of the Aristotelian Society* **108**(1): 289–317.

Block, N. (2011). "The Higher Order Approach to Consciousness is Defunct." *Analysis* **71**(3): 419–431.

Block, N., Flanagan, O. J., and Guzeldere, G., eds. (1997). *The Nature of Consciousness*. Cambridge, MA, The MIT Press.

Braddon-Mitchell, D., and Jackson, F. (2007). *Philosophy of Mind and Cognition: An Introduction*. Oxford, Blackwell.

Brogaard, B. (2010). "Degrees of Consciousness." Unpublished paper.

Brown, R., et al. (2019). "Understanding the Higher-Order Approach to Consciousness." *Trends in Cognitive Sciences* **23**(9): 754–768.

Byrne, A. (1997). "Some Like It HOT: Consciousness and Higher-Order Thoughts." *Philosophical Studies* **86**: 103–129.

Carnap, R. (1937). *The Logical Syntax of Language*. London, Routledge and Kegan Paul.

Carnap, R. (1967). *The Logical Structure of the World*. Berkeley, University of California Press.

Chalmers, D. J. (1995a). "The Puzzle of Conscious Experience." *Scientific American*, December 1995: 62–68.

Chalmers, D. J. (1995b). "Facing Up to the Problem of Consciousness." *Journal of Consciousness Studies* **2**(3): 200–219.

Chalmers, D. J. (1996). *The Conscious Mind: In Search of a Fundamental Theory*. New York, Oxford University Press.

Chalmers, D. J. (2002). "Consciousness and its Place in Nature." In D. J. Chalmers (ed.), *Philosophy of Mind: Classical and Contemporary Readings*. New York, Oxford University Press.

Chalmers, D. J. (2010). *The Character of Consciousness*. New York, Oxford University Press.

Chalmers, D. J. (2015). "Panpsychism and Panprotopsychism." In T. Alter and Y. Nagasawa (eds.), *Consciousness in the Physical World: Perspectives on Russellian Monism*. New York, Oxford University Press: 246–276.

Chalmers, D. J. (2018). "The Meta-problem of Consciousness." *Journal of Consciousness Studies* **25**(9–10): 6–61.

Chomsky, N. (1986). *Knowledge of Language: Its Nature, Origin, and Use*. Westport, CT, Praeger Publishers.

Chomsky, N. (2009). "The Mysteries of Nature: How Deeply Hidden?" *The Journal of Philosophy* **106**(4): 167–200.

Churchland, P. M. (1981). "Eliminative Materialism and the Propositional Attitudes." *Journal of Philosophy* **78**: 67–90.

Churchland, P. S. (1983). "Consciousness: The Transmutation of a Concept." *Pacific Philosophical Quarterly* **64**: 80–95.

Churchland, P. S. (1986). *Neurophilosophy: Toward a Unified Science of the Mind/Brain*. Cambridge, MA, MIT Press.

Churchland, P. S. (1996). "The Hornswoggle Problem." *Journal of Consciousness Studies* **3**(5–6): 402–408.

Cleve, J. V. (1983). "Conceivability and the Cartesian Argument for Dualism." *Pacific Philosophical Quarterly* **64**(1): 35–45.

Cohen, M., and Dennett, D. C. (2011). "Consciousness Cannot Be Separated From Function." *Trends in Cognitive Sciences* **15**(8): 538–364.

Conee, E. (1985). "Physicalism and Phenomenal Properties." *Philosophical Quarterly* **35**: 296–302.

D'Ambrosio, J. (2019). "A New Perceptual Adverbialism." *Journal of Philosophy* **116**(8): 413–446.

D'Ambrosio, J., and Stoljar, D. (2021). "Two Notions of Resemblance and the Semantics of 'What It's Like.'" *Inquiry*. Available at https://doi.org/10.1080/0020174X.2022.2075453

Dasgupta, S. (2015). "The Possibility of Physicalism." *The Journal of Philosophy* **111**: 557–592.

Dennett, D. C. (1990). "Quining Qualia." In W. G. Lycan (ed.), *Mind and Cognition*. Oxford, Blackwell: 519–548.

Dennett, D. C. (1991). *Consciousness Explained*. Boston, Little, Brown and Co.

Dennett, D. C. (1993). "The Message Is: There Is No Medium." *Philosophy and Phenomenological Research* **53**(4): 889–931.

Dennett, D. C. (1995). "The Unimagined Preposterousness of Zombies." *Journal of Consciousness Studies* **2**(4): 322–326.

Dennett, D. C. (2005). *Sweet Dreams: Philosophical Obstacles to a Science of Consciousness*. Cambridge, MA, MIT Press.

Descartes, R. (1641/1986). *Meditations on First Philosophy: With Selections From the Objections and Replies*. Translated by John Cottingham. Cambridge, Cambridge University Press.

Doerig, A., Schurger, A., and Herzog, M. H. (2020). "Hard Criteria for Empirical Theories of Consciousness." *Cognitive Neuroscience* **12**(2): 41–62.

Drayson, Z. (2015). "The Philosophy of Phenomenal Consciousness." In S. Miller (ed.), *The Constitution of Phenomenal Consciousness*. Amsterdam, John Benjamins: 273–292.

Dretske, F. (2000). *Perception, Knowledge and Belief: Selected Essays*. Cambridge, Cambridge University Press.

Flanagan, O. (1992). *Consciousness Reconsidered*. Cambridge, MA, MIT Press.
Frankish, K. (2017). *Illusionism as a Theory of Consciousness*. London, Imprint Academic.
Gennaro, R. J., ed. (2004). *Higher-Order Theories of Consciousness: An Anthology*. Amsterdam, John Benjamins Publishing Company.
Gennaro, R. J. (2005). "The HOT Theory of Consciousness: Between a Rock and a Hard Place." *Journal of Consciousness Studies* 12: 3–21.
Gennaro, R. J. (2012). *The Consciousness Paradox: Consciousness, Concepts and Higher-order Thoughts*. Cambridge, MA, MIT Press.
Gennaro, R. J. (2016). *The Routledge Handbook of Consciousness*. New York, Routledge.
Gertler, B. (2007). "In Defense of Mind-Body Dualism." In Joel Feinberg and Russ Shafer-Landau (eds.), *Reason and Responsibility*, 13th ed. Belmont, CA, Wadsworth: 285–296.
Godfrey-Smith, P. (2016). *Other Minds: The Octopus and the Evolution of Intelligent Life*. New York, Farrar, Straus and Giroux.
Goff, P. (2017). *Consciousness and Fundamental Reality*. New York, Oxford University Press.
Goldman, A. (1993). "Consciousness, Folk-Psychology, and Cognitive Science." *Consciousness and Cognition* 2: 364–382.
Goodale, M. A. (2014). "How (and Why) the Visual Control of Action Differs from Visual Perception." *Proceedings of the Royal Society B* 281: 1–9. http://doi.org/10.1098/rspb.2014.0337
Goodale, M. A., and Milner, A. D. (1992). "Separate Visual Pathways for Perception and Action." *Trends in Neuroscience* 15: 20–25.
Graziano, M. (2019). *Rethinking Consciousness: A Scientific Theory of Subjective Experience*. New York, Norton and Company.
Harman, G. (1990/1997). "The Intrinsic Quality of Experience." In Ned Block et al. (eds.), *The Nature of Consciousness*. Cambridge, MA, The MIT Press: 663–675.
Horgan, T. (1984). "Jackson on Physical Information and Qualia." *Philosophical Quarterly* 32: 127–136.
Husak, D. (2016). *Ignorance of Law: A Philosophical Inquiry*. Oxford, Oxford University Press.
Irvine, E. (2012). *Consciousness as a Scientific Concept*. Dordrecht, Springer.
Jackson, F. (1982). "Epiphenomenal Qualia." *The Philosophical Quarterly* 32(127): 127–136.
Jackson, F. (1986). "What Mary Didn't Know." *The Journal of Philosophy* 83(5): 291–295.
James, W. (1890). *Principles of Psychology*. New York, Dover.
Jennings, C. D. (2020). *The Attending Mind*. Cambridge, Cambridge University Press.

Kind, A. (2003). "What's So Transparent About Transparency?" *Philosophical Studies* **115**: 225–244.
Kind, A. (2007). "Restrictions on Representationalism." *Philosophical Studies* **134**: 405–427.
Kind, A. (2008). "How to Believe in Qualia." In E. Wright (ed.), *The Case for Qualia*. Cambridge, MA, MIT Press: 285–298.
Kind, A. (2013). "The Case Against Representationalism About Moods." In U. Kriegel (ed.), *Current Controversies in the Philosophy of Mind*. New York, Routledge: 113–134.
Kind, A. (2015). "Pessimism About Russellian Monism." In T. Alter and Y. Nagasawa (eds.), *Consciousness in the Physical World: Perspectives on Russellian Monism*. Oxford, Oxford University Press: 401–421.
Kind, A. (2018). "The Mind-Body Problem in 20th Century Philosophy." In A. Kind (ed.), *Philosophy of Mind in the Twentieth and Twenty-First Centuries*. New York, Routledge: 53–77.
Kind, A. (2020). *Philosophy of Mind: The Basics*. New York, Routledge.
Koch, C. (2012). *Consciousness: Confessions of a Romantic Reductionist*. Cambridge, MA, MIT Press.
Koch, C., Massimini, M., Boly, M., and Tononi G. (2016). "Neural Correlates of Consciousness: Progress and Problems." *Nature Reviews Neuroscience* **17**(5): 307–321. doi:10.1038/nrn.2016.22. PMID: 27094080.
Kriegel, U. (2007). "Consciousness: Phenomenal Consciousness, Access Consciousness, and Scientific Practice." In P. Thagard (ed.), *Handbook of the Philosophy of Psychology and Cognitive Science*. Amsterdam, Elsevier.
Kripke, S. (1980). *Naming and Necessity*. Cambridge, MA, Harvard University Press.
LeDoux, J. (2019). *The Deep History of Ourselves: The Four-Billion-Year Story of How We Got Conscious Brains*. New York, Penguin Random House.
Lee, A. Y. (2020). "Does Sentience Come in Degrees?" *Animal Sentience*: 1–2.
Lee, A. Y. (2021). "Modelling Mental Qualities." *Philosophical Review* **130**(2): 263–298.
Lee, A. Y. (2022). "Degrees of Consciousness." *Nous*. https://doi.org/10.1111/nous.12421
Levine, J. (1983). "Materialism and Qualia: The Explanatory Gap." *Pacific Philosophical Quarterly* **64**: 354–361.
Lewis, D. K. (1988). "What Experience Teaches." *Proceedings of the Russellian Society* **13**: 29–57.
Lewis, D. K. (1994). "Reduction of Mind." In S. Guttenplan (ed.), *A Companion to the Philosophy of Mind*. Oxford, Blackwell.
Lewis, D. K. (1995). "Should a Materialist Believe in Qualia?" *Australasian Journal of Philosophy* **73**(1): 140–144.
Locke, J. (1689/1975). *An Essay Concerning Human Understanding*. Edited with an introduction by Peter H. Nidditch. Oxford, Oxford University Press.

Lycan, W. (1996). *Consciousness and Experience*. Cambridge, MA, MIT Press.
Lycan, W. (2019). "Representational Theories of Consciousness." In E. N. Zalta (ed.), *The Stanford Encyclopedia of Philosophy*, Fall 2019 ed. Available at https://plato.stanford.edu/archives/fall2019/entries/consciousness-representational/
McGinn, C. (1989). "Can We Solve the Mind-Body Problem?" *Mind* 98(391): 349–366.
Mindt, G. (2017). "The Problem with the 'Information' in Integrated Information Theory." *Journal of Consciousness Studies* 24: 130–154.
Montero, B. (1999). "The Body Problem." *Noûs* 33(2): 183–200.
Montero, B. (2001). "Post-Physicalism." *Journal of Consciousness Studies* 8(2): 61–80.
Montero, B. (2010). "A Russellian Response to the Structural Argument Against Physicalism." *Journal of Consciousness Studies* 17(3–4): 70–83.
Moore, G. E. (1903/1965). "The Refutation of Idealism." In *Philosophical Studies*. Totowa, NJ, Littlefield, Adams & Co.: 1–30.
Mørch, H. H. (2014). "Panpsychism and Causation: A New Argument and a Solution to the Combination Problem." *Department of Philosophy, Classics, History of Art and Ideas*. PhD. Oslo, University of Oslo.
Mørch, H. H. (2018). "Is the Integrated Information Theory of Consciousness Compatible With Russellian Panpsychism?" *Erkenntnis* 84: 1065–1085.
Mørch, H. H. (2019). "Is Consciousness Intrinsic? A Problem for Integrated Information Theory." *Journal of Consciousness Studies* 26(1–2): 133–162.
Nagel, T. (1974). "What Is It Like to Be a Bat?" *The Philosophical Review* 83(4): 435–450.
Nemirow, L. (1990). "Physicalism and the Cognitive Role of Acquaintance." In William G. Lycan (ed.), *Mind and Cognition*. Oxford, Blackwell.
Nida-Rümelin, M. (1995). "What Mary Couldn't Know: Belief About Phenomenal States." In T. Metzinger (ed.), *Conscious Experience*. Thorverton, Imprint Academic.
Orwell, G. (1962). *Homage to Catalonia*. Harmondsworth, Penguin.
Papineau, D. (2001). "The Rise of Physicalism." In C. Gillett and B. Loewer (eds.), *Physicalism and Its Discontents*. Cambridge, Cambridge University Press.
Papineau, D. (2021). *The Metaphysics of Sensory Experience*. Oxford, Oxford University Press.
Pautz, A. (2019). "What Is the Integrated Information Theory of Consciousness." *Journal of Consciousness Studies* 26(1–2): 188–215.
Pavese, C. (2017). "Know-how and Gradability." *Philosophical Review* 126(3): 345–383.
Quine, W. V. O. (1960). *Word and Object*. Cambridge, MA, MIT Press.

Quine, W. V. O. (1969). *Ontological Relativity and Other Essays.* New York, Columbia University Press.
Rabin, G. (2020). "Fundamentality Physicalism." *Inquiry* **65**(1): 77–116.
Rosenberg, G. (2004). *A Place for Consciousness.* Oxford, Oxford University Press.
Rosenthal, D. (2005). *Consciousness and Mind.* New York, Oxford University Press.
Rosenthal, D. (2011). "Exaggerated Reports: Reply to Block." *Analysis* **71**(3): 431–437.
Russell, B. (1921). *The Analysis of Mind.* New York, The Macmillan Company.
Russell, B. (1927/1954). *The Analysis of Matter.* New York, Dover Publications.
Russell, B. (1948). *Human Knowledge: Its Scope and Limits.* London, Allen and Unwin.
Schlicht, T. (2012). "Phenomenal Consciousness, Attention and Accessibility." *Phenomenology and the Cognitive Sciences* **11**(3): 309–334.
Searle, J. (1980). "Minds, Brains, and Programs." *Behavioral and Brain Sciences* **3**: 417–457.
Shoemaker, S. (1980). "Absent Qualia Are Impossible." *Philosophical Review* **90**: 581–599.
Shoemaker, S. (1982). "The Inverted Spectrum." *Journal of Philosophy* **79**(July): 357–381.
Shoemaker, S. (1996). *The First-Person Perspective and Other Essays.* Cambridge, Cambridge University Press.
Siegel, S. (2011). *The Contents of Visual Experience.* New York, Oxford University Press.
Simon, J. (2017). "Vagueness and Zombies: Why 'Phenomenally Consciousness' Has No Borderline Cases." *Philosophical Studies* **174**(8): 2105–2123.
Solomon, R. (1976). *The Passions.* New York, Anchor Press/Doubleday.
Stoljar, D. (2001). "Two Conceptions of the Physical." *Philosophy and Phenomenological Research* **62**(2): 253–281.
Stoljar, D. (2005). "Physicalism and Phenomenal Concepts." *Mind & Language* **20**(5): 469–494.
Stoljar, D. (2006). *Ignorance and Imagination: The Epistemic Origin of the Problem of Consciousness.* New York, Oxford University Press.
Stoljar, D. (2007). "Two Conceivability Arguments Compared." *Proceedings of the Aristotelian Society* **107**(1): 27–44.
Stoljar, D. (2010). *Physicalism.* London and New York, Routledge.
Stoljar, D. (2015). "Russellian Monism or Nagelian Monism?" In T. Alter and Y. Nagasawa (eds.), *Consciousness in the Physical World: Perspectives on Russellian Monism.* New York, Oxford University Press.
Stoljar, D. (2016). "The Semantics of 'What It's Like' and the Nature of Consciousness." *Mind* **125**(500): 1161–1198.

Stoljar, D. (2017). *Philosophical Progress: In Defence of a Reasonable Optimism*. New York, Oxford University Press.
Stoljar, D. (2019). "In Praise of Poise." In A. Pautz and D. Stoljar (eds.), *Blockheads!: Essays on Ned Block's Philosophy of Mind and Consciousness*. Cambridge, MA, MIT Press: 511–536.
Stoljar, D. (2020a). "Chalmers v Chalmers." *Nous*: 469–487.
Stoljar, D. (2020b). "Panpsychism and Non-Standard Materialism: Some Comparative Remarks." In W. Seager (ed.), *The Routledge Handbook of Panpsychism*. New York, Routledge.
Stoljar, D. (2021). "Physicalism." In E. N. Zalta (ed.), *The Stanford Encyclopedia of Philosophy*, Summer 2022 ed. Available at https://plato.stanford.edu/archives/sum2022/entries/physicalism/
Strawson, G. (2006). "Realistic Monism: Why Physicalism Entails Panpsychism." In A. Freeman (ed.), *Consciousness and Its Place in Nature: Does Physicalism Entail Panpsychism?* Exeter, Imprint Academic.
Strawson, G. (2019). "Underestimating the Physical." *Journal of Consciousness Studies* **26**: 228–240.
Tegmark, M. (2015). "Consciousness as a State of Matter." *Chaos, Solitons & Fractals* **76**: 238–270.
Tononi, G. (2008). "Consciousness as Integrated Information: A Provisional Manifesto." *The Biological Bulletin* **215**(3): 216–242.
Tononi, G. (2018). "Why Scott Should Stare at a Blank Wall and Reconsider (or the Conscious Grid." *Shtetl-Optimized: The Blog of Scott Aaronson*. Available at https://scottaaronson.blog/?p=1823
Tononi, G., and Koch, C. (2015). "Consciousness: Here, There and Everywhere?" *Philosophical Transactions of the Royal Society* **370**: 1–18.
Tye, M. (1995). *Ten Problems of Consciousness*. Cambridge, MA, The MIT Press.
Tye, M. (2000). *Consciousness, Color, and Content*. Cambridge, MA, The MIT Press.
Watzl, S. (2017). *Structuring Mind*. Oxford, Oxford University Press.
Wierzbicka, A. (2010). *Experience, Evidence, and Sense: The Hidden Cultural Legacy of English*. New York, Oxford University Press.
Williamson, T. (2000). *Knowledge and Its Limits*. New York, Oxford University Press.
Wilson, J. M. (2006). "On Characterizing the Physical." *Philosophical Studies* **131**(1): 61–99.
Wishon, D. (2015). "Russell on Russellian Monism." In T. Alter and Y. Nagasawa (eds.), *Consciousness in the Physical World*. New York, Oxford University Press: 91–120.
Wittgenstein, L. (1980). *Remarks on the Philosophy of Psychology, Volume I*. Chicago, University of Chicago Press.
Yablo, S. (1993). "Is Conceivability a Guide to Possibility." *Philosophy and Phenomenological Research* **53**(1): 1–42.

Yancy, G. (2008). "Elevators, Social Spaces, and Racism." *Philosophy and Social Criticism* **34**(8): 843–876.

Zylke, J., and Bauchner, H. (2020). "Mortality and Morbidity: The Measure of a Pandemic." *Journal of the American Medical Association* **324**(5): 458–459. Available at https://jamanetwork.com/journals/jama/fullarticle/2768085

Index

Aaronson, Scott, 115–17
ability hypothesis, 27–8
Absent Qualia argument, 31
abstract laws, 130
access consciousness, 14–15, 83–5, 88–91, 116
acquaintance hypothesis, 28–9
ad hominem arguments, 188–9
agnosticism, 7
Analysis of Matter (Russell), 46, 49
anxiety, 4, 39–41
a posteriori claims, 145
argument(s): Absent Qualia argument, 31; ad hominem arguments, 188–9; Bat argument, 23–5, 82; clear and distinct conception, 8–10, 32; deductive arguments, 8; defined, 8; from hallucination, 121–3, 126; inductive arguments, 8; knowledge argument, 23, 25–30, 104–5; nomological properties argument, 126–9; structure and dynamics argument, 167–9, 172, 179–82, 186; sufficiently comprehensive conception, 9, 32; Zombie Argument, 30–4. *See also* conceivability argument
Armstrong, David, 43
artificial intelligence, 12
Asimov, Isaac, 33–4
associated feelings, 74–6, 98
atheism, 7
Atler, Torin, 167

awakeness. *See* wakefulness
awareness, 14–15, 17, 20, 22, 43–5, 86

Babbie, Earl, 60
Bartlett, Daniel, 52
Bat argument (Nagel), 23–5, 82
Beha, Christopher, 52
being conscious, 44, 80–1, 125–6
Berkeley, George, 6
Bicentennial Man (Asimov), 33–4
Blackburn, Simon, 148
Block, Ned, 13–14, 31
Bloom, Paul, 52, 191–2
book of nature example, 97

Chalmers, David: fundamental theory, 117; on neuroscience, 183–4; physicalism and, 184–5; physics and, 46; protophenomenal monism, 48; psychological consciousness and, 15, 20–3; Russellian monism and, 163–4, 166–7; structure and dynamics argument, 167–9, 172, 179–82, 186; Zombie Argument, 30–4
Churchland, Patricia, 21–2
clear and distinct conception, 8–10, 32
cognitive phenomenology, 18
color thought experiment (Jackson), 23, 25–30
coma state, 14–15, 72, 77

combination problem, 50, 160, 162–3, 166
compatibility problem: epistemic view and, 113, 120–1, 135–6, 144, 146–9, 186–7; ignorance hypothesis and, 131, 138–40, 147, 189; introduction to, 64–7, 135–6; meta-problem and, 105; mind-body problem and, 92; for phenomenal consciousness, 114–15; pretty hard problem of consciousness, 117; science of consciousness, 131; standard presentation of, 171
complementation, 77–8
conceivability argument (CA): demanding standard for conceiving, 142–3; dualism and, 7–10, 99–101; dualism 2.0 and, 169–70; eliminativism and illusionism, 101–2; epistemic view, 94–8, 103–6, 138–44, 158, 164, 194; feelings and, 93; ignorance hypothesis and, 95–6, 103–4; introduction to, 31–3; introspection and, 102, 109–10; knowledge argument and, 104–5; metaphysics of consciousness, 144–8; meta-problem solution through, 105; no-explanation-of-consciousness objection, 112–14; ordinary book *vs.* book of nature, 97; panpsychism and, 99–101; persistence objection, 107–8; phenomenal consciousness and, 92–109; against physicalism, 92–4, 110–12; physical properties and, 94–6; premises and, 92–7, 111, 141–2; relevance objection, 107; revelation objection, 108–9; Russellian monism and, 106, 169–70; standard physicalism and, 102–3; variations of, 105–6; zombie example, 98
conceptualization, 60–1

The Conscious Mind (Chalmers), 117
consciousness: access consciousness, 14–15, 83–5, 88–91, 116; attempts to define, 66–7; complications to debate, 70–8; degrees of, 123–6, 131; explanation of, 112–14, 116–17; explanatory gap, 20, 25, 146; hard problem of consciousness, 20, 64, 117, 136, 183; introduction to debate, 63–8; introspection and, 91; metaphysics of, 144–8; nature of, 3–4, 18, 31, 67, 138, 146, 157, 196; neural correlates of, 18–19, 59; no-explanation-of-consciousness objection, 112–14; philosophical questions about, 91–114; physicalist net and, 13, 23–34, 180; pretty hard problem of, 117; psychological consciousness, 15, 20; root word, 77–8; science of, 115–31; self-consciousness, 14; theories of, 35–51; unconsciousness, 14–15, 17, 43–4, 77; unified consciousness, 50. *See also* higher-order theory of consciousness; phenomenal consciousness
consciousness problem, 3–4, 13–22, 35, 146–7
conscious states: access-conscious states and, 89–91; epistemic view and, 113; explanation of consciousness, 112; introspection and, 88; overview of, 71–2; phenomenally conscious states, 16–17, 33, 37n6, 39, 44, 55, 82, 90–1; philosophy of consciousness, 129–31; physicalism and, 120; psychological state and, 44, 66, 71–3, 78–82, 196–7
conscious subjects, 66, 71
contingent fact, 110

deductive arguments, 8
degrees of consciousness, 123–6, 131
demanding standard for conceiving, 142–3

Democritus, 150
Dennett, Daniel, 32
Descartes, Rene, 5–8, 10, 13, 105, 150
dispositional properties, 106, 157–9, 161–5, 167–8, 172
doubt/doubting act, 5–7
dreams, 17, 37, 43, 141
dualism: conceivability argument for, 7–10, 99–101; as default view, 191–2; defense of, 177–9, 186–92; defined, 11, 45; introduction to, 7; property dualism, 10; standard physicalism and, 178–9, 195
dualism 2.0: conceivability argument and, 169–70; future development of, 61–2; ignorance is no defense, 135–54, 193, 198–200; introduction to, 155–6; irreducibly of, 53–8; mathematics and, 170–1, 173; overview of, 52–62; phenomenal consciousness and, 53–8, 61–2; Russellian monism and, 53–4, 156–60, 169–70; science and, 58–61; set of options and, 171–3
dualism-physicalism divide: epistemic view and, 151; introduction to, 4–6, 35; Russellian monism and, 45–51, 164–6

echolocatory experience, 24–5, 82
elevator example, 15
eliminativism, 11n1, 101–2, 147, 147n1, 156, 171–2
emotional experience, 40, 187
empirical laws, 67–8, 100, 117–18, 120, 130
epiphenomenalism, 55, 190–1
epistemic view: burden of proof, 148–53, 197–8; compatibility problem and, 113, 120–1, 135–6, 144, 146–9, 186–7; conceivability argument and, 94–8, 103–6, 138–44, 158, 164, 194; conscious states and, 113; considerations of simplicity, 151–2; defense of, 193–4; denial of physicalism and, 150; dualism-physicalism divide and, 151; future *vs.* past success, 150–1; ignorance hypothesis and, 136, 152, 194; ignorance is no excuse, 193, 198–200; introduction to criticism, 136–8; metaphysics of consciousness, 144–8; non-Russellian epistemic view, 179–86, 189; presumption of physicalism and, 152–3; reasons to support, 138–45; you're-not-done response, 144–7, 193, 196–7
experience: conscious experience, 4, 15, 19–21, 24; defined, 70–1; echolocatory experience, 24–5, 82; emotional, 40, 187; indirect experience, 16; knowledge argument and, 26, 28–9; mind and matter in, 49; particular experiences, 145; perceptual, 16, 43; phenomenal consciousness and, 19–21, 23, 33, 41–7, 61, 70–1; properties of, 16; thought experiments and, 26; transparency of, 38; of unified consciousness, 50; Zombia argument and, 30–1
explanation of consciousness, 112–14, 116–17
explanatory gap, 20, 25, 146
extraordinary phenomenal properties, 158

factual knowledge, 27–9
the feeling he had when (TFW), 130
feelings: associated feelings, 74–6, 98; bundling together of, 50; combination problem and, 162; conceivability argument and, 93, 101–2; defined, 73; eliminativism and, 101; intensity of, 125; of pain, 68–9, 82, 125, 165, 197; panpsychism and, 47; perception of, 74–6; phenomenal consciousness and, 17, 70–1, 90–1; psychological state and, 72; of shock, 130; TFW (the feeling when), 73–5

first-order theory, 42
functionalism, 12–13, 31, 180

Gertler, Brie, 9
gluons, 56
Goodale, Melvyn, 16–17

hallucinations, 17, 37, 121–3, 126, 128
hard problem of consciousness, 20, 64, 117, 136, 183
Harman, Gilbert, 38
Hempel, Carl, 57
Hempel's Dilemma, 57
higher-order account, 79–82, 85–8
higher-order theory of consciousness: access consciousness and, 88–90; defined, 36, 91; introduction to, 4; overview of, 42–5, 78–83; phenomenal consciousness and, 44–5; phenomenal consciousness vs., 81–2, 85–7, 92
homunculi-headed robot scenario, 31
HOP (higher-order perception) theory, 42–3
HOT (higher-order thought) theory, 42–3, 80

idealism, 6, 151
identity theory, 11–12, 147–8, 180
ignorance hypothesis: compatibility problem and, 131, 138–40, 147, 189; conceivability argument and, 95–6, 103–4; epistemic view and, 136, 152, 194; introduction to, 64, 67; laws of consciousness and, 120, 130–1; physical properties and, 152; science of consciousness, 120, 130–1, 196
ignorance is no defense, 135–54, 193, 198–200
illusionism, 101–2
implausibility, 100–1
indirect experience, 16
inductive arguments, 8
information processing, 20–1
integrated information theory (IIT), 115–17, 124

intentional content, 36–42
introspection: conceivability argument and, 109–10; consciousness and, 91; defined, 81, 109–10; as experience, 16, 23; feelings and, 125; higher-order account and, 81–2, 88–9, 91; knowledge based on, 108–9; metaphysical character and, 106
"I" thinking, 6

Jackson, Frank, 23, 25–30
James, William, 50
jealousy, 15, 17–18

Kant, Immanuel, 161, 185
knowledge argument, 23, 25–30, 104–5
Koch, Christof, 115

Latinisms, 71, 115–16
laws of consciousness (LCT), 117, 118–31
Lewis, C. I., 16
Lewis, David, 27–8
Locke, John, 31
logical possibility, 8, 31, 58
Lycan, William, 41

Malcolm, Norman, 77–8
materialism, 6, 11n1, 147, 162–3, 166
mathematics, 54, 59, 96, 113, 170–1, 173, 189–90
Meditations on First Philosophy (Descartes), 5, 7
mental causation, 55
mental states: functionalism and, 12–13; phenomenal consciousness and, 15–18, 22, 35–6, 43–4; physicalism and, 11–13; representationalism and, 36–42
metaphysics of consciousness, 144–8
Milner, David, 16
mind-body problem: defined, 64; functionalism, 12–13, 31, 180; introduction to, 3–5; nature of

Index

mind, 3, 13, 18; overview of, 5–6, 13; philosophy of mind and, 13, 26, 61, 84, 112, 199; physicalism and, 3–4; taxonomy of, 6; theories of consciousness, 35–51. *See also* dualism; physicalism
modal knowledge, 94
moods, 39–41
Moore, G. E., 38
motivations, 43, 55, 120–1, 169–70
multiple realizability, 12
mysterianism, 106

Nagel, Thomas, 18, 23–5, 82, 92
Naming and Necessity (Kripke), 103
nature of consciousness, 3–4, 18, 31, 67, 138, 146, 157, 196
nature of mind, 3, 13, 18
necessary condition, 111, 181–2, 190
neural correlates of consciousness, 18–19, 59
neural processes, 4
neuroscience, 19–22, 26, 107, 183–4
neutral monism, 6, 47, 49, 159, 172
neutral monist Russellian monism, 159
New York Times, 52
no-explanation-of-consciousness objection, 112–14
no-fundamental-mentality (NFM), 181–2, 184, 186, 189–90
nomological properties argument, 126–9
non-dispositional properties, 157–64, 167–8, 172
non-physicalism, 53, 187
non-Russellian epistemic view (NRE), 179–86, 189
non-standard physicalism: failure of, 178; non-Russellian epistemic view and, 179–86, 189; Russellian monism and, 164, 166–7. *See also* epistemic view
not-physicalism objection, 110–12
noumena, 161, 185

old fact/new guise hypothesis, 29
operationalization, 60–1

ordinary book example, 97
ordinary phenomenal properties, 100–1, 158–9, 165, 170
Oxford Dictionary of Philosophy (Blackburn), 148

PANIC theory, 38–9
panprotopsychist Russellian monism, 158–64, 172
panpsychism/panpsychists: conceivability argument and, 99–101; feelings and, 47; Russellian monism and, 46–7, 158–63, 167
particular experiences, 145
percepts/perceptions, 16–19, 44, 74–6
perceptual experience, 16, 43
persistence objection, 107–8
phenomenal account, 68–73, 79–81, 85, 87, 90, 92, 125–6
phenomenal character, 36–9, 41–2
phenomenal concept strategy, 103
phenomenal consciousness: access consciousness and, 90–1; access consciousness *vs.*, 85–7; compatibility problem for, 114–15; conceivability argument and, 92–109; conscious subjects, 71; defined, 91; dualism 2.0 and, 53–8, 61–2; epiphenomenalism, 55, 190–1; experience and, 19–21, 23, 33, 41–7, 61, 70–1; feelings and, 17, 70–1, 90–1; higher-order theory of consciousness and, 44–5, 81–2, 85–7, 92; mental states and, 15–18, 22, 35–6, 43–4; metaphysical structure, 76; notion of feeling, 68–9; overview of, 14–18, 68–9; perception and, 74–6; percepts/perceptions and, 16–19, 44, 75; problematic notion, 101; problem of, 22–34, 135–6; as psychological property, 73–4; representationalism and, 36–9, 41–2; in robots, 34; terminology of, 70–1; unproblematic notion, 101

phenomenality, 54, 56, 58, 169, 181, 186, 189–91
phenomenally conscious states, 16–17, 33, 37n6, 39, 44, 55, 82, 90–1
phenomenal monism, 46–8, 50
phenomenal properties: extraordinary phenomenal properties, 158; notion of feeling, 69; ordinary phenomenal properties, 100–1, 158–9, 165, 170; panprotopsychism and, 162; panpsychist Russellian monism, 158
philosophy of mind, 13, 26, 61, 84, 112, 199
PhilPapers survey (2020), 187
physicalism: burden of proof, 148–53, 197–8; Chalmers, David and, 184–5; conceivability argument against, 92–4, 110–12; consciousness and, 67; defense of, 152–3, 177–9; defined, 6, 11–12, 45, 181–2; denial of, 150; higher-order theory of consciousness and, 44–5; identity theory, 11–12, 147–8, 180; ignorance is no defense, 135–54, 193, 198–200; Knowledge Argument and, 23, 25–30; laws of consciousness and, 119–20; mental states and, 11–13; metaphysics of consciousness, 144–8; mind-body problem and, 3–4; not-physicalism objection, 110–12; as objective, 34; overview of, 11–13; premises and, 27, 102–3; scientific theory of mind and, 12; t-physical properties, 48–9; true/not-true debate, 65. *See also* dualism-physicalism divide; epistemic view; non-standard physicalism; standard physicalism
physicalist net, 13, 23–34, 180
physicalist Russellian monism, 159–60
physical monism, 47–51
physical possibility, 8
physical properties: conceivability argument and, 94–5, 141–2; ignorance hypothesis and, 152; necessary condition, 111, 181–2, 190; non-Russellian epistemic view and, 179–86, 189; structure and dynamics argument, 180–1; sufficient condition, 69, 111, 182
physical theory, 48–9, 56–8, 105, 157, 162, 168–9, 172, 181–4, 189
plausibility, 30, 41–4, 153, 171, 194–6
pluralists/pluralism, 67, 78, 88, 91–2, 114
The Practice of Social Research (Babbie), 60
premises: combination problem and, 162; conceivability argument and, 92–7, 111, 141–2; conscious states, 121–2; defined, 8–9; degrees of consciousness argument, 124–5; existence of God, 7; knowledge argument and, 28–9, 104; nomological properties argument, 126, 128; physicalism and, 27, 102–3; structure and dynamics argument and, 181–2; Zombie argument and, 31–3
pretty hard problem of consciousness, 117
Principles of Psychology (James), 50
problematic notion, 101
property dualism, 10
protophenomenality, 49
protophenomenal monism, 47–8, 50
psychological consciousness, 15, 20–3
psychological state: access consciousness and, 84–91; conscious states and, 44, 66, 71–3, 78–82, 196–7; feelings and, 72; hallucinations, 17, 37, 121–3, 126, 128; Zombie argument and, 98

qualia, 15–16, 23, 31, 58, 71, 83

relationalism, 76, 122–3
relevance objection, 107, 196
representational content, 36
representationalism: defined, 36; intentional content and, 36–42;

introduction to, 4, 35; mental states and, 36–42; moods and, 39–41; overview of, 36–42; phenomenal consciousness and, 36–9, 41–2
revelation objection, 108–9
Rosenberg, Gregg, 47
Russell, Bertrand, 6, 46, 49, 105, 106
Russellian monism (RM): combination problem and, 50, 160, 162–3, 166; conceivability argument and, 106, 169–70; defined, 6, 36; dispositional properties and, 106, 157–9, 161–5, 167–8, 172; dualism 2.0 and, 53–4, 156–60, 169–70; eliminativism, 101–2, 147n1, 156, 171–2; false advertising, 164–6; introduction to, 4, 35; neutral monism, 6, 47, 49, 159, 172; non-dispositional properties and, 157–64, 167–8, 172; non-Russellian epistemic view (NRE), 179–86, 189; non-standard physicalism and, 164, 166–7; overview of, 45–51; panprotopsychist, 158–64, 172; panpsychism and, 46–7, 158–63, 167; phenomenal monism, 46–8, 50; physicalists and, 159–60; physical monism, 47–51; protophenomenal monism, 47–8, 50; structure and dynamics argument, 167–9, 172, 179–82, 186

science of consciousness: argument from hallucination, 121–3, 126; degrees of, 123–6; ignorance hypothesis, 120, 130–1, 196; integrated information theory, 115–17; laws of consciousness, 117, 118–31; nomological properties argument, 126–9; without laws of consciousness, 128–30
scientific theory of mind, 11n1, 12
second-order theory, 42
self-consciousness, 14
sense data, 83

sense-datum theory, 76, 101–2, 109, 121–2
Solomon, Robert, 40
speculative metaphysics, 112
spookiness, 5, 54–8, 62, 150, 153, 170–1, 190, 192
standard physicalism: conceivability argument and, 102–3; defense of, 187; defined, 156; dualism and, 178–9, 195; Russellian monism and, 164–7, 171–2
structure and dynamics argument, 167–9, 172, 179–82, 186
sufficient condition, 69, 111, 182
sufficiently comprehensive conception, 9, 32

Team Body Project, 52
Tegmark, Max, 115
TFW (the feeling when), 73–5
theism, 53
Toklas, Alice B., 71, 158, 165–6
Tononi, Giulio, 115–17
t-physical properties, 48–9
transparency of experience, 38
Tye, Michael, 38–9

unconsciousness, 14–15, 17, 43–4, 77
unified consciousness, 50
Universal Declaration of Human Rights, 149
unproblematic notion, 101

via negativa, 168–9
vision for action, 17
vision for perception, 16–17
Vogt, Karl, 150

wakefulness, 14–15, 17
"what it's like" phrase, 82–3
Wierzbicka, Anna, 77
Wilson, Jessica, 168–9
Wittgenstein, Ludwig, 82–3

Yancy, George, 15
you're-not-done response (YND), 144–7, 193, 196–7

Zombie Argument, 30–4, 98

For Product Safety Concerns and Information please contact our EU representative GPSR@taylorandfrancis.com
Taylor & Francis Verlag GmbH, Kaufingerstraße 24, 80331 München, Germany

www.ingramcontent.com/pod-product-compliance
Lightning Source LLC
Chambersburg PA
CBHW052017290426
44112CB00014B/2274